Social Media and Public Relations

Social media is having a profound, but not yet fully understood impact on public relations. In the 24/7 world of perpetually connected publics, will public relations function as a dark art that spins (or tweets) self-interested variations of the truth for credulous audiences? Or does the full glare of the Internet and the increasing expectations of powerful publics motivate it to more honestly engage to serve the public interest?

The purpose of this book is to examine the role of PR by exploring the myriad ways that social media is reshaping its conceptualization, strategies, and tactics. In particular, it explores the dichotomies of fake and authentic, powerless and powerful, meaningless and meaningful. It exposes transgressions committed by practitioners—the paucity of digital literacy, the lack of understanding of the norms of social media, naivety about corporate identity risks, and the overarching emphasis on spin over authentic engagement. But it also shows the power that closely networked social media users have to insert information and opinion into discussions and force "false PR friends" to be less so.

This timely, challenging, and fascinating book will be of interest to all students, researchers, and practitioners in Public Relations, Media, and Communication Studies.

Judy Motion is Professor of Communication at the University of New South Wales, Australia.

Robert L. Heath is Professor Emeritus at the University of Houston, USA.

Shirley Leitch is Dean and Professor of Communication at the Australian National University, Australia.

Routledge New Directions in Public Relations and Communication Research

Edited by Kevin Moloney

Routledge New Directions in Public Relations and Communication Research is a new forum for the publication of books of original research in PR and related types of communication. Its remit is to publish critical and challenging responses to continuities and fractures in contemporary PR thinking and practice, and its essential yet contested role in market-orientated, capitalist, liberal democracies around the world. The series reflects the multiple and interdisciplinary forms PR takes in a post-Grunigian world; the expanding roles which it performs, and the increasing number of countries in which it is practised.

The series will examine current trends and explore new thinking on the key questions which impact upon PR and communications including:

- Is the evolution of persuasive communications in Central and Eastern Europe, China, Latin America, Japan, the Middle East and South East Asia developing new forms or following Western models?
- What has been the impact of postmodern sociologies, cultural studies and methodologies which are often critical of the traditional, conservative role of PR in capitalist political economies, and in patriarchy, gender and ethnic roles?
- What is the impact of digital social media on politics, individual privacy and PR practice? Is new technology changing the nature of content communicated, or simply reaching bigger audiences faster? Is digital PR a cause or a consequence of political and cultural change?

Books in this series will be of interest to academics and researchers involved in these expanding fields of study, as well as students undertaking advanced studies in this area.

Motion, Heath, and Leitch have done excellent work in the past and this is no exception. The area of social media and public relations has long needed an authoritative and critical text and *Social Media and Public Relations* fills that void.

Michael L. Kent, *Professor, University of Tennessee Knoxville, USA*

Social Media and Public Relations provides an insight into a growing area of focus in social media while tying in emerging trends and historical perspectives in public relations. This book helps explore the current issues, risks, opportunities, and challenges involving social media from the audience perspective, which can be applicable for practitioners and researchers – adding a needed area of discussion in social media research and practice within public relations.

Karen Freberg, *Assistant Professor, University of Louisville, Kentucky, USA*

Social Media and Public Relations disrupts the notion that social media has ameliorated public relations. Motion, Heath, and Leitch question the relationship between public relations and social media to reveal the complexities and tensions between social media cultures and the promotion-oriented goals of public relations. Sharply written and scrupulously documented, this is a must read for scholars, practitioners, and students interested in the future of social media in public relations.

Adam J. Saffer, *Assistant Professor, The University of North Carolina at Chapel Hill, NC, USA*

Social Media and Public Relations

Fake friends and powerful publics

Judy Motion, Robert L. Heath and Shirley Leitch

Routledge
Taylor & Francis Group

LONDON AND NEW YORK

First published 2016
by Routledge
2 Park Square, Milton Park, Abingdon, Oxon OX14 4RN

and by Routledge
711 Third Avenue, New York, NY 10017

Routledge is an imprint of the Taylor & Francis Group, an informa business

© 2016 Judy Motion, Robert L. Heath and Shirley Leitch

The right of Judy Motion, Robert L. Heath and Shirley Leitch to be identified as authors of this work has been asserted by them in accordance with sections 77 and 78 of the Copyright, Designs and Patents Act 1988.

Trademark notice: Product or corporate names may be trademarks or registered trademarks, and are used only for identification and explanation without intent to infringe.

British Library Cataloguing in Publication Data
A catalogue record for this book is available from the British Library

Library of Congress Cataloging in Publication Data
Motion, Judy.
Social media and public relations : fake friends and powerful publics / Judy Motion, Robert L. Heath, Shirley Leitch. -- 1 Edition.
pages cm. -- (Routledge new directions in public relations & communication research)
Includes bibliographical references and index.
1. Social media. 2. Public relations. I. Heath, Robert L. (Robert Lawrence), 1941- II. Leitch, Shirley, 1960- III. Title.
HM742.M68 2015
302.23'1--dc23
2015021332

ISBN: 978-0-415-85626-3 (hbk)
ISBN: 978-0-203-72779-9 (ebk)

Typeset in Bembo
by GreenGate Publishing Services, Tonbridge, Kent

Contents

Preface

As we began this project, we knew that we would have to overcome two obstacles, at least. One was the study of a topic that was in its formative stages. Given that social media are continuing to develop, as are the patterns of users, we would be writing on a topic for which little historical perspective was available. We knew that it would be challenging to know what was going on and how people and public relations practitioners were using and responding to social media trends. Scholars, practitioners, social media developers, and skilled users were deeply engaged in making something happen. In the midst of all of that uncertainty, we were confronted with the notion that social media were (or were constrained from) being used for sociopolitical activism, terrorism, and marketing. As we immersed ourselves in social media, we joined various communities and sought to understand not only public relations practices but also gain insights into user perspectives. Social media became a distraction, a fascination, and at times, a procrastination technique. As critical scholars, our attention was drawn to the cultural clash between the promotional cultures of public relations and participatory cultures of social media; the shift in power/ knowledge relations; and the ways in which sociality played out in various social media. At the heart of our inquiry was a concern for democratic principles and equity practices. It seemed to us that social media was driving a cultural transformation in which identities were formed and performed as users engaged in collaborative relationships, exchanged information and meanings, and shared their everyday lives more publicly. We have sought to document, theorize and critique these cultural changes and the ways in which public relations seeks to influence such processes.

The second problem was time and geography. What seemed to be a workable timetable failed for many reasons, and distance led to the difficulties of coordinated work. On this last point, we decided that each of us would be the lead author on various chapters, but no one would have the task of making style and presentation totally consistent. Each of the authors had special interests, read each other's chapters, and made comments. Most importantly, rather than severely differing over matters we tended to help one another make points clearer and more forcefully. We shared articles, cases, and encouragement.

In that spirit, rather than having the book read like something that was an edited work, we agreed to acknowledge the individual chapters and the writer who was primarily responsible for them, but the work is ours as a team. Judy led Chapters 1, 2, 7 and 12, and co-authored Chapter 5 with Bob, who also authored Chapters 6, 9, 10 and 11. Shirley authored Chapters 3, 4 and 8. However well we presented the technical elements of social media, we do believe that we shared a critical perspective, a pragmatic sense of the possibilities and limits of social media, and confidence that something important is happening, something that needs early on a critique of purpose and practice. This book represents the culmination of many years of critical discussions about public relations and its role in society. We believe that communication, through the practice of public relations, can make society more fully functioning, and a better place to live. But we also know that swords have two edges and cut both ways.

Acknowledgements

Our very sincere thanks to the many people who have contributed to this book. So many wonderful students, academic colleagues and practitioners have supported our work over the years—we are deeply appreciative of your warm generosity. We would also like to acknowledge the series editor, Kevin Moloney, who encouraged us to tackle this topic and Sinead Waldron, the editorial assistant, whose encouragement and constant assistance was invaluable. It is important for us to thank people who have contributed to our individual chapters:

Judy: Thank you so much to Dan O'Reily-Rowe who helped me get started, Kathleen Williams and Susanne Pratt for the scholarly provocations and encouragement, Madeleine my inspiring cheerleader and muse, and my beloved Tony whose complete disregard for social media served as a valuable counterbalance.

Bob: Having advised public relations students in the 1990s that the Web would be their playground, I thank those students, and colleagues, who helped make my prediction come true. Thanks also for explaining to me how social media work, and how people relate to them. Thanks to my four grandchildren, I am at the cutting edge of technological and social use among youths.

Shirley: I dedicate my contributions to this book to: Summer—who taught me all I know about social media; Jeanette, David, Ian, Dianne, Tony and Gail—for the many, wonderful dinners at which they indulged my social media obsession; Leo and Oscar—for their boundless joie de vivre; and NJ—for always seeing the possibilities.

1   Identify the problems

Social media and public relations

Social media has opened up new possibilities and raised many questions for public relations practitioners and academics. In the world of perpetually connected publics, is public relations to be a dark art that spins (or tweets) the truth for credulous publics? Or is this the time to conceptualize public relations under the full glare of the Internet and the expectations of increasingly powerful publics? These questions speak to both the continuing relevance and ethical basis of public relations. Answering them depends upon our better understanding of the fundamental shifts that social media has wrought. Such analysis also must be cautious to examine actual changes in practices and influences, and not merely get caught up in designer or practitioner promotions of what social media are and can accomplish.

The purpose of this book is to increase our understanding of the role of public relations in social media through an exploration of the myriad ways that social media is reshaping the core concepts and practices of public relations. These concepts include authenticity, power, knowledge, social capital, dialogue, relationships, sharing, meaning, risk, transparency, and truth, as they are played out in a social media contexts. Our intention is not to create a series of dialectics that pit one notion or definition against another. Instead, we seek to offer a series of problematizations and multiple theoretical insights into the implications of changes that have been driven by working in social media ecologies for public relations practice, scholarship, and pedagogy.

Problematization is a method of inquiry, interrogation and interpretation that we adopt to query how particular meanings and practices have come to dominate. The aim of problematization is to examine the "assumptions, the familiar, unchallenged, unconsidered modes of thought that we accept" (Foucault, 1988, p. 154). One such problematization is considering whether social media are just another channel or a unique channel. Also, we can muse about social media with a lens provided by Marshall McLuhan: Is social media a message or merely a medium?

A starting point for adopting problematization as our mode of inquiry and critique is questioning our ways of thinking about and making sense of the relationship between public relations and social media. Here we pose a set of questions that are designed to open up possibilities, identify vulnerabilities and examine common transgressions:

- What is the nature of the relationship between public relations and social media?
- How do power relations play out within the practices of public relations in social media?
- What are the implications of public relations practices within social media contexts for identity and relationships?
- In what ways does social media open up or reconfigure discursive possibilities for public relations?
- Does social media increase transparency or merely give it one more kaleidoscopic twist?

The potential for an improved, engaged form of public relations within social media spaces needs to be considered in conjunction with contemporary scholarship. Public relations, Heath (2001) suggested, is a rhetorical practice concerned with influencing meaning production and sense-making. Meaning oriented approaches have primarily interpreted public relations efforts as attempts to fix certain meanings and overturn others (Motion and Leitch, 1996). In contrast, relational approaches (Ferguson, 1984; Hutton, 1999; Ledingham and Bruning, 1999) have interpreted public relations as a strategic relationship building and management process. Within both of these approaches public relations is often theorized as an instrumental resource for corporate advancement; either from functionalist perspectives in which the role of public relations is understood to be about improving the effectiveness of public relations at achieving strategic goals, or from critical perspectives that aim to identify and change inequitable power relations (Trujillo and Toth, 1987). Functionalist perspectives are criticized for serving the interests of status quo, elitist power relations, falling into the trap of isolating problems from their societal contexts, and attempting to achieve a type of "scientific" certainty, which is illusory. Critical perspectives are accused of unconstructive negativity and of lacking relevance and utility for public relations practice. The problem with these generalizations is that although they capture the weaknesses of each approach, they do not acknowledge that increasingly the boundaries between these two approaches are blurring and shifting as scholars work across multiple theories and themes (Motion et al., 2013).

More recently, Heath (2010, p. 1) identified three dominant paradigms of public relations that he termed "management adjustive, discourse engagement and normative/critical/ethical." These conceptualizations of public relations, we suggest, may be usefully applied to understand the role of public relations in social media. The management adjustive paradigm takes into consideration current developments in the very dynamic nature of managerial theory and practice about organizational responsiveness to complexity and chaos. Do organizations organize to communicate or communicate to organize? An issues management approach underpins the paradigm and emphasizes a proactive philosophy that aligns multidimensional, layered and textual interests to develop mutually beneficial relationships through managerial processes and societal engagements.

Within the discourse engagement paradigm, public relations strategies are increasingly played out within engagement and participative communication processes that open up dialogic spaces and allow publics to reframe and debate salient issues (De Bussey, 2010; Hughes and Demetrious, 2006; Motion and Leitch, 2008). Key ideas that are applied within the discourse engagement paradigm include change, power relations, legitimacy, and cocreated meanings. The discourse engagement paradigm challenges the pseudoscientific promotional practices that seek to close down debate and generate acceptance or acquiescence. Engagement theory forces academics and practitioners to abandon a prevailing assumption that dominant coalitions' elites can dominate discourse processes to predetermined ends. Such linear thinking is giving way to a much more fluid paradigm that sees public relations as flow through engagement.

Within the normative/critical/ethical paradigm an emphasis is placed on the responsibilities and societal obligations of public relations and the potential for building harmony and resolving discord. A significant corpus of public relations research now focuses beyond the organization to individual, national, and societal imperatives that intersect historical, philosophical, political, cultural, technological and environmental concerns. Emergent multidisciplinary and multidimensional approaches include, for example, postmodern (Holtzhausen, 2000; McKie 2001, 2010), poststructuralist (Motion and Leitch, 2009), and postcolonial critiques (McKie and Munshi, 2007), themes of power, globalization, diversity and change (Bardhah and Weaver, 2011; Curtin and Gaither, 2007; Edwards and Hodges, 2011; Heath et al., 2010; Sriramesh and Verčič, 2009), and ethics and corporate responsibility (Cheney and Christensen, 2001; L'Etang, 1995). The guiding principles of proactive adjustment, collaborative communication, and responsible behavior that Heath (2010) identified for public relations practice also apply to participation in social media spaces. Heath's (2010) suggestion that an organization should reflectively adjust its behavior to focus on mutual interests and benefits that meet societal ideals and expectations, communicate collaboratively through discourse to develop shared meanings, and behave ethically, could form philosophical guidelines for organizations seeking to develop social media policies and open up significant possibilities for expanding what is understood as public relations and how it is practiced in these spaces.

Defining social media

Teasing out terminological distinctions and deploying current social media expressions is essential for public relations professionals, scholars and educators. Social media terminology is constantly changing as technologies evolve and practices change—what was once known as Web 2.0 or "new media" is now commonly referred to as social media or, more formally, social network sites (boyd and Ellison, 2008). The evolution of Web 2.0 into an assemblage of Internet applications that facilitate "participation, connectivity, user-generation, information sharing, and collaboration" (Henderson and Bowley, 2010) informs many of the definitions of social media. The technologies, platforms and applications that underpin social media may also be itemized to provide an integrated, inventory-oriented definition, for example:

> The notion of social media is associated with new digital media phenomena such as blogs, social networking sites, location-based services, microblogs, photo- and video- sharing sites, etc., in which ordinary users (i.e. not only media professionals) can communicate with each other and create and share content with others online through their personal networked computers and digital mobile devices.
>
> (Bechmann and Lomborg, 2013, p. 767)

The interactive, participatory characteristics of social media may prove a more useful and stable definitional feature; definitions that itemize the technologies, platforms and applications have the potential to rapidly date.

The social meaning of digital technologies, according to Stadler (2012, p. 242) is "shaped and reshaped by how they are embedded into social life" . Conversely, Castells (2009) observed that digital technologies are transforming the way that society is organized and characterized the reorganized structure as a networked society. For public relations professionals, engagement with networks that operate in a mediated space requires an understanding of networked practices and how they fit into a wider societal context (boyd, 2007). Within social media spaces users form or join networked communities to engage in social interactions and share and filter content such as textual information or conversations, photos, pictures or videos (boyd, 2007). Social media is, fundamentally, a space for connecting and conversing with people.

In addition to understanding the implications of a restructured, networked social life, public relations professionals need to take into account deinstitutionalization, user-driven content, networked interactive communities and Web 2.0 features (Bechmann and Lomborg, 2013). Media organizations no longer control content delivery and channels of distribution, a phenomenon that is referred to as deinstitutionalization. Bechmann and Lomborg (2013) explained that "most theories of social media suggest some degree of collapse or oscillation between producer and audience when users create content"—in contrast to the "media producer-text-audience model" (p. 766). As a consequence, user-created content is reconfiguring the role (and possibly power) of traditional media institutions such as print or television news organizations. The role of intermediaries has become less significant or is changing, and (as will be discussed in Chapter 4 in relation to authenticity) may actually lead publics to devalue communications as inauthentic precisely because intermediaries are involved. The sources and types of value that public relations may offer for users within deinstitutionalized social media spaces is therefore problematic. However, although the decentralized structure has impacted on traditional media, Castells (2009) notes that deinstitutionalization is only partial—social media spaces are owned and controlled by corporate social media institutions. The notion that deinstitutionalization has created an empowered user or powerful publics is therefore also open to question.

Bechmann and Lomborg (2013) distinguish between user-centric and industry centric perspectives:

> Social media are either addressed in terms *economic and socio-political value creation in an industry perspective*, that is, power, exploitation and business revenues, or in terms of *value creation as sense making in a user–centric perspective*, that is creative explorations of self and the management of social relationships in everyday life.
>
> (Bechmann and Lomborg, 2013, p. 766)

They argue that these two perspectives operate with very different conceptions of producer/user nexus, stating that, as a result, "the user is simultaneously an empowered, productive agent, and a target for companies to exploit" (Bechmann and Lomborg, 2013, p. 767). Exploitation of this duality enables public relations to continue to operate as a persuasive mechanism rather than capitalizing on the deliberative and democratic features of social media. The disparity between the ways in which public relations practitioners imagine their publics and the reality of how these publics see themselves and actually behave is another emerging issue. Rosen (2006) suggested that "the people formerly known as the audience are simply *the public* made realer, less fictional, more able, less predictable."

Contests for online presence and power have been further complicated by this dramatic shift from spectatorship to participation and the increased expectations of publics in the interactive environment of web 2.0. Castells (2009) suggested that within this era of mass self-communication the forms of power in networked society are being fundamentally transformed. Public relations content producers may have even less control than when journalists mediated their messages. Social media participants are not passive or malleable audiences. It was always a mistake to think of publics in this way but even more so in digital contexts. Online publics are not there to listen and applaud but to engage and follow their own interests (Solis, 2012). Although spin may occasionally succeed within social media spaces, we contend that overall it is an extremely risky communicative modality. Social media publics have expectations and norms about appropriate communication and have a space for voicing such expectations at volume.

Sharing, John (2013) suggests "is the fundamental and constitutive activity of Web.2.0 in general, and social network sites (SNS) in particular" (p. 167). Social media is predicated on user participation and sharing—a radical shift from traditional media-generated content and control to user-generated content, agency and influence (Jenkins et al., 2013). Thus, part of the discursive context of social media is the paradox of space that is simultaneously public and private and reconfigures power relations through sharing practices. John

(2013) explains that there are two logics of sharing—a distributive and a communicative logic—users circulate and generate content and engage in relational practices. John (2013) argues that the term "sharing" carries "positive connotations of equality, selflessness and giving" (p. 176) but that it has been co-opted by the social media industry as a rhetorical device to promote and increase participation. So it seems that by promoting social media as spaces for positive social relations—for "sharing and caring"—they have inadvertently made it very difficult for commercial promotional practices to succeed. Commercial intrusions are unwelcome, lack value and offer negligible meaningfulness for users. Public relations theory must, then, recognize and attempt to reconcile the tensions inherent in operating across organizational, public sphere and private spaces. The notion of social media as a potential avenue for distributing promotional material is very appealing for public relations professionals but it clashes with the relational practices of users.

For many users, social media is a space for presentation of the self (Goffman, 1959) that involves curation of personal information, images, feelings and emotions. While social media sites are owned for the most part by private sector organizations, they tend to be popularly regarded as either public sphere (Goldberg, 2011; Papacharissi, 2002) or personal spaces. Commercial and promotional messages are perceived as an intrusion (Marwick and boyd, 2011) and sit incongruously alongside relationship connections and self-disclosure. Although social media companies may attempt to harness the positive connotations of sharing for economic gain by monetizing user activities (John, 2013, p. 177), and while users may appear to accept and legitimate such attempts by sharing content, at the same time users resent blatant commercial intrusions within social media spaces. Herein lies the dilemma for public relations—social media participants may sometimes accept promotional content—but it is unclear how that sharing is relational in the sense of giving of oneself or equitable power relations.

Sharing carries a risk that the "relative lack of structured constraints on modes of expression may present a vulnerability to strategic behavior on the part of participants" (Stirling, 2008, p. 280). The popularity of sharing negative or activist content that goes viral makes social media a risky space for undertaking promotional efforts. (Although negative viral exposure may be also be viewed as a business opportunity for those working in crisis management!)

Public relations professionals who contravene expectations and norms by promoting commercial interests are perceived as "fake friends" which in turn gives rise to instances of identity politics, brand critique and activism along with their implications for the power relations between organizations and their publics. A "social norm of personal authenticity" (Marwick and boyd, 2011, p. 11) prevails in social media and transgressions that attempt to project an identity that is perceived as fake may be subject to exposure and identity correction by journalists, customers or activist groups such as *Anonymous* who may "occupy" or even disable sites.

Social media publics expect that authenticity and truth claims will also be balanced by communication that is creative, engaging and entertaining

(Livingstone, 2008; Marwick and boyd, 2011; Couldry, 2012). Creative content in social media frequently derives from or constitutes popular culture. The principles that underpin popular culture reflect a concern with "the everyday, the intimate, the immediate..." (Jenkins et al., 2002, p. 3). These may not be the usual concerns of public relations but in line with Jenkins's (2006) suggestion that social media has brought this layer of cultural production to the fore, cultural and social competencies for public relations in social media need to be rethought.

Working within the nexus of popular culture and social media or, what Jenkins (2006) refers to as, a "participatory culture," affords opportunities for new identities, meanings, and collaborative practices. Social media is an ideal space for what Callon et al. (2001/2009) refer to as a "dialogic democracy" in which citizens not only participate but also identify, weigh up and contribute to societal decision-making. From this perspective, the aims of public relations would be to: organize public debate; support the formation of publics and identities; explore what is at stake; generate problems and questions; and work with dynamic interests and expectations, rather than ensure that certain policies and strategies are accepted (Callon et al., 2001/2009). Moving beyond the socialization role of seeking to constitute societal norms, promote commercial practices and influence practices of the self to a more political role of deliberative, democratic communication would challenge public relations to shift from a control to a facilitative mode of communication. This shift would be marked by a reframing of who defines the issues, what may be said, who may speak, the positions from which they may speak, the viewpoints that may be presented, and the interests, stakes and institutional domains that are represented (Foucault, 1972). Understanding the forces and dynamics that underpin creativity within social media contexts and the possibilities for a more participatory and engaged form of public relations practice are pressing issues for public relations practitioners and scholars.

Such emphasis on the nature of social media can be amplified by noting its differences from "traditional" mass media. Traditional mass media are owned properties of content, channel, and process. Having editorial boards and journalistic assignments, for instance, media organizations could "determine" the news. And large, powerful corporate or governmental organizations could battle that "ownership." Public relations practitioners could ask to meet with editorial boards and even emphasize the advertising dollars that a client was spending. Standard journalism ethics and processes presumed that "both sides" of a story should be presented. If a company was being attacked, it could respond to the criticism. Journalists were supposed to be "fair and balanced," making no editorial judgments other than getting the information without bias to readers who then could make enlightened decisions.

Owned media determined whose voices were heard, how loudly, and in what ways. As did powerful corporations and trade associations with hordes of practitioners and cozy relationships (even in a battle between hacks and flacks). Governmental agencies could shape news reports and determine the salience of some issue. Governments could, especially with controlled media, present a narrative as the only one. They could prevent competing narratives, or at least do that within the media.

Social activists engaged in social movements could call for power to the people, but that often required the creation of alternative "owned" media. Whereas they championed themselves as the "voice of the people," they were presented as "agitators." That appellation marginalized alternative voices no matter how loud they were.

Social media turned that equation on its head. They not only gave voice to the often "voiceless" but they also allowed corporate, media, and governmental organizations the opportunity and challenge to "narrow" cast messages to quite small but important populations. That was due to the fact that such populations could not only voice opinions and place facts (such as pictures) into play, but they could ask questions. Web sites and then apps became locations for like-minded individuals to congregate as they might in a coffee shop.

Chapter descriptions

In the opening chapter we introduce readers to the key concepts that underpin our exploration of social media and public relations and to the challenges that arise at the intersection between these sets of concepts. We position these concepts within the evolving social media landscape and consider how public relations might also evolve and change in order to maintain relevance. In doing so, the ongoing relevance of the major public relations paradigms is brought into question (Edwards, 2012; Heath, 2010). Throughout the book we explore whether a new paradigmatic orientation—one centered on connectivity, engagement and creativity—may be required (Leitch and Motion, 2010).

Within Chapter 2 we offer a practice-oriented context for making sense of the relationship between social media and public relations focusing on the influence of social media affordances, rules and cultures on organizational attempts to navigate social media. For public relations, the diverse expressive cultures of social media represent a significant challenge to traditional power relations. The ability to manage and control discourse is seriously constrained, publics resist corporate intrusions and participatory cultures demand new modes of operating based on sharing and reciprocity. Concerns about managing social media are channeled into the creation of social media policies and provide insights into the types of sociocultural and political priorities that organizations use to open up or close down employee and citizen engagement. Analysis of a range of social media policies suggests two key strategies are at play—policies function as interdictions or as useful guidelines that establish common principles by safeguarding organizational reputation and ethical standards. Engagement and conversational principles are notably absent in the sample of policies analyzed.

Chapter 3 considers the increasing centrality of social media for communicating corporate identity and for developing the social capital associated with a particular corporate identity. The direct, personal and voluntary character of the communication between organizations and their publics that is enabled by social media stands in stark contrast to the traditional media which social media has replaced. Social media has afforded myriad new communication opportunities, such as crowdsourcing, which may be deployed to increase both social and economic capital. However, as will be discussed in later chapters, the use of social media for public relations purposes is not without significant risks and corporate identity work is no exception. Indeed, a new industry has sprung up around the need to protect corporate reputations and rescue damaged reputations from attacks that occur within social media contexts. Social media may just as easily provide a means for damaging reputations as they do for developing reputations. Despite the apparent dangers, many organizations have been slow to engage with social media. Opting out of engagement may not prove to be the wise option, especially when the conversation relates to issues of high importance to the organization.

The point of departure for Chapter 4 is that legitimating ideas by establishing the truth of certain facts or perspectives on issues or events lies at the heart of effective public relations practice. This apparently simple precept is made complex by the inherent slipperiness of the concept of truth. Additional layers of complexity are added when the concept is played out in the green fields of social media in which the rules of engagement are still largely undecided. In order to better understand what it might mean to "speak the truth" through social media, this chapter turns the spotlight on the three core dimensions of truth claims—transparency, power/knowledge and authenticity. In the light of this analysis, it becomes clear that many of our established understandings of effective or ethical practice are challenged or turned on their heads. The various national codes of conduct that govern public relations practice, which largely pre-date social media, are revealed as inadequate mechanisms to guide or regulate practice. Similarly, the diffusion of power/knowledge through networks of communication means rethinking public relations as engagement within streams of communication rather than as a centralized, controlled or even controllable activity. Indeed, the temporal shifts engendered by social media have put an end to the time-limited campaign. The enormity of this development has yet to be fully grasped by those who theorize, teach or practice public relations. The third dimension of truth claims, authenticity, is also hugely problematic for public relations. The involvement of public relations professionals in social media enables popular social media sites—which may have millions of followers—to function while at the same time, devaluing these same sites in the eyes of followers by reducing their authenticity. Truth, then, emerges from our analysis as something of a paradox.

Critiques of directional modes of conceptualizing and analyzing public relations practices form the focus of Chapter 5. The aim is to explore how organizations connect, interact and engage with social media publics. We analyze a number of public relations campaigns' social media examples that suggest one-way communication may be equally, if not more, influential in social media spaces. The analysis ranges across entertaining diversions, storytelling and conversational instances of public relations that point to the need to prioritize meaning, engagement and social impact rather than directional considerations. The chapter then broadens out to a governance-oriented discussion of public engagement principles and practices and their implications for public relations in social media. Power relations sit at the heart of this discussion and we examine how engagement techniques may be used to disrupt institutional determinism, organizational power and intentionality in order to effect social impact or change.

Chapter 6 seeks to avoid a Pollyanna approach to social media that would suggest that they are inherently a panacea to resolve personal and societal problems and fill the need for collaborative problem-solving. They have become a tool that is firmly embedded in daily lives in ways that reveal the needs for publics to engage in content production and co-production. Friends and families can connect, relationally and socioemotionally, in ways that enrich lives and strengthen social bonds. For instance, grandparents can obtain pictures, chat, and text in ways that reduce time/space distances. Thus, we might be at the brink of a global village as broad as the world and as narrowly focused as a living room or a room in a rest care facility. But, intimate details, and even video and pictures, can be used to bully and can reveal seams of discord between police and targeted groups of citizens. Is the discourse structure and content of the global village of social media, therefore, better, worse, or about the same as that of the traditional village? Does it matter whether gossip occurs at the card game, over the backyard fence, or on social media? Identities become rituals and spirals that are played out, and perhaps social media shortens time and reduces distances, but may not otherwise reshape the dynamics of the village. Strangers still come to town, and sometimes are menacing as, for instance, they lure young people to join terrorists. In such villages, rules abound and impressions are managed, as are relationships.

We then turn, in Chapter 7, to a discussion of the ways in which civil society groups may seek to open up and engage in conversations with organizations. The term "critical public engagement" is applied to describe these efforts and the various forms of resistance, popularization and politicization that civil society groups deploy to escalate controversy. Attempts to destabilize the rhetorical power and legitimacy of fossil fuel are informed by a critical discourse approach. Three key campaigns form the focus of our critique of critical public engagement: the Greenpeace campaign targeting the Lego-Shell cobranded relationship; the Tate Modern-BP sponsorship arrangement and the 350.org-led divestment campaigns. Social media functions as an alternative discursive space for dissenting voices, discursive interventions and the re-establishment of connections between particular organizations and their questionable practices.

Chapter 8 considers the major information privacy and regulation issues that arise through the use of social media. The changing configurations of communication power within social media contexts are our starting point. Social media has enabled "mass self-communication," which means that individuals with access to an Internet enabled device are able to share their ideas with the nearly 3 billion other people who have similar access (Castells, 2007). This phenomenon has been celebrated as "liberation technology" because of its enormous democratic potential (Diamond, 2010). However, social media participation occurs within the broader context of the Internet, which is itself enmeshed in a web of power relations that includes nation states, international bodies, commercial entities, activists, terrorists, and criminal networks. There is no global agreement on the regulation of the Internet or on data privacy issues that impact on the conduct of public relations through social media. In this regard, the chapter considers the Edward Snowden case at some length, due to its importance in shaping our thinking about privacy on the Internet. The Snowden case highlights four major issues for public relations practice. The first is that social media sites are almost certainly caught up in the general surveillance of Internet traffic that is being undertaken by governments. The second issue is that while social media may appear to exist "in the cloud," the physical location of servers remains an important consideration when it comes to regulation and control of the Internet. The third issue is that the data streams that feed into social media sites also pass through geographical locations where they may be subject to monitoring, control, collection and storage. The final issue highlighted by the Snowden case is that individual data may not matter as much as the aggregation of metadata, which may be used to track the relationships and communications of individuals and groups. All of these issues come into play whenever we set up a social media site and invite participation from our publics.

Risk is acknowledged as a, perhaps the, universal condition of human society and collective deliberation in Chapter 9. Concerned voices now call this a risk society, because of technology advances and related public health costs. As a tool for emergency management messaging, and as an arena to contest risk, the challenge is to determine how this medium, as a tool and message, facilitates or hinders efforts to maximize the shared gains and narrowly allotted costs of technology advance and risk-bearing. Social media, like all previous societies, allow for risk-related contacts, such as "mommy sites," and discourses that are usefully relevant to children's health, well-being, and nurturing, for instance. Organizations of all types have participated in such discourse, but it seems to be driven by individuals (and communities of interest) who shape the discourse to fit their self-interests, altruism, and identities. As such, social media may become risk management empowering. Advocates can put messages, about organic foods, for instance, into the public arena in ways that bypass and confound corporate interests that would prefer that such topics are not made the subject of public discussion. Such discourse can keep alive the dynamics of the precautionary principle which presumes that if unintended consequences are not well known, and controlled for, then caution is preferred as a brake on change management. Social media may make such discourse more authentic because it is less subject to power/knowledge control.

Chapter 10 wrestles with the notion of competing zones of meaning and the tangles of deliberative democracy which continue to be a work in progress.

The years after World War II are especially important because this was an era of social change and technological advances, of which the computer—first used for naval gunnery and code breaking—was one. Issues are contested as a foment and discourse for social and public policy change. Issues became the grist of power/ knowledge debates that occur increasingly in cyberspace. Advocacy could be seen as democratized since social media allowed for more voices to enter the issue discourse arenas. Public relations became more issue oriented and rhetorically engaged. The dynamics of legitimacy became far more apparent, are widely debated, and subjected to discourse variety. Thus, in such discourse, minds and senses of reality changed, individuals' identities became more cluttered and uncertain, and society became increasingly entrenched zones of meaning. A key question is persistently seeking answer: Have societies advanced along the lines of what experts call deliberative democracy, or is all of that clatter merely a tangle of friendly and faux voices? As much as some favor a progressive interpretation of current events, others await the pudding to see what it proves.

The tensions between public and private arenas as a space where users play in cyberspace feature in Chapter 11. In this arena, or arenas, clashes occur between individuals, as well as spokespersons who advocate on behalf of corporate, nonprofit (including NGOs), and governmental organizations. As much as individuals might believe this space is democratic, it may be rigged against interests, even large segments of a population. The paradox of the private and public is such that they often blur because what was shared in private can quickly become public, in matters of social change management. Likewise, that which is presumed to be public can become reshaped for the interest of power segments. As much as that is a factor in the rage that occurs that seeks to foment social movement agitation, it also relates to texting, bullying, and sexting. Attacks on authority can boomerang. Agitators' plans, made ostensibly in private, can quickly become public, allowing for authority backlash. Incentives to collaborate can be reshaped to support power interests, seemingly advanced on behalf of the "people." Community, even that on social media, can become a pawn of public policy decision-making. Thus, the tensions of public and private reveals the seams in society that result from power struggles in all other communicative infrastructures. Social media, in terms of public policy battles, are not a panacea but a playing ground.

Our ambition with this writing project was to open up diverse possibilities for critically problematizing and theorizing the relationship between public relations and social media. Social media, as an assemblage of discursive spaces, poses significant challenges for an industry that has traditionally pushed its messages into the ether. Navigating the cultural transformation that social media has shaped highlights the tensions between the promotional culture of public relations and the participatory cultures of social media. Very different power relations circulate within social media that demand truth, authenticity and meaningful engagement. Institutional determinism is destabilized and the discursive power of organizations is disrupted and redistributed in ways that are not always predictable or even positive. Ultimately, our vision for the future of public relations in social media is democratic—an embrace of participatory politics and the possibilities for positive social change that have equity as a fundamental value.

References

Bardhah, N. and Weaver, C.K. (eds) (2011). *Public Relations in Global Cultural Contexts: Multi-Paradigmatic Perspectives*. New York: Routledge.

Bechmann, A. and Lomborg, S. (2013). Mapping actor roles in social media: Different perspectives on value creation in theories of user participation. *New Media & Society*, 15(5), 765–781.

Beck, U. (1986/1992). *Risk Society: Towards a New Modernity*. London: Sage.

Belanger, F. and Crossler, R. (2011). Privacy in the digital age: A review of information privacy research in information systems. *MIS Quarterly*, 35(4), 1017–1041.

boyd, d. (2007). Social Network Sites: Public, Private, or What? *Knowledge Tree* 13, May. http://kt.flexiblelearning.net.au/tkt2007/?page_id=28.

boyd, d. and Ellison, N. B. (2008). Social network sites: Definition, history, and scholarship. *Journal of Computer Mediated Communication*, 13(1), 210–230.

Callon, M., Lascoumes, P., and Barthe, Y. (2001/2009). *Acting in an Uncertain World: An Essay on Technical Democracy*, Trans. G. Burchell. Cambridge, Ma: MIT Press.

Castells, M. (2007). Communication, power and counter-power in the network society. *International Journal of Communication*, 1(1), 238–266.

Castells, M. (2009). *Communication Power*. Oxford: Oxford.

Cheney, G. and Christensen, L.T. (2001). Public relations as contested terrain: A critical response. In R.L. Heath (ed.), *Handbook of Public Relations*. Thousand Oaks, CA: Sage, pp. 167–182.

Couldry, N. (2012). *Media, Society, World: Social Theory and Digital Media Practice*. Cambridge: Polity.

Curtin, P.A. and Gaither, T.K. (2007). *International Public Relations: Negotiating Culture, Identity, and Power*. Thousand Oaks, CA: Sage.

Davies, S. (1977). Re-engineering the right to privacy: How privacy has been transformed from a right to a commodity. In P. Agre and M. Rotenberg (eds.). *Technology and Privacy: The New Landscape*, pp. 143–165. Cambridge, MA: MIT Press.

De Bussy, N. (2010). Dialogue as a Basis for Stakeholder Engagement: Defining and Measuring the Core Competencies. In R.L. Heath (ed.), *The Sage Handbook of Public Relations* (2nd ed.). Thousand Oaks, CA: Sage, pp. 127–144.

Diamond, L. (2010). Liberation technology. Journal of Democracy, 21(3), 69–83.

DiStaso, M. and Bortree, D. (2012). Multi-method analysis of transparency in social media practices: survey, interview and content analysis. *Public Relations Review*, 38, 511–514.

DiStaso, M., McCorkindale, T., and Wright, D. (2011). How public relations executives perceive and measure the impact of social media in their organizations. *Public Relations Review*, 37, 325–328.

Edwards, L. (2011). Public relations and society: A Bourdieuvian perspective. In L. Edwards and C. Hodges (eds.). *Public Relations, Society and Culture: Theoretical and Empirical Explorations*, pp. 61–74. London and New York: Routledge.

Edwards, L. (2012). Defining the "object" of public relations research: A new starting point. *Public Relations Inquiry*, 1(1), 7–30.

Edwards, L. and Hodges, C.E.M. (eds) (2011). *Public Relations, Society and Culture: Theoretical and Empirical Explorations*. Oxford, UK: Routledge.

Elmer, P. (2011). Public relations and storytelling. In L. Edwards and C. Hodges (eds.). *Public Relations, Society and Culture: Theoretical and Empirical Explorations*, pp. 47–60. London and New York: Routledge.

Fairclough, N. (1992). *Discourse and Social Change.* Cambridge: Polity Press.

Fairclough, N. (1995). *Critical Discourse Analysis.* Boston: Addison Wesley.

Ferguson, M.A. (1984). Building theory in public relations: Interorganizational relationships as a public relations paradigm. Paper presented to the Public Relations Division, Association for Education in Journalism and Mass Communication Annual Convention, August, Gainesville, FL.

Foucault, M. (1972). *The Archaeology of Knowledge* (A. M. Sheridan Smith, trans.). London: Routledge.

Foucault, M. (1988). Technologies of the self. In L. Martin, H. Gutman, and P. Hutton (eds.). *Technologies of the Self: A Seminar with Michel Foucault*, pp. 16–48. Amherst: University of Massachusetts.

Goffman, E. (1959). *The Presentation of Self in Everyday Life.* New York: Doubleday.

Goldberg, G. (2011). Rethinking the public/virtual sphere: The problem with participation. *New Media and Society*, 13(5), 739–754.

Green, A. (2010). *Creativity in Public Relations.* London: Kogan Page.

Heath, R. L. (ed.) (2001). A rhetorical enactment rationale for public relations: The good organization communicating well. In *Handbook of public relations*, pp. 31–50. Thousand Oaks, CA: Sage.

Heath, R.L. (ed.) (2010). Mind, self, society. In *The Sage Handbook of Public Relations*, pp. 1–4. Thousand Oaks, CA: Sage.

Heath, R. and Palenchar, M. (2008). *Strategic Issues Management.* Sage.

Heath, R.L., Motion, J., and Leitch, S. (2010). Power and public relations: Paradoxes and programmatic thoughts. In R.L. Heath (ed.), *The Sage Handbook of Public Relations* (2nd ed.), pp. 191–204. Thousand Oaks, CA: Sage.

Henderson, A. and Bowley, R. (2010). Authentic dialogue? The role of "friendship" in a social media recruitment campaign. *Journal of Communication Management*, 14(3), 237–257.

Holtzhausen, D. R. (2000). Postmodern values in public relations. *Journal of Public Relations*, 12(1), 93–114.

Hughes, P. and Demetrious, K. (2006). Engaging with stakeholders or constructing them? Attitudes and assumptions in stakeholder software. *Journal of Corporate Citizenship*, 23, 93–101.

Hutton, J.G. (1999) The definition, dimensions and domain of public relations. *Public Relations Review*, 25(2), 199–214.

Ibrahim, Y. (2008). The new risk communities: Social networking sites and risk. *International Journal of Media and Cultural Politics*, 4(2), 245–253.

Jenkins, H. (2006). *Convergence Culture: Where Old and New Media Collide.* New York: New York University Press.

Jenkins, H., McPherson, T., Shattuc, J., and Durham, N.C. (2002). *Hop on Pop: The Politics and Pleasures of Popular Culture.* Durham: Duke University Press.

Jenkins, H., Ford, S., and Green, J. (2013). *Spreadable Media: Creating Value and Meaning in a Networked World.* New York: New York University Press.

John, N.A. (2013). Sharing and Web 2.0: The emergence of a keyword. *New Media & Society*, 1461444812450684.

Jordan, J. (2005) A virtual death and a real dilemma: Identity, trust, and community in cyberspace. *Southern Communication Journal*, 70(3), 200–218.

Ledingham, J.A. and Bruning, S.D. (1999). Relationship management in public relations: Dimensions of an organization-public relationship. *Public Relations Review*, 24(1), 55–65.

Leitch, S. and Neilson, D. (2000). Bringing publics into public relations: New theoretical frameworks for practice. In R. Heath. (ed.). *Handbook of Public Relations*. Thousand Oaks, CA: Sage.

Leitch, S. and Motion, J. (2010). Publics and public relations: Effecting change. In R. Heath (ed.). *The Sage Handbook of Public Relations*. Thousand Oaks, CA: Sage.

L'Etang, J. (1995). Ethical corporate social responsibility: A framework for managers. *Journal of Business Ethics*, 14(2), 125–132.

Livingstone, S. (2008). Taking risky opportunities in youthful content creation: teenagers' use of social networking sites for intimacy, privacy and self-expression. *New Media and Society*. 10(3), 393–411.

Marwick, A. and boyd, d. (2011). I tweet honestly, I tweet passionately: Twitter users, context collapse and the imagined audience. *New Media and Society*, 13(1), 114–133.

McKie, D. (2001). Updating public relations: "New science" research paradigms, and uneven developments. In R. Heath (ed.), *Handbook of Public Relations*. Thousand Oaks, CA: Sage, pp. 75–91.

Mckie, D. and Munshi, D. (2007.) *Reconfiguring Public Relations: Ecology, Equity and Enterprise*. Oxford, UK: Routledge.

Motion, J. and Leitch, S. (1996). A discursive perspective from New Zealand: Another world view. *Public Relations Review*, 22(3), 297–309.

Motion, J. and Leitch, S. (2007). A toolbox for public relations: The oeuvre of Michal Foucault. *Public Relations Review*, 33, 263–268.

Motion, J. and Leitch, S. (2008). The multiple discourses of science-society engagement. *Australian Journal of Communication*, 35(3), 29–40.

Motion, J. and Leitch, S. (2009). On Foucault: A toolbox for public relations. In O. Ihlen, B. van Ruler, and M. Fredriksson (eds), *Public Relations and Social Theory: Key Figures and Concepts*. New York: Routledge, pp. 83–102.

Motion J., Davenport S., Leitch S., Merlot L. (2013). Corporate Reputation and the Discipline of Public Relations. In C. Carroll (Ed.), The Handbook of Communication and Corporate Reputation, pp. 62-71. Chichester: Wiley-Blackwell.

Papacharissi, Z. (2002). The virtual sphere: The internet as a public sphere. *New Media and Society*, 4(1), 9–27.

Rosen, J. (2006). The people formerly known as the audience. Press Think. Retrieved 1 September 2015 from http://archive.pressthink.org/2006/06/27/ppl_frmr.html

Solis, B. (2012). *The End of Business as Usual*. New Jersey: Wiley.

Sriramesh, K. and Verčič, D. (eds) (2009) The Global Public Relations Handbook: Theory, Research and Practice (2nd ed.). New York: Routledge.

Stadler, F. (2012). Between democracy and spectacle: The front end and back end of the social web. In M. Mandiberg (ed.). *The Social Media Reader*, pp. 242–256. New York: New York University Press.

Stirling, A. (2008). "Opening up" and "closing down" power, participation, and pluralism in the social appraisal of technology. *Science, technology & human values*, 33(2), 262-294.

Trilling, L. (1971). Sincerity and Authenticity. Cambridge, MA: Harvard University Press.

Trujillo, N. and Toth, E.L. (1987). Organizational perspectives for public relations research and practice. *Management Communication Quarterly*, 1(2), 199–281.

Verhoeven, P., Tench, R., Zerfass, A., and Vercic, D. (2012). How European PR practitioners handle digital and social media. *Public Relations Review*, 38, 162–164.

2 "Don't do anything stupid"

Social media affordances, policies, and governance agendas

The unmanageable nature of social media interactivity and sharing acts as a deterrent for organizations that need or want to very carefully manage their communication and avoid potential controversy. An understanding of the utility or communicative practices of various platforms—commonly referred to as affordances (Treem and Leonardi, 2012)—is essential for the development of a social media profile and an appreciation of the role that social media policies may play in the governance of social media participation. The chapter opens with an overview of the affordances of various social media platforms, followed by an analysis of the purpose of social media policies and a discussion of social media policy controversies.

Social media affordances

It is important to note that social media does not refer to a type of technology; rather, it reflects the *use* of technologies. As boyd and Ellison (2007) note, while "key technological features" of social networking sites "are fairly consistent, the cultures that emerge around [them] are varied" (p. 201). The challenge, then, is not only to understand the use of these networks or platforms—it is also to understand the types of cultures that shape and are shaped by participation in various sites. The reasons and purposes behind social networking sites also vary:

> Most sites support the maintenance of pre-existing social networks, but others help strangers connect based on shared interests, political views, or activities. Some sites cater to diverse audiences, while others attract people based on common language or shared racial, sexual, religious, or nationality-based identifies. Sites also vary in the extent to which they incorporate new information and communication tools such as mobile, connectivity, blogging, and photo/video-sharing.
>
> (boyd and Ellison 2007, p. 210)

Consequently, social networking sites can mirror interactions that exist outside of social media. Thus, while new connections can be made between individuals and groups, it is more likely that many social network interactions are between those who are already familiar with one another. The term "social networking sites" serves as a reminder that the key functions of social media are relational and conversational.

Social (and mobile) media are integral to contemporary communication. Mobile devices and phones in particular are sites of cultural production and consumption that enable us enact and interpret our worlds (Goggin, 2006). The ubiquitous nature of social media—what boyd (2012) refers to as an "always-on lifestyle"—is driving a cultural transformation that is disrupting traditional relationships between public relations and society. The danger, for public relations, is that it may end up simply talking to the ether (or itself) if the affordances of various platforms are not well understood and the complexities and challenges of various expressive cultures are not appreciated. The affordances of each platform or network, as well as the cultures associated with them, are contrasted with public relations objectives and explained below.

Social networks

A social network is a web site for building social relations among people who share interests, activities and connections. Facebook, for example, allows for users to create a profile, update their "status" which involves broadcasting links or personal information to their friends, add friends and share networks they are a part of, communicate with others, share media, and engage with brands and organizations through groups and "pages." Individual's Facebook pages are a way to stay in touch with friends, upload photographs, and share information and links with their networks. Within social networks, cultures of connecting, messaging, and sharing predominate. Sociality—or relationship maintenance—was a founding principle for social networks—but teens report that they are now more likely to use social media for connecting and messaging (A teenager's view on social media, 2015).

Examples

Facebook, Google+

Strengths

Social networks offer an important opportunity for individuals and organizations to increase communication reach. An ongoing presence can allow organizations to build customer loyalty and advocacy as well as drive traffic to "owned" platforms such as web sites. Social network sharing can also improve organizations' search presence through direct and indirect links.

Bortee and Seltzer (2009) claim that social networking sites have the potential to "produce positive outcomes such as increasing the number of stakeholders who interact with the organization by growing the organization's social network" (p. 318), particularly in instances where the organization initiates dialogue. Consequently, while uploading content, and maintaining existing content is important to the success of a presence on Facebook, so too is utilizing multimedia to stimulate conversation. Moreover, the importance of having the content on a Facebook page moderated and maintained ensures not only that stakeholders are publicly engaged with, but also that unrelated or unnecessary content can be removed in a timely manner.

Weaknesses

Key challenges are that social networks are owned by third party media organizations and that the driving rationale for social media networks is to monetize their investments. For general users, algorithms designed by the social media corporations determine how newsfeeds occur, based on a complex mix of mediatized, promotional and personal content. Individuals and organizations have to comply with the rules of a network or risk deletion if the rules are transgressed. It also means that the rules may change over time. Social networks require constant presence and resources to create the content expected by a community. As there is an assumption that these networks are staffed 24/7, a stream of complaints about the organization that would normally be resolved in private, may rapidly become public and can create an element of negative backlash if a network is not monitored. A delay in responding to questionable content on an organization's Facebook page has the potential to create controversy. Facebook pages can also be subject to "trolling"—a term that refers to the act of individuals or organized groups deliberately hijacking or diverting the purpose of a page by posting controversial or malicious comments. For example, in 2010, animal rights activist group PETA (People for the Ethical Treatment of Animals) organized Facebook users to post on fashion designer Donna Karan's Facebook page (PETA, 2014). The users changed their profile picture (the avatar for their account) to a letter and posted in a sequence that would spell out "DK BUNNY BUTCHER" in reference to Donna Karan's use of fur in their garments. Screenshots (images of the webpage) were shared widely, and still appear on PETA's web site along with a video titled "Donna Karan Bunny Butcher" (PETA, 2014). The updates from users sparked conversation and debate between Donna Karan's fans on Facebook.

Microblogging

A microblog is a type of web service that allows users to publish a short text message, updates or converse. The expressive cultures of microblogs often emulate fandom cultures—there are those who lead the conversation and those who follow—and the interactions may be instantaneous, brief and random. More recently, however, concerns about negativity—from complaints to abusive cyberbullying—within some microblog cultures has gained attention and signaled the need for greater governance of social media. These issues are, of course, not restricted to microblogging but recent Twitter cases have been particularly serious (Topping, 2014). Responses to abusive behavior include prosecution, public shaming, sharing, and even reporting the offenders to their mothers (True, 2014). Although flagging is the most common technical mechanism for reporting offensive content to an online platform, Crawford and Gillespie (2014) have called for greater public deliberation as a mechanism of governing negative cultures and behaviors.

Examples

Twitter, Sina Weibo (China)

Strengths

Microblog engagements may be quick and easy and become more conversational in nature due to the limited character allowance. Twitter, for example, is a microblogging service that allows users to post updates of 140 characters or less. Users "follow" other users in order to subscribe to their updates, and on their homepage they will receive their own updates of a stream of all the other Twitter users they subscribe to. Twitter is commonly used via a social media management "dashboard" (on either mobile or desktop devices) such as Hootsuite that allows greater customization of Twitter's appearance and may enable users to integrate their social media networks.

Twitter may be used to communicate with other individuals, organizations or companies or to "the public at large" (boyd et al., 2010: 1). Users follow individual's conversations rather than topic feeds, resulting in a nonlinear representation of discussions. As Twitter feeds also update in real time, the updates in a conversation may be asynchronous. Many discussions may occur at once (boyd et al., 2010) and conversations do not need to be directly participated in by users.

An important element of the use of Twitter that is unique is "retweeting." Retweeting is a term to describe the facility to share or "retweet" another user's update. This can be achieved without the user having any relationship to the user of the original tweet. For organizations, retweeting is often the goal, as it can have a far reach outside of the account's followers:

> While retweeting must be seen as the act of copying and rebroadcasting, the practice contributes to a conversational ecology in which conversations are composed of a public interplay of voices that give rise to an emotional sense of shared conversational context. For this reason, some of the most visible Twitter participants retweet others and look to be retweeted. This includes users of all kinds, but notably marketers, celebrities and politicians.
>
> (boyd et al., 2010: 1)

Common examples of what people retweet can include an opinion they agree with, a call for information, something humorous, or for "social action" (boyd et al., 2010: 7). Retweeting is most effective when the retweeter is broadcasting to a large network, or is attempting to draw together disparate groups—however, users are most likely to retweet information that is similar to topics they already tweet about and to their notions of "self-image and self-promotion" (boyd et al., 2010: 7).

Crawford (2009) explains that listening is integral to the uses and popularity of Twitter and that users do not only post information, they use Twitter as constant "noise" in the background, choosing to pay greater detail at various times. Crawford (2009) identifies three ways that corporations might usefully employ listening in their social media presence on Twitter:

> being seen to participate in a community and hearing people's opinions; utilizing a rapid and lower-cost form of customer support (as opposed to the telephones); and gaining a dispersed global awareness of how a brand is discussed and the patterns of consumer use and satisfaction.
>
> (pp. 531–532)

Facebook and Twitter may be used as "giant focus groups" (Crawford, 2009, p. 352), where both negative and positive criticisms are taken into account. Twitter may be useful for organizations to participate in community dialogue.

Three broad categories of Twitter users may be identified: "*information sources* post news and tend to have a large base of 'followers'," "*friends* is a broad category that encompasses most users, including family, co-workers and strangers," and "*information seekers* tend to be users who may post rarely but who follow others regularly"(Honeycutt and Herring, 2009). The dissemination and consumption of news forms an important part of the use of Twitter, and is a reason for following particular users and the content that they post.

Like the major social networks, microblogging services can improve an organization's search engine optimization (SEO), particularly in the short term around events, news, etc. and drive traffic to an organization's owned media

Weaknesses

Microblogs have limited value in conveying complicated ideas because message content is restricted to 140 characters. Messages may also have a limited "top of mind" lifespan because once they have left the feed, they are forgotten.

Video services

Video-hosting or sharing web sites allow users to upload, view, post comments and share video content.

Examples

YouTube, Vimeo, Vine, Instagram

Strengths

Video sharing services may be considered social media because they offer interactive and dialogical opportunities. YouTube is a mass-market video sharing service whereas Vimeo and Vine (a Twitter-owned service) are considered niche and creative. Instagram is a more recent video and photo sharing service now owned by Facebook. YouTube is the second largest search engine globally and thus has a large pre-existing audience interested in consuming content. All of the video-sharing web sites have well-established mobile platforms—Vine, Vimeo and Instagram are mobile-designed applications and YouTube has now established a successful mobile platform. YouTube, and to an extent Vine, are high word of mouth channels, with YouTube videos being shared sustainably across other social platforms. YouTube was launched in 2005 primarily as an entertainment and educational video-sharing site. There are many uses for YouTube including as an archive, a place to watch teasers and trailers for upcoming releases, to watch amateur created content, and to watch music videos (Burgess and Green, 2009; Hilderbrand, 2007). Since its launch, YouTube has become the primary site to watch videos or to share content with friends or strangers. As with most social media sites, YouTube serves entirely disparate purposes for its producers and consumers. Its content is varied and its users vary from being part of a community, to being a user who watches videos and never logs in.

YouTube can be considered social media as it involves interaction, and the blurring of the boundaries between producer and consumer (Müller, 2009: 126). Interaction is built into YouTube's architecture; users are able to rate a video (this has changed over time from a "star" ranking to a "thumbs up/down" function), they are able to comment on the video, and the views that a video receives (often through sharing) will impact on the video's popularity and the ease with which it is found.

Burgess and Green (2009) examined the most popular videos uploaded to YouTube and identified that YouTube is not only a repository for video content—the ability to participate has been integral to YouTube's success. YouTube hosts both amateur and professionally made content that anyone may comment on and interact with.

Hilderbrand (2007) argues that YouTube is a "portal of cultural memory" in its culture of archiving and sharing past clips. But just as YouTube may function as a place to share and store videos, it is also a site for parody and criticism. As Müller (2009) notes, it is common practice on YouTube to critique the content and the technical ability demonstrated in video clips. Videos may become popular on YouTube because they are being mocked, rather than enjoyed.

In contrast, both Vimeo and Vine are considered niche sites where people share creative ideas and form communities. Vimeo is particularly focused on creative, high quality videos but offers less visibility, whereas Vine has short creative clips—no longer than six seconds. Instagram offers a 15-second video duration.

Weaknesses

Original video content can be expensive to create when compared to other social activities. Vine provides limited video duration of 6 seconds, Instagram is 15 seconds duration and Vimeo limits the amounts of videos that may be uploaded each week.

Professional networking

A professional network is a service that is focused on business interactions and relationships.

Examples

LinkedIn

Strengths

Professional networking services such as LinkedIn offer individuals an opportunity to invite others who share professional business interests to join their network. LinkedIn may be used by individuals to curate professional contact details, communicate with their network, engage in self-promotion and endorse their own or other networked members' products, brands or organization. LinkedIn claims to have 300+ million members in over 200 countries and territories (LinkedIn, 2014), which makes it a very useful mechanism for promoting business-to-business products and internal communications. It is possible to buy targeted contact lists and use networks as a type of database to conduct surveys. LinkedIn is a more professional environment which means that there is far less negative sentiment and users are more professional in general.

Weaknesses

LinkedIn has a limited user base compared to Facebook or YouTube. There may be limited engagement because people are conscious of their personal professional brand and often prefer to share minimally rather than say the wrong thing.

Photo services

Photo services are online, mobile social networking services for sharing visual images (photos and videos). Instagram has a number of affordances that appeal to youth cultures in particular—there is more control over the newsfeeds, it is less commercialized, higher quality and more focused on content (A teenager's view on social media, 2015).

Examples

Pinterest, Instagram, Flickr

Strengths

Both Pinterest and Instagram provide a visual platform for quick and easy photo sharing that is increasingly used by marketers to create brand awareness and promote products. Pinterest functions as a type of noticeboard for discovering, "pinning" up, and curating other users' content—so it is a valuable tool for business to business marketing. The key demographic is women. Although the Pinterest focus is collecting and collating content, Instagram is a more traditional platform for users to share original visual content. Pictures taken via mobile devices may be uploaded via Instagram to create brand awareness and promote products. Instagram uses hashtags in the same way that Twitter does for users to follow trends and topics, so it allows captions and may be useful for event support.

Weaknesses

Visual platforms require continual image content to remain active. Instagram is currently quite siloed from owned media channels. Neither platform has the volume seen on Facebook.

Bookmarking and aggregation sites

Recommendation-based news, entertainment and social networking services.

Examples

StumbleUpon, Reddit

Strengths

When content is relevant and shared by users high media value accrues. Reddit can be used to start a movement or bring a celebrity to an audience, particularly around launches. The lack of overt brand influence gives these types of platforms an authenticity that can sometimes be lacking elsewhere.

Weaknesses

Aggregation sites do not take kindly to overt marketing so it may be risky for public relations to use these sites.

Apps (applications)

"Apps" is an abbreviation of "application" software. Although apps are generally understood to be information retrieval or entertainment computer programs designed for mobile devices, apps may also offer social networking opportunities. The advantage of custom designed apps is that they offer tailored functionality and may integrate connectivity. Mobile applications help users by connecting them to Internet services quickly, provide customized information and marketing and public relations opportunities. Apps, Goggin (2011) suggests, have constituted an important new platform, or area, for cultural development and innovation. Thus Goggin (2011) argues that "there needs to be scrutiny of the terms upon which culture circulates in the apps arena, what kinds of power relations exist and what kinds of freedom are permitted" (p. 155).

Examples

Google maps, Skype, TripAdvisor

Expressive participatory cultures

An understanding of social media as a range of discourse arenas with particular affordances and expressive cultures has significant implications for public relations. Particular cultures have discursive expectations, norms and implicit boundaries that limit the possibilities for promotion or politics. Compounding this challenge are the complexities inherent in the shared identities, meaning creation and sense-making systems, and power relations of expressive cultures and networks. Public relations interventions in social media encounter a number of risks—they may be perceived as unwelcome intrusions and be subject to public attack. There is also the risk that public relations representatives may misjudge what is acceptable. There is an inherent clash, we suggest, between the promotional culture of public relations that seeks to advance client interests and the participatory cultures of social media. Public relations has survived and thrived in traditional media because it supplies content for news organizations—however, in user-driven social media milieu the value of public relation is less obvious. A key challenge for public relations is to determine what it has to offer and how to participate in social media. Business as usual may be adequate for "owned" social media spaces but public relations has few strategic options in the public, culturally constituted, discursive arenas of social media. Within these arenas the ability to manage and/or control discourse is severely restricted. Social media users' explorations of contemporary issues and practices shape the platforms they participate in as particular cultural zones of meanings with their own social order. As a consequence, promotional activities that do not comply with the norms of shared zones of meaning are likely to be resisted. Fundamental shifts in power relations are taking place within social media that place social networks at the heart of our online lives and provide marginalized or less powerful voices with a forum for expression (Jenkins et al., 2013). Publics are assuming power and actively shaping the ways in which sociality plays out in social media networks and communities. Many publics are also advocating for equity and democracy as part of a broader cultural transformation that has significant implications for public relations. New modes of operating and sensitivities to diverse values are called for as public relations practitioners traverse diverse social media platforms and engage with multiple individuals, networks, organizations and communities. Regulation of public relations practices in social media milieu are also critical for meaningful engagement with empowered, expressive, social media cultures.

Social media policies

Social media policies are designed to establish organizational communication priorities and principles, and to regulate the online communication practices of organizational members. For organizations that have concerns about the unmanageable and sometimes uncontrollable nature of social media, well-designed social media policies provide a measure of reassurance and establish governance mechanisms for assigning responsibility and accountability. From a critical public relations perspective, social media policies provide insights into how organizations attempt to manage how they are perceived and the communication practices they favor. Broader communication and media agendas underpin policy documents and prescribe how meaning production and circulation are to be coordinated, how power relations are to be navigated and negotiated, and how organizational identities are to be shaped and policed.

In this chapter we examine a range of social media policies from media organizations and public relations firms in order to identify the communication philosophies that drive the governance of social media and the potential vulnerabilities organizations seek to mitigate. As a starting point for our critique, we undertook a thematic analysis of the social media policies. The social media policies were selected on the basis of the availability and the international profile of the organizations. This purposive sampling method is not intended to be generalizable; it is intended to open up analysis and critique of how social media policies act as governance mechanisms and/or strategies for facilitating conversation and engagement. In doing so, we highlight the modes of governance, surveillance, regulation, engagement or normalization that play out in such policies. We are particularly interested in understanding how social media issues are framed within policy documents, the principles, priorities, rules and norms that underpin preferred modes of communication, the expectations relating to the navigation of personal and professional boundaries, and the types of conditions that facilitate or restrict agency. Fundamental questions that we ask in relation to our analysis of social media policies include: "What do these policies mean?"; "What is at stake here?"; "Whose interests are being served?"; and "Do these policies open up or close down discursive possibilities?"

A generic guideline

The first policy-related document we discuss is an open-source, social media disclosure toolkit. Social media.org, a "brands-only" membership organization for corporations that represent client brands with at least US$1 billion in revenue, offers a toolkit of checklists to help member organizations educate their employees on how to interact with the social media community and to comply with the law. The toolkit was originally designed in 2008 and continuously evolves with feedback and participation (see Social Media.org, nd) The fundamental considerations for organizations to "stay safe" ethically and legally, according to the Social Media.org Disclosure Best Practices Toolkit, are as follows:

1   Require disclosure and truthfulness in social media outreach
2   Monitor the conversation and correct misstatements
3   Create social media policies and training programs.

A series of checklists is provided to assist organizations to develop social media policies, create a training tool, and establish a baseline of best practices. Best practice advice and guidelines are offered that relate to truthfulness and honesty in all social media communications; techniques for navigating the boundaries between personal and professional social media participation; open disclosure; and strategies for proactive ethical and legal compliance in outreach campaigns. Checklists for monitoring social media outreach and responding to misstatements are also included. Creative flexibility in artistic situations is supported in the suggestion that "delay," but not dishonesty, in disclosure may be acceptable for creative freedom; however, a number of conditions are stipulated. The document concludes with a series of general best practice guidelines for creating an "atmosphere of ethical, transparent disclosure" (Social Media.org, nd). Principles that underpin the prescriptive character of the guidelines are clearly oriented towards ethical and legal compliance and protecting the public interest. The toolkit/checklists offer a practical set of suggestions and questions that may be applied to assist in the development of a social media policy.

Code of ethics or corporate reputation?

Many media organizations tend to open their social media policies with a reference to the organization's code of ethics, professional conduct or news values and principles. For example, the Associated Press (AP), which is an independent, nonprofit news co-op owned by 1400 American newspapers (Associated Press, 2012), opened its policy document with a statement that the guidelines are based on the AP "Statement of News Values and Principles." From the outset the policy established the importance of ethical and professional standards. The stated purpose of the policy is to "advance the AP's brand and employees' personal brands on social networks" (Associated Press, 2012).

Emphasis on brand advancement suggests a concern with corporate identity, reputation and commercial imperatives. Employees are reminded that "staffers may not express opinions on controversial issues of the day," a proviso to safeguard the reputation of AP as an independent, neutral news source.

The notion that social media policy should be ethically based was echoed in the *Los Angeles Times* blog titled *Readers' Representative Journal* (Times updates social media guidelines, 2009). In a very recent revision of the Ethics Guidelines the stated objective is to reflect "a principled news organization" that is "above reproach" (*Los Angeles Times* Ethics Guidelines, 2014). Employees were reminded that although methods may change, standards do not and that the ethics guidelines provided the statement of principles and standards.

In contrast, Reuters, an international news agency owned by Thomson Reuters, states that "we are committed to aggressive journalism in all its forms including the field of computer assisted reporting, but we draw the line at illegal behavior" (Reporting from the internet and using social media, 2013). This statement is striking in its openness about the competitive approach. It is however, tempered by the following statement, "internet reporting is nothing more than applying the principles of sound journalism to the sometimes unusual situations thrown up in the virtual world. The same standards of sourcing, identification and verification apply" (Reporting from the internet and using social media, 2013). The statement implies that breaking the news is the first priority, to be followed by journalistic standards. CNN's "policy regarding personal writings online" (Sheila, 2008) states that most important to remember is "unless given permission by CNN management, CNN employees are to avoid taking public positions on the issues and people and organizations on which we report" (Sheila, 2008). Here the priority is media neutrality.

The social media policies of many international public relations organizations were not publicly available on their own web sites but a web site titled Social Media Governance (http://socialmediagovernance.com/policies/) provided access to a selection which we have analyzed. Hill and Knowlton Strategies, which was founded over 80 years ago, describes its role as strategic communications rather than public relations, and claims to be one of the world's largest communications groups with over 87 international offices. Hill and Knowlton Strategies have a number of social media policies including "Blogging policies and guidelines"; a "Collective conversation code of conduct"; and "Personal use of media" principles. Although the reference to collective conversations in the title indicates an understanding of the shifts that social media has wrought, the code of conduct covers the following topics: criticizing clients or colleagues, respecting other opinions, breaching your employment contract, acknowledging and correcting mistakes, preserving the original post, deleting comments disclosing conflicts of interests, accuracy, linking and deleting posts. These are important journalistic and ethical considerations—but they do not take into account or embody conversational considerations such as sharing, listening, turn taking that moderate power relations and the cultural contexts that influence meaning production and sense-making. Hill & Knowlton's blogging policies and guidelines document opens with the following statement:

> Hill & Knowlton views personal websites and weblogs (blogs) positively. Blogs are powerful tools that are influencing reputation. They form part of some much wider changes taking place in online media that will increasingly affect our business and our clients brands. By experimenting with the medium—personally or on behalf of the company—our staff will learn more and be able to advise our clients better and more credibly.
>
> (Blogging policies and guidelines, 2005)

The intent here, it is possible to argue, is to make it clear that blogging forms part of the job description—and that experimenting with social media platforms is essential. The "Collective conversational code of conduct" is designed to be applied in tandem with the "Blogging policies and guidelines."

Navigating boundaries

Across the various social media policies that we examined, there are two key trends. The first trend is a set of rules about what is appropriate in terms of navigating the boundaries between professional and personal social media engagement and the second trend is an expectation that employees will apply common sense. Many organizations explicitly state that employees must declare when they are engaging as an employee and when engagement is personal. Distinctions about representation—identifying professional roles and personal views—is a key issue when navigating personal and professional boundaries.

The BBC, for example, allows employees to acknowledge their employer and their work publicly, but within personal social media activities employees must identify that the views they express are their own. AMP3PR, a New York-based fashion and lifestyle public relations firm offers its employees a set of guidelines for personal usage that broadly covers issues relating to confidentiality, authenticity, respect, full disclosure of sponsorship and acknowledging sources. The guidelines are not so much about managing personal—professional boundaries—they are designed to offer advice about social media norms and to protect the organization's reputation.

Hill and Knowlton's guidelines on the personal use of social media need to be taken into account when employees can be identified as a Hill & Knowlton employee or use company resources for personal use of social media. Employees are reminded that clients may read social posts and that criticism could result in the company losing clients, and consequently, that employee losing their job. It is suggested that the same rules that apply in conversations with journalists and others apply in online situations. Confidentiality and legal constraints are emphasized, along with appropriateness and identification of personal or professional views. The guidelines are clearly oriented towards protecting Hill & Knowlton reputation and business first. Employee responsibilities are a key feature of social media policies.

The Public Relations Society of America (PRSA) states that "personal use of social media unrelated to the PRSA is at an individual's discretion" (PRSA, 2011) and offers a series of considerations to be taken into account that establish clear boundaries between personal and professional social media activities, urge caution in relation to sensitive issues and prioritize PRSA legal compliance and safeguards.

The Australian Broadcasting Corporation (ABC), an editorially independent, state-owned and funded national public broadcast organization, state that personal and professional usage should not "bring the ABC into disrepute, imply ABC endorsement or personal views and disclose confidential information obtained through work" (ABC, 2013).

Issues relating to sensitive issues, confidentiality and posting proprietary material inform many of the guidelines relating to personal social media usage. A key concern for journalists and public relations practitioners is the disclosure of political affiliations. Media organizations seem more likely to forbid disclosure of political affiliations and postings that express political views (see, for example, the AP in order to safeguard perceptions of neutrality or independence). If political affiliations are permitted they must be clearly labeled as personal views.

Judgement

The BBC discusses three social media activities that it is concerned with—personal use, core news, and editorial and journalistic roles. The striking advice from the BBC in the first section about personal social media activities is that "there are particular considerations to bear in mind. They can all be summarized as: 'don't do anything stupid'" (Hamilton, 2011). In comparison with most social media policies, this guideline is clear, simple and direct. The expectation is that BBC journalists should be able to exercise judgment about what comprises stupidity.

Jeff Bercovici, who writes for the Forbes Magazine "tech beat," suggests, along similar lines to the BBC, that many organizations have settled on an informal approach to guidelines for employees: "just don't embarrass us" (Bercovici, 2012). He argues that an informal approach is not just preferable, it is inevitable and suggests that social media policy should be condensed into the following phrase: "don't be an idiot. And if you must say something idiotic, don't tweet it." His argument is that organizations do not need complicated social media policies—he suggests that if someone is going to be unwise then they should do it quietly and not make it something for their employer to manage.

Bercovici was referring to an incident in which a freelance writer at the *New York Times* wrote controversial Twitter messages. The public editor, Margaret Sullivan responded by reaffirming the principles that apply to social media usage, emphasizing the public, shareable nature of social media, the need for appropriate thoughtful behavior—namely civility and fairness. Sullivan (2012) stated that if in doubt, the question to ask was whether a particular action might damage the *New York Times'* reputation—if so, then it was "probably a bad idea."

Discussions with postgraduate students about what they considered should be a set of policy guidelines for social media usage yielded this gem of advice: "If your grandmother wouldn't like it, don't do it." Whether the advice is interdictions about avoiding stupidity or idiocy or a recommendation about adhering to family values, policies that are judgment based are derived from a set of values or principles that communicate social expectations.

The principles that underpin many policies relate to respect for an organization's reputation and its publics; confidentiality, sensitivity and discretion; authenticity, honesty, and self-disclosure; and consideration for others. Rather than interdictions about stupidity and idiocy, it may be more productive to encourage flexibility and responsibility in social media engagement and emphasize caution, consideration (kindness and sensitivity) and honesty.

Learning from policy controversies

Within this section, we discuss and analyze social media controversies that are particularly salient for illustrating the types of issues that may evolve from policy development. Controversy erupted in 2014 when the Australian government changed the Public Service Commission social media policy to compel public service workers to "dob in" or report coworkers who criticize government policy online. The policy was changed to warn staff that if they post critical political commentary online, they may be in breach of the Public Service Act. Even if the posting is made in the employee's own name or a private social media site, it may be considered a breach of the Act. Within the policy, employee loyalty and demonstration of allegiance to the governing political party seem to be the principles being promoted. However, a closer reading of the policy suggests that the key principle is actually impartiality and that the policy is designed to avoid accusations of bias or even corruption:

> The APS Values stipulate that the APS is, among other things, "apolitical, performing its functions in an impartial and professional manner", but this does not mean that APS employees must be apolitical in their private affairs. Rather, it means that employees should avoid behaving in a way that suggests they cannot act apolitically or impartially in their work.

Although employees are not required to be apolitical in their private lives, there is an expectation that personal online practices will not impact on the workplace. For employees, the problem is that it is not always clear what has the potential to have a political impact or how to safeguard the boundary between public and private identities. Exactly what constitutes impartiality and professionalism is imprecisely defined and places employees in a precarious position in regard to social media usage. "Judgment" becomes the determining factor. In a critical *Canberra Times* editorial, questions were asked about whether an individual's opinion is of consequence and would really impact on political processes. The editor stated, "The public service's default position is that any strong political view is a potential danger. This moral panic is clearly absurd…" (*Canberra Times*, 2014). Issues about the evidence to support the view that strong political views were a danger were introduced and questions about suppression of political freedom of expression were raised. The Public Service Workers Union interpreted the policy change as an attempt to silence workers and promoted the principle of freedom of speech. This policy change instantiates the problems when two closely related principles collide. Principles about a citizen's right to an impartial public service have to be weighed against an employee's right to freedom of speech. The complication is that both principles relate to democratic rights and issues of sound governance. Teasing out how to prioritize these democratic rights needs to be given further consideration. This example points to the difficulties in designing workable social media policies and the importance of complexities that may be involved. The Codes of Ethics that underpin many media and public relations policies offer a useful set of guidelines for employees. Although social media policies may be interpreted as a gag they can also act as frameworks for positive cultural change. In this instance, the individual's right to freedom of speech may be subjugated to a broader community commitment.

A second social media policy controversy that gained international coverage in 2012 was the Sky News social media policy that restricted Twitter usage by prohibiting employees from retweeting rivals' tweets or tweeting messages about nonwork subjects. The policy also stated that journalists "should stick to their own beat" and pass stories onto the news desk rather than tweet the news. The issue that drove the policy was reputedly a problem over verification of stories (Cellan-Jones, 2012). Neal Mann (@fieldproducer), the Sky News digital editor, was widely regarded as a leading Twitter pioneer in the United Kingdom with over 44,880 followers (Beaujon, 2012). Imposition of the Twitter restrictions effectively meant that Mann would be limited in how he could report news. Mann resigned from Sky News and, as a consequence, a Twitter campaign entitled "save@fieldproducer" was started. However, because Mann was offered a position at the *Wall Street Journal* Digital Network's social team as an editor the campaign faltered and he has continued to tweet the news. This controversy illustrates the problem that restrictive social media policies may create—the extraordinary following that Neal Mann had garnered was an important source of visibility for Sky News and an indicator of the popularity of social media. It also suggests that many may prefer news in brief—in Twitter form. Mann played an important role in alerting followers to trending news items by promoting stories via his tweets. The value of his followers was also lost on Sky News—Mann had what may, in effect, be referred to as a significant fan base. Yet, the importance of plurality in hybrid environments that traverse traditional and social media environments and the value of connectivity was not recognized or valued by Sky News. This policy also reminds us that although before Web 2.0 there was broad acceptance of the belief that "content was king" on the Internet, which led to massive increases in the value of content-rich companies such as Time Warner, that is not always the case in a social media environment. Public relations—as a major producer of content—was well-positioned to prosper in a content-centered environment. However, to date, none of the predictions about the role of Internet content have been realized. Instead, the interactivity enabled by Web 2.0 has dethroned content. If there is a new king, we would argue, it is the connectivity enabled by social media. As Solis (2012, p. 46) states "Connected consumers no longer start their online experience by visiting destinations; they visit their streams." There are myriad streams of connectivity but at the time of writing Facebook, YouTube and Twitter clearly lead.

Conclusion

Appropriate engagement within social media is dependent on an understanding of the rules, affordances and cultures of social media networks. Knowing how sharing and conversations work within the diverse networks means that transgressions are less likely. More importantly, an understanding of the cultural transformation that social media is shaping is essential for public relations. Not only are the practices related to sociality being transformed but, as publics assume power, the ability of public relations to control discourse is constrained. The promotional culture of public relations clashes with the participatory cultures of social media. New modes of meaningfully engaging with social media publics are required. Careful governance policies and regulation of social media practices form part of the cultural adjustments that public relations has to consider. Analysis of social media policies suggests that two key strategies are at play—policies may serve as interdictions that outline what is forbidden or they may function as useful guidelines that establish common principles and standards. What was notably absent was discussion of engagement and conversational principles—how engagement and conversational efforts translate into social media seems to be neglected. Social media policies play an important role in protecting corporate brands and reputation—the analysis confirmed that organizational reputation was certainly as important as ethical considerations. It is possible to argue that social media policies support organizational power/knowledge mechanisms and impose a regime of surveillance. It is equally possible to argue that social media policies are an important governance mechanism that provides safeguards for those engaged in social media. Social media policies, negative or positive, do provide insights into the types of sociocultural and political priorities that organizations use to open up or close down employee and citizen engagement.

References

A teenager's view on social media (2015). *Backchat.* Retrieved 5 February 2015 from https://medium.com/backchannel/a-teenagers-view-on-social-media-1df945c09ac6

ABC (2013). Personal use of social media. 18 October. Retrieved 10 October 2014 from http://about.abc.net.au/reports-publications/personal-use-of-social-media-guidance-note/

Associated Press (2012). Social Media Guidelines for AP Employees. Retrieved 15 August, 2014 from www.ap.org/company/about-us

Beaujon, A. (2012). Neal Mann (@fieldproducer) joins *Wall Street Journal* as social media editor. *Poynter*, 23 April. Retrieved 10 October 2014 from www.poynter.org/latest-news/mediawire/171385/neal-mann-fieldproducer-joins-wall-street-journal/

Bercovici, J. (2012). "Don't be an idiot": The only social media policy that matters. Forbes. Retrieved 15 August 2014 from , www.forbes.com/sites/jeffbercovici/2012/10/12

Bortee, D. and Seltzer, T. (2009). Dialogic strategies and outcomes: An analysis of environmental advocacy groups' Facebook profiles. *Public Relations Review*, 35(3), 317–319.

boyd, d. (2012). Participating in the always-on lifestyle. In M. Mandiberg (ed.), *The Social Media Reader*, pp. 71–76. New York: New York University Press.

boyd, d. and Ellison, N. (2007). Social network sites: Definition, history, and scholarship. *Journal of Computer-Mediated Communication*, 13(1): http://jcmc.indiana.edu/vol13/issue1/boyd.ellison.html

Boyd, D., Golder, S., and Lotan, G. (2010). Tweet, tweet, retweet: Conversational aspects of retweeting on Twitter. In *System Sciences (HICSS), 2010 43rd Hawaii International Conference on*, pp. 1–10. IEEE.

Burgess, J. E. and Green, J. B. (2009). The entrepreneurial vlogger: Participatory culture beyond the professional-amateur divide. *YouTube Reader*, 89–107.

Canberra Times (2014). Moral panic plagues the bureaucracy. Editorial, 14 April. Retrieved 16 April 2014. www.canberratimes.com.au/comment/ct-editorial/moral-panic-plagues-the-bureaucracy-20140413-36l6x.html

Cellan-Jones, R. (2012). Tweeting the news. BBC Technology News, 8 February. Retrieved 15 August 2014 from www.bbc.com/news/technology-16946279

Crawford, K. (2009). Following you: Disciplines of listening in social media. *Continuum: Journal of Media & Cultural Studies*, 23(4), 525–535.

Crawford, K. and Gillespie, T. (2014). What is a flag for? Social media reporting tools and the vocabulary of complaint. *New Media & Society*, 1–19.

Hamilton, C. (2011). Updated social media guidance for BBC journalists. BBC News: The Editors [web log], 14 July. Retrieved 10 October 2014 from www.bbc.co.uk/blogs/legacy/theeditors/2011/07/bbc_social_media_guidance.html

Hilderbrand, L. (2007). YouTube: Where cultural memory and copyright converge. *Film Quarterly*, 61(1), 48–57.

Hill and Knowlton. (2005). Marketing Technology: Collective conversations code of conduct. Retrieved 8 May 2014 from http://blogs.hillandknowlton.com/niallcook/hks-policies/collective-conversation-code-of-conduct/

Honeycutt, C. and Herring, S. C. (2009). Beyond microblogging: Conversation and collaboration via Twitter. In *System Sciences, 2009. HICSS'09. 42nd Hawaii International Conference on*, pp. 1–10. IEEE.

Goggin, G. (2006). *Cell Phone Culture: Mobile Technology in Everyday Life*. Oxon: Routledge.

Goggin, G. (2011). Ubiquitous Apps: Politics of Openness in Global Mobile Cultures. *Digital Creativity*, 22(3), 148–159.

Jenkins, H., Ford, S., and Green, J. (2013). *Spreadable Media: Creating Value and Meaning in a Networked Culture.* New York: New York University Press.

LinkedIn (2014). About us. Retrieved 7 October, 2014 from www.linkedin.com/about-us?trk=hb_ft_about

Los Angeles Times Ethics Guidelines (2014). *Los Angeles Times,* 16 July. Retrieved 10 October 2014 from http://touch.latimes.com/#section/-1/article/p2p-59154719/

Müller, E. (2009). Where quality matters: discourses on the art of making a YouTube video. *YouTube Reader,* 126–139.

PETA (2014). Donna Karan, Bunny butcher. Retrieved 6 October, 2014. www.peta.org/videos/donna-karan-bunny-butcher/

PRSA (2011). *Social Media Policy.* Retrieved 8 May, 2014 from http://socialmediagovernance.com/policies/

Reporting from the internet and using social media (2013). *Handbook of Journalism: Reuters.* Retrieved 8 May 2014 from http://handbook.reuters.com/index.php?title=Reporting_from_the_internet

Sheila (2008). CNN's new rules for personal blogging. *Gawker* [weblog], 4 August. Retrieved 18 August 2014 from http://gawker.com/5032920/cnns-new-rules-for-personal-blogging

Social Media.org. (nd). Disclosure best practices toolkit. Retrieved 8 May 2014 from http://socialmediagovernance.com/policies/)

Solis, B. (2012). *The End of Business as Usual.* New Jersey: Wiley.

Sullivan, M. (2012). After an outburst on Twitter, The Times reinforces its social media guidelines. *New York Times.* Retrieved 15 August 2014, http://publiceditor.blogs.nytimes.com/2012/10/17

Times updates social media guidelines. (2009). *Readers Representative Journal* [web log], 19 November. Retrieved 8 May 2014 from http://latimesblogs.latimes.com/readers/2009/11/updated-social-media-guidelines.html

Topping, A. (2014). Jane Austen Twitter row: Two plead guilty to abusive threats. *Guardian,* 8 January. Retrieved 7 April 2015 from www.theguardian.com/society/2014/jan/07/jane-austen-banknote-abusive-tweets-criado-perez

Treem, J. W. and Leonardi, P. M. (2012). Social media use in organizations: Exploring the affordances of visibility, editability, persistence, and association. *Communication Yearbook,* 36, 143–189.

True, E. (2014). The gaming journalist who tells on the internet trolls—to their mothers. *Guardian,* 28 November. Retrieved 7 April 2014 from www.theguardian.com/culture/australia-culture-blog/2014/nov/28/alanah-pearce-tells-on-her-internet-trolls-to-their-mothers

3 Create yourself

Corporate identity for interconnected publics

A fundamental precept of public relations holds firm within digital media contexts—organizations do not have a choice about whether or not they have a corporate identity. Instead, the choice for organizations lies in the degree to which they actively engage in the creation and management of identity. A similar precept is emerging in relation to social media—organizations do not have a choice about their social media presence, only how actively they engage with and how well they manage that presence. The two are also converging, with social media emerging as one of the most important sites within which corporate identities are formed, enacted, challenged and destroyed. In this chapter, we argue that a central problem for organizations that have yet to understand or proactively engage with social media is the growing impact of social media on corporate identity.

Unmanaged, unmonitored social media streams pose an enormous risk to the reputation, operation and value or share price of organizations. Despite the risk, many organizations have been slow to develop social media policies, monitor their profiles or "mentions," or introduce even the most rudimentary measures of their social media performances (Verhoeven et. al., 2012). This lack of action suggests that these organizations, along with the public relations practitioners they employ, are still in the early stages of coming to terms with the power and possibilities of social media (Diga and Kelleher, 2009). Lack of action is also indicative of a profession in which the senior ranks were educated prior to the advent of social media and, in many instances, have yet to accept or understand it. There is an urgent need for the development of appropriate theory and well-validated tools by public relations researchers to support the profession as it enters uncharted territory.

Ironically, perhaps, it is the desire to avoid risk that may lead organizations to avoid engaging with social media and, in the process to open themselves up to a whole gamut of new risks. The fundamental reason for avoiding social media is the fear that arises from the limited ability to control communication (Verhoeven et. al., 2012). Lack of control is equated with higher risk and, therefore, as something to be avoided. However, as one public relations executive stated, organizations place themselves at greater risk if they "ignore social media and ... allow conversations to happen without awareness or participation" (DiStaso et al., 2011, p. 326). Social media cannot be managed by avoidance precisely because of the significant risks that it poses for the management of corporate identity. This is not to argue that all organizations must seek to build a profile through social media. Rather, it is to argue that some degree of engagement—albeit simply through systematic monitoring of "mentions"—is essential. We begin this chapter with a discussion of corporate identity before moving on to consider the ways in which this identity may be played out within social media contexts, and the challenges and opportunities posed for public relations.

Corporate Identity

Corporate identity management is a core public relations function as well as one of its most complex areas of responsibility. Given the strong link between the corporate identity and the corporate brand, it is also a core function of corporate level marketing (Keller and Aaker, 1998). The most widely promulgated definition of corporate identity, known as the Strathclyde statement, reads in part:

> Corporate identity management is concerned with the conception, development, and communication of an organization's mission, philosophy and ethos. Its orientation is strategic and is based on a company's values, cultures and behaviors … When well-managed, an organization's identity results in loyalty from its diverse stakeholders. As such, it can positively affect organizational performance, e.g. its ability to attract and retain customers, achieve strategic alliances, recruit executives and employees, be well positioned in financial markets, and strengthen internal staff identification with the firm.
>
> (Balmer and Greyser, 2003, p. 37)

A clearly communicated corporate identity thus constitutes an organizational asset that may add value in multiple ways by differentiating an organization in what may be a market crowded with competitors (Balmer, 2001).

Corporate identity management was traditionally viewed as an organization-centric activity involving the development of strict rules that governed all areas of corporate communication activity. However, in a digital age characterized by interconnectivity and decentralization, such "command and control" systems inevitably break down (Leitch and Richardson, 2003). As Martyn Thomas, of media consultancy *FRANk Vizeum*, reflects:

> The big issue for many clients is control and how they manage any negative comments. You can't use the old paradigm of "push" in the new space. It's not about running a campaign. It's about being in the conversation and building a long-term asset.
>
> (Knowledge@Australian School of Business, 2014)

The metaphor of "being in the conversation" is an apt one for social media work. A corporate identity may be seen as a more or less loose amalgam of all of the conversations that are occurring in multiple sites and with multiple publics. Most of these conversations will have been initiated by publics rather than by the organization, many will be online, and some will be occurring without the participation of organizational representatives. From a social media perspective, being part of the conversation with publics means being actively involved in the many conversations about the organization that occur in social media contexts.

A useful way to think about corporate identity, then, is that it is the outcome of what Motion and Leitch (2002, p. 58) term "Multiple Identity Enactments" or MIEs (see Figure 3.1), which comprise every interaction or conversation that an organization has with its publics or which members of the organization's publics have with one another. Publics make sense of an organization within particular contexts and through a variety of relationships with the organization. These MIEs may be direct as, for example, when a customer (*relationship*) has a positive interaction (*sensemaking*) in a retail store with an employee (*context*). MIEs may be mediated as, for example, when a shareholder or supplier (*relationship*) reads bad news (*sensemaking*) about the organization's environmental performance in a news story or learns about the organization's shoddy products from a friend (*context*). Increasingly, both direct and indirect MIEs will be virtual and occur through web sites or social media. Indeed, for many organizations, virtual interactions will be the sole or primary means of interaction or engagement with publics.

The concept of MIEs draws attention to the dynamic character of corporate identity. This dynamism means that corporate identities are not fixed but are constantly in a state of "becoming" or flux (Ainsworth and Hardy, 2004). Tsoukas and Chia (2002, p. 567) suggest that change is the norm for all organizations and that change involves "the reweaving of actors' webs of belief and

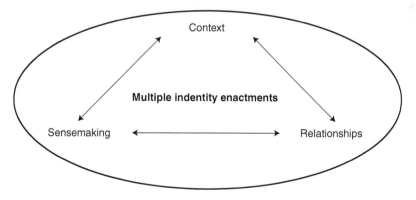

Figure 3.1 Multiple Identity Enactments

(Adapted from Motion and Leitch, 2002, p. 59)

habits of action to accommodate new experiences obtained through interactions." Building on Tsoukas and Chia, we contend that such interactions may also be seen as MIEs which have the potential to challenge or change public perceptions of an organization. These challenges—along with any resulting changes—may come from anywhere and will not necessarily be consistent with one another.

Some MIEs will inevitably be negative or misaligned with an organization's desired identity (Balmer, 2003). Others will enhance the value of the corporate brand, potentially in ways not envisioned by the organization itself. Within the context of the Internet, one of the potential issues for organizations is that the negative MIEs may come to dominate over the positive. For this reason, a niche industry has grown up that specializes in ensuring that the negatives gain less prominence. For example, the web site of Brand.com™ includes a number of "online band management case studies" that recount the company's successes. One case study features an individual whose DUI mug shots found their way onto the Internet. As a result, every Google search of the client's name featured these highly embarrassing images. Brand. com™ responded by publishing a series of positive images over a series of months, which had the effect of "pushing down" the DUI images in the order of search results. Google searches of their client's name now feature these more positive images, while the DUI images appear only after scrolling through three or more pages of search results—something few people do. Given the widespread sharing of images that occurs through social media, knowledge of how to "push down" negative images and stories in search engines is likely to be an increasingly in-demand skill. As the first generation to go through adolescence on the Internet moves into adulthood and working life, the likelihood that impulsive teenage posts and the mistakes of the past come back to haunt many is high.

Wikipedia pages are another common site for negative posts that are potentially damaging to the corporate identities of organizations or to the reputations of individuals. For example, another Brand.com™ case study describes the situation facing a client who had a distinguished career as an athlete before being convicted on recreational drug charges. Subsequently the drug charges came to dominate his Wikipedia page, while his achievements both prior to and after the charges were minimized. The company outlined how they had worked with the editors of Wikipedia to ensure that the pages relating to the client were more balanced, including both his athletic achievements and his subsequent criminal record. The goal was not to conceal the drug charges but to ensure that this incident was not the sole focus of the client's profile.

Given that Wikipedia is the constantly changing product of multiple contributors and editors, it is not possible to control Wikipedia pages. However, it is possible to be actively engaged with relevant Wikipedia pages to ensure that balanced and fair views are represented. On its page of "Strengths, weaknesses and article quality," Wikipedia states that:

Wikipedia is written by open and transparent consensus—an approach that has its pros and cons. Censorship or imposing "official" points of view is extremely difficult to achieve and usually fails after a time. Eventually for most articles, all notable views become fairly described and a neutral point of view reached. In reality, the process of reaching consensus may be long and drawn-out, with articles fluid or changeable for a long time while they find their "neutral approach" that all sides can agree on. Reaching neutrality is occasionally made harder by extreme-viewpoint contributors. Wikipedia operates a full editorial dispute resolution process, one that allows time for discussion and resolution in depth, but one that also permits disagreements to last for months before poor-quality or biased edits are removed. A common conclusion is that Wikipedia is a valuable resource and provides a good reference point on its subjects.

(http://en.wikipedia.org/wiki/Wikipedia:About)

A Wikipedia page is, therefore, always a work-in-progress and one which may contain the views of a broad range of contributors. For example, the page on General Motors carries information about the company's environmental policies as well as the statement that "The EPA and others have listed General Motors as a particularly egregious polluter" (http://en.wikipedia.org/wiki/General_motors)—or at least it did at the time of writing. No doubt further changes and edits will have been made to the page by the time you are reading this chapter. The page is heavily referenced and General Motors appears to have been very actively engaged with the text. The result is neither the suppression of negative information and opinions about the company nor a one-sided view of the historical performance of the company in a range of areas. Rather, the site presents a range of information and views likely to wholly please neither the company nor its detractors. Ensuring that the organization or client's perspective is well represented within such online contexts is a goal that is both ethical and realistic for public relations practice.

The inherent messiness of social media does pose an ongoing challenge to public relations practice—especially for those who are accustomed to time-bound campaigns over which they have a high degree of control. According to Kristen Boschma, the head of online and social media for Australian Telecommunications company, Telstra:

> Social media requires you to have extremely thick skin and extremely big ears…. It's not only that you act: it's also that you have to be seen to act—and you have to be clear that it's not with corporate spin. Social-media aficionados have finely tuned antennae to corporate spin or weasel words. Keeping it real is the fundamental point.
>
> (Knowledge@Australian School of Business, 2014)

Messiness may well be a key component "keeping it real," with slick, one-dimensional representations of organizations unlikely to resonate with publics or build social capital. In the next section, we discuss the relationship between corporate identity and social capital as it is played out within social media contexts.

Social capital

Through public relations, organizations seek to establish and maintain beneficial relationships with publics which enhance corporate identity and, as Ihlen (2005) argues, constitute the organization's social capital. According to Fieseler and Fleck (2013, p. 761):

> The benefits derived from the possession of social capital allow individuals and organizations to achieve ends that would not otherwise be possible or would incur additional costs...

At the level of individuals, everyday actions, such as chatting with neighbors, sharing a meal, or loaning a book, may be seen as activities that increase social capital. At the level of organizations, spending time with customers, providing consistently high quality services, and supporting charities, may also be seen to grow social capital. The social capital created by organizations through positive engagement with their publics may be seen as a valuable resource and an intangible asset. When an organization experiences trouble, as, for example, when it has to recall a faulty product, the extent of its social capital reserves will likely influence its ability to recover and continue to operate. However, when an organization breaks faith with its publics, by for example, producing products using sweatshop or slave labor, they may rapidly exhaust their social capital and cause ongoing damage to their corporate identity. However, social capital is, of course, a metaphor and as such should be treated with caution. It does not sit on a balance sheet and nor is it amenable to simple calculations based on deposits, withdrawals and interest rates. There is simply no guarantee that social capital will be available during times of need.

Ihlen (2005) defines the metaphor of social capital in terms of the size of social networks and the resources embedded within networks that can be accessed by network members to support actions. This definition, which incorporates the important concept of networks, draws extensively on the work of Bourdieu (1986) and Lin (2002). Both Bourdieu and Lin were writing before the rise of social media, which has massively expanded and amplified social networks and, potentially, the social capital of both the individuals and organizations that engage within them. Moreover, as Ihlen (2005) has identified, Bourdieu, who is a foundational theorist for the concept of social capital, was not interested in organizations. Instead, his work focused on social capital formation and flows between individuals. This individual focus may help to explain the neglect of Bourdieu's work within the public relations literature, which is largely concerned with the strategies and activities of organizational actors.

Ihlen (2005, p. 493) also reminds us that social capital should be understood as one of three forms of capital, with the full set including economic capital and cultural capital. Economic capital, which is the most widely understood form of capital, includes money, property and other assets with a monetary value. Cultural capital, like social capital, is intangible and comprises the knowledge and skills that individuals have acquired through formal and informal education. These three forms of capital interact in a dynamic way so that, for example, increasing one's cultural capital through education may enhance one's social capital by enabling access to new social networks. Similarly, a negative economic event, such as bankruptcy may lead to exclusion from social networks and, thereby, reduce social capital. There may also be tension between the capitals. For example a wealthy individual who lacks education may find it more difficult to build social capital and may find themselves excluded from the networks of equally wealthy individuals. The three forms of capital must therefore be viewed as an interrelated set rather than in isolation from one another. These complex interrelationships apply as much at the level of organizations as they do at the level of individuals. Indeed, as Ihlen (2005, p. 493) reminds us, organizational power is anchored in particular configurations of the three forms of capital.

Social capital within social media

In thinking specifically about social capital formation (and expenditure) within the context of social media, it is helpful to consider it from both a structural and a relational perspective (Fieseler and Fleck, 2013). Viewed from a structural perspective, social capital may be understood as the totality of the relationships between the members of a network as well the totality of linkages between networks. Viewed from a relationship perspective, social capital may be seen to flow directly between members of a network or indirectly, via members who have relationships that span multiple network connections and who broker social capital flows between them. The relational dimension of social capital thus has both direct and indirect dimensions. Some networks are clearly more valuable than others due to what Ihlen (2005) terms the volume of social capital they contain or have access to.

Through social media networks, individuals and organizations are able to establish and maintain many more relationships than would have been previously possible. For the most part these large networks of relationships are made up of a myriad of "weak ties" (Wellman et al., 2001). Social media is well suited to supporting this plethora of weak ties, which, collectively may be of enormous value. For example, Facebook has become the underlying infrastructure that supports millions of extended family and personal relationships. Facebook contributions build social capital and also enable people to draw down social capital during times of need. However, the power of social media to build social capital is many times greater for organizations. The large social media networks that surround many organizations enable them to extend their capacity and capabilities. When organizations need to communicate with their publics, the social media networks in which they have previously invested resources and within which they have built up social capital, provide ideal communication vehicles. Here it is important to distinguish between communicating through one's own social media networks and simply using social media as a vehicle for communication using paid placements. That is, messages posted on an organization's Facebook page are very different from advertisements that appear uninvited on the Facebook pages of individuals. In the former case, the audience has opted in to receive organizational communication and therefore has a pre-existing relationship, albeit only a weak tie. In the latter case, the communication is more likely to be perceived as a form of spam or as an unwelcome intrusion in a space that users may perceive as private.

One increasingly popular means of both building and accessing the valuable social capital contained within an organization's social media networks is known as "crowdsourcing." Crowdsourcing is a term that is generally believed to have been coined by the editors of *Wired Magazine* in 2005. In a later blog post, one of those editors, Jeff Howe (2006) defined crowdsourcing as follows:

> Simply defined, crowdsourcing represents the act of a company or institution taking a function once performed by employees and outsourcing it to an undefined (and generally large) network of people in the form of an open call. This can take the form of peer-production (when the job is performed collaboratively), but is also often undertaken by sole individuals. The crucial prerequisite is the use of the open call format and the large network of potential laborers.

Howe acknowledges that the concept builds on earlier work by Surowiecki (2003) about the so-called "wisdom of crowds," which refers to the way in which decisions or conclusions based on aggregated data drawn from groups are likely to be more effective or accurate than are decisions made or conclusions drawn purely on an individual basis. Howe (2006) also gives credit to a much earlier work by Charles Mackay entitled *Extraordinary Popular Delusions and the Madness of Crowds*, which dates from the Victorian era.

While crowdsourcing may take many different forms, it generally involves soliciting ideas, products or services from the "crowd." From an organizational perspective, the crowd comprises anyone and everyone who is not a formal organizational member. Though most crowdsourcing involves the Internet and is, therefore, limited to those with Internet connections, other modes of communication, including billboards, have been effectively used. The act of crowdsourcing innovation may enable an organization to access the skills and ideas of millions of people who are not on the payroll. Indeed, the very act of engaging in crowdsourcing may build social capital by drawing publics into a very direct relationship with an organization. It may also serve to build the corporate reputation of organizations as tech-savvy, open to innovation and connected to their publics.

Through crowdsourcing, organizations can directly engage their publics in a variety of tasks. It may be used to make decisions, in which case it is often known as "crowdvoting." Perhaps the most well-known example of this subgroup is Threadless.com. This company has based its business model on crowdvoting. Site users contribute ideas for T-shirt designs and other site users vote on which designs are then available for sale. In addition, through their purchase choices, site users (known as "threadfriends') may also "vote" for designs to receive large cash prizes. For example, the site launched what it called a "Parody Design Challenge Showdown" and then invited users to determine which of the four most popular designs should win a US$10,000 prize. They invited site users to participate through the following message:

> Threadfriends, we need your help! After launching our $10k Parody Design Challenge in February, we received so many awesomely awesome submissions that we simply couldn't choose a final winner by ourselves. We've managed to whittle the abundance of radness down to the four finalists below, but now we're passing the baton to you! What do you need to do? Simply purchase your fave finalist design!
> (Retrieved 1 May 2014 from www.threadless.com/10k-parody-challenge)

Sites such as Threadless.com function as hybrid ecommerce and social media sites, with their own committed group of site users who share design ideas as well as make purchases.

At the time of writing, the mysterious disappearance of a Malaysian Airways flight MH370 with the loss of 239 lives, was dominating both traditional and social media. One US-based satellite imagining company, DigitalGlobe, entered the search for the jet using a crowdsourcing modality. DigitalGlobe invited the public to log onto its crowdsourcing site, tomnod.com, and comb through satellite imagery of more than 3,000 square kilometers of ocean in search of debris. A company spokesperson posted the following message to all those who participated via its Facebook site (retrieved 1 May 2014 from www.facebook.com/Tomnod):

> To everyone on the Tomnod team, a huge THANK YOU for the amazing response to our search for #MH370. Together we searched more than 1,000,000km2 of satellite imagery and tagged millions of possible clues. Search teams and analysts investigated all the promising leads we discovered but the plane has still not been found. As the search of the ocean surface winds down and our campaign comes to an end, we mourn with the families and friends of everyone on board MH370. Although this search has ended, Tomnod's mission to crowdsource the world continues. We're always launching new campaigns to explore satellite images and reveal information about our amazing planet .... We'd love for you to continue to be part of the Tomnod team.

The final message in this post is a clear example of the way in which organizations may seek to develop social capital through their crowdsourcing activities within social media.

Social media, social capital and corporate identity: A virtuous circle

Overall, social media may be seen as an ideal medium for communicating corporate identity and for developing the social capital associated with a particular corporate identity. The direct, personal and voluntary character of the communication between organizations and their publics that is enabled by social media stands in stark contrast to the traditional media which social media has replaced. The crowdsourcing examples cited above, illustrate just a few of the myriad of creative ways in which social media has been used to grow social and, in some cases, economic capital. However, as will be discussed in later chapters, the use of social media for public relations purposes is not without significant risks and corporate identity work is no exception. Indeed, the advent of services such as that provided by Brand.com, serve as a strong warning to both organizations and individuals that social media may just as easily provide a means for damaging reputations as they do for developing reputations.

References

Ainsworth, S. and Hardy, C. (2004). Discourse and identities. In S. Clegg, C. Hardy, T. Lawrence and W. Nord. (eds.). *The Sage Handbook of Organizational Discourse*, pp. 153–173. London: Sage.

Balmer. J. (2001). Corporate identity, corporate branding and corporate marketing: Seeing through the fog. *European Journal of Marketing*, 35, 3/4 (2001), 248–291.

Balmer, J. (2003). Corporate brands: What are they? What of them? *European Journal of Marketing*, 37 (7/8), 972–997.

Balmer, J. and Greyser, S. (2003). *Revealing the Corporation: Perspectives on Identity, Image, Reputation, Corporate Branding, and Corporate-Level Marketing*. London and New York: Routledge.

Bourdieu, P. (1986). The forms of capital. In J. G. Richardson (ed.). *Handbook of Theory and Research for the Sociology of Education*, pp. 242–258. New York: Greenwood.

Diga, M. and Kelleher, T. (2009). Social media use, perceptions of decision-making power, and public relations roles. *Public Relations Review*, 35, 44–442.

DiStaso, M., McCorkindale, T., and Wright, D. (2011). How public relations executives perceive and measure the impact of social media in their organizations. *Public Relations Review*, 37, 325–328.

Fieseler, C. and Fleck, M. (2013). The pursuit of empowerment through social media: Structural social capital dynamics in CSR-Blogging. *Journal of Business Ethics*, 118, 759–775.

Ihlen, O. (2005). The power of social capital: Adapting Bourdieu to the study of public relations. *Public Relations Review*, 31, 492–496.

Howe, J. (2006). Crowdsourcing: A definition. http://crowdsourcing.typepad.com/cs/2006/06/crowdsourcing_a.html. Accessed 5 pm. 01/05/2014.

Keller, K. and Aaker, D. (1998). The impact of corporate marketing on a company's brand extensions. *Corporate Reputation Review*, 1(4), 356–378.

Knowledge@AustralianSchoolofBusiness (2014). Social media: Is your corporate image really out of control?. http://knowledge.asb.unsw.edu.au/article.cfm?articleid=1106 Accessed 4:04 pm 31/01/2014.

Leitch, S. and Richardson, N. (2003).Corporate branding in the new economy. *European Journal of Marketing*, 37(7/8), 1065–1079.

Lin, N. (2002). *Social Capital: A Theory of Social Structure and Action*. Cambridge University Press

Motion. J. and Leitch, S. (2002). The technologies of corporate identity. *International Studies of Management & Organization*, 32(3), 45–64.

Surowiecki, J. (2003) *Wisdom of Crowds : Why the Many Are Smarter Than the Few, and How Collective Wisdom Shapes Business, Economies, Societies, and Nations*. New York: Double Day.

Tsoukas, J. and Chia, R. (2002). On organizational becoming: Rethinking organizational change. *Organization Science*, 13(5), 567–582.

Verhoeven, P., Tench, R., Zerfass, A., and Vercic, D. (2012). How European PR practitioners handle digital and social media. *Public Relations Review*, 38, 162–164.

Wellman, B., Haase, A. Q., Witte, J. and Hampton, K. (2001). Does the Internet increase, decrease or supplement social capital? Social networks, participation, and community commitment. *American Behavioral Scientist*, 45(3), 436–455).

4   Speak the truth

Transparency, power/knowledge, and authenticity

In this chapter we examine the ways in which truth claims are established and circulated within social media. Our analysis centers on what are arguably the three core dimensions of truth claims—transparency (Rawlins, 2009), power/knowledge (Foucault, 1980), and authenticity (Trilling, 1971). Before moving on to analyze each of these core dimensions in depth, we first consider the place of truth (and related concepts) in public relations in terms of the requirements placed on practitioners by the various professional associations in Western democracies. Our purpose in this first section, then, is to better understand the standards of behavior to which the profession itself professes to adhere as well as the underlying rationale and context of these standards. The codes tend to be silent on the medium of communication and so there are no specific references to social media to be considered. Rather, the codes are intended to set out broad principles and expected standards of behavior that are to be applied regardless of the medium.

One profession—many codes of conduct

The popular characterization of public relations as "spin" is sharply at odds with the profession's own codes of conduct or ethics, which tend to emphasize honesty, truth, and transparency. However, there are nuanced but important differences in the ways different nations have conceptualized the requirement for truthfulness in public relations practice. For example, the Public Relations Society of America's (PRSA) Statement of Professional Values states that "We adhere to the highest standards of accuracy and truth in advancing the interests of those we represent and in communicating with the public." In Australia, the PRIA Code of Ethics states that "Members shall not knowingly disseminate false or misleading information and shall take care to avoid doing so inadvertently." The PRSA code is the stronger of the two because it advances a clear responsibility for the "highest standards of accuracy and truth." In contrast, the PRIA code contains a somewhat lower standard of not "knowingly" disseminating information that is "false or misleading." This lower standard is also evident in the Code of Conduct of the UK's Chartered Institute of Public Relations (CIPR), whereby members are simply required to check the "reliability and accuracy of information before dissemination." Given these differences, it is worth delving a little further into the PRSA Code of Ethics.

A core principle that underpins the PRSA Code of Ethics is that "Protecting and advancing the free flow of accurate and truthful information is essential to serving the public interest and contributing to informed decision making in a democratic country." This statement reflects the political culture of its country of origin. The right to freedom of speech is firmly embedded in the First Amendment to the US Constitution, where it has provided the foundation for a raft of contemporary judicial decisions in relation to, for example, defamation, censorship, indecency, and privacy. The PRSA Code references and overtly upholds this tradition of free speech and enjoins its members to do the same. Moreover, in positioning public relations practice as contributing to "informed decision making in a democratic country," the Code establishes an implied duty for practitioners to serve a broader set of interests beyond those of their clients or employers. In contrast, while the preamble to the PRIA Code of Ethics states that "PRIA is mindful of the responsibility which public relations professionals owe to the community as well as to their clients and employers," there is nothing in the Code to explain what this broader responsibility is or the basis and purpose of its existence. The CIPR Code of Conduct is even less forthcoming and makes no mention of words such as "community" or "democracy." It may be that practitioners in the US are no more or less likely to engage in public relations practices that uphold democratic decision-making than are their counterparts in other countries. Nonetheless, the PRSA Code of Ethics explicitly requires such behaviour while the codes operating in some other Western democracies do not. These omissions have the effect of reducing the efficacy of such Codes for promoting a broader debate about the roles and responsibilities of public relations practitioners.

The issues that potentially arise due to the neglect, within some Codes of Conduct or Ethics, of the role of public relations in society are, we suggest, amplified in social media. The Codes appear to be rooted in a transmission model of communication, as exemplified by their use of words such as "dissemination" and "information." Social media is inherently interactive, involving engagement with publics within streams of communication. In order to be relevant for social media contexts, we would argue that the codes therefore need to consider public relations practice from an engagement rather than a transmission perspective (Leitch and Motion, 2010). Within social media contexts, public relations practitioners may engage in ongoing discussions or debates, with their contributions serving to shape, contest or support various ideas, positions or perspectives on events and issues. This more conversational role for public relations could be better reflected within, for example, the PRSA Code in relation to its core value of "advocacy," where it states:

> We serve the public interest by acting as responsible advocates for those we represent. We provide a voice in the marketplace of ideas, facts and viewpoints to aid informed public debate.

This statement could be reframed to take account of the exponential increase in: the size, reach and number of different "marketplaces;" the number of "ideas, facts and viewpoints" promulgated; the volume with which the Internet enables voices to be heard; and the speed with which such contributions may be shared globally.

One further element of the various professional codes, which it is helpful to consider here, is the way in which the codes deal with the concept of transparency. For the most part, transparency is considered somewhat narrowly in terms of the relationship between practitioners and their clients or employers, rather than in relation to the broader concept of truth or to the rights of publics to access information. For example, the CIPR Code of Conduct includes a section entitled "Transparency and conflicts of interest," which deals with the financial aspects of the relationship and requires, for example, "Disclosing to employers, clients or potential clients any financial interest in a supplier being recommended or engaged." However, both the PRIA and PRSA codes go further in terms of requiring practitioners to publicly disclose the identity of the clients or employers by whom they are funded. The PRIA Code, for example, states "Members shall be prepared to identify the source of funding or any public communication they initiate or for which they act as a conduit."

A major reason for concern with transparency in the relationship between practitioners and their clients or employers is that one of the most negative accusations levelled against public relations relates to its involvement with so-called "front organizations." According to Fitzpatrick and Palenchar (2006, p. 203), front organizations "are created to pursue public policy objectives for organizations that disguise their connection" rather than to serve the interests of democracy by creating an informed citizenry, In short, "[f]ront organizations intend to lead both citizens and lawmakers to draw particular conclusions based on partial evidence or misinformation that supports these conclusions" (Leitch and Davenport, 2011, pp. 1502–3). This concern is explicitly referenced in the PRSA Code in a section entitled "Disclosures of information" which provides the following examples of improper conduct:

- Front group: A member implements "grass roots" campaigns or letter-writing campaigns to legislators on behalf of undisclosed interest groups.
- A member deceives the public by employing people to pose as volunteers to speak at public hearings or participate in "grass roots" campaigns.

The reason for these inclusions in the PRSA Code is likely to be the extent to which such activities have been documented in the US and, in the process, brought public relations in that nation into disrepute (Stauber and Rampton, 1995). Requirements for transparency in the client-practitioner relationship are therefore intended to protect both the public interest and the interests of the public relations profession more broadly. In the next section we consider the concept of transparency in more depth, as the first of three dimensions of truth claims within public relations practice.

Transparency

The interactive character of social media would seem to be ideally suited to aid transparency in public relations practice. Certainly, DiStaso and Bortree (2012) found that public relations practitioners believed that the use of social media could improve transparency and enable their publics to make better informed decisions. However, in their detailed analysis of award-winning social media campaigns, these researchers found little evidence that public relations practitioners were putting this belief into practice. One of the difficulties may be the lack of a shared understanding of the concept or its execution. While many organizations lay claim to transparency in their communications, they are not necessarily in agreement as to what transparency means in practice. Moreover, as discussed above, the professional codes of conduct or ethics have tended to take a narrow view of transparency. There are, however, multiple ways of thinking about this important concept and, as a corollary, multiple different ways of implementing transparency in practice.

In this chapter, we draw on Rawlins (2009, p. 75) definition of transparency in organizational communication as:

> The deliberate attempt to make available all legally releasable information—whether positive or negative in nature—in a manner that is accurate, timely, balanced and unequivocal, for the purpose of enhancing the reasoning ability of publics and holding organizations accountable for their actions, policies, and practices.

We choose to use this multifaceted definition of transparency because it moves the concept from a transmission paradigm to an engagement paradigm. Within the mechanistic and widely discredited transmission paradigm, the decision-making power resides solely with the organization in terms of determining what information will be provided, to whom, at what time, and in what formats. Within an engagement paradigm, power is shared, at least to some extent, with the organization seeking to understand and meet the information needs of their publics. Given the inherently interactive character of social media, the engagement paradigm would seem to offer a far more useful model for public relations practice (Leitch and Motion, 2010).

Interactivity is not, however, the same thing as transparency. Coombs and Holladay (2011) argue that the sheer scale of the Internet has lulled us into believing that a kind of "pseudo-panopticon" is in operation. The panopticon was a means of surveillance imagined by Jeremy Bentham and, more recently, popularized through the work of Foucault (1977). It was envisaged as a system of ensuring that every cell within a prison could be monitored from a single point, with prisoners aware of the possibility of surveillance but unsure when they were actually being watched. To the extent that the Internet enables multiple viewpoints to be aired, including the viewpoints of activists, whistle-blowers and other individuals or organizations who question the status quo, the ability of any one entity—be it a government or a major corporation—to conceal information or mislead the public is curtailed. However, through their research on corporate social responsibility (CSR), Coombs and Holladay come to the view that the extent of this curtailment has been overstated:

> In reality, we argue that a pseudo-panopticon is being constructed through the confluence of discourses about CSR reporting and transparency coupled with the purported power of internet-based communication to expose wrongdoing. The assumptions of panopticism lead the public to place unwarranted confidence in corporate CSR reporting. The discourse of transparency creates the impression that CSR reporting is accurate because the internet would be used to expose any irresponsible corporate conduct.
>
> (Coombs and Holladay, 2011, p. 213)

In essence, they contend that the efficacy of the Internet as a panopticon that exposes wrongdoing is limited and our belief in its supposed powers may be leading us into a false sense of security. It is also interesting to consider the concept of the panopticon from the perspective of our discussion on privacy and regulation later in this book. Given the revelations by Edward Snowden and others of the extensive surveillance of digital communications that is undertaken by government agencies, such as the NSA, conceptualizing the Internet as a panopticon may be less about citizen surveillance of organizations than it is about organizational surveillance of citizens. Certainly, Goldberg (2010, p. 740) makes a strong case that participation in social media is not a trivial matter because it "embeds users within relations of power" that have potentially far reaching and unforeseen consequences.

Coombs and Holladay (2011) conclude that one underlying cause for our misguided complacency in relation to the utility of the Internet as a panoptic aid to organizational transparency, is the commonly held view that transparency means disclosure. They point to the work of McGongale and Vella (2007) on "defensive competitive intelligence," which may be understood as the dissemination of information that it is difficult to understand. If organizations disclose information that is not meaningful then they cannot be said to have engaged in transparent communication. Coombs and Holladay (2011) also argue that organizations can overdisclose by releasing massive amounts of information. Especially information that is not in digital and therefore searchable form. In doing so organizations may rightly conclude that any potentially damaging or embarrassing information is likely to be lost in a sea of data or else only discovered long past the point at which disclosure could be damaging. Organizations may also disclose information that appears as neutral or objective but is actually a carefully crafted presentation that is designed to support particular conclusions and avoid others. Disclosures that are difficult to understand, difficult to locate, or partial and self-serving cannot be said to render organizations more transparent.

The definition of transparency as an active process offered by Rawlins (2009) is supported by Coombs and Holladay's (2011) research. They argue that one of the problems with commonly held understandings of transparency is that it is seen as a quality that organizations possess rather than as a set of processes through which organizations engage with others. Conceptualized in this way, transparency may be understood as the processes through which organizations make and negotiate truth claims with their publics. To the extent that these processes enable publics to make sense of the organization and the impact of its activities on their lives and on society and the environment more generally, the organization may be said to engage in transparent communication practices.

This last point is relevant to the assumption that discourse, including that engaged in by public relations practitioners, is best when it fosters enlightened choices. Enlightenment presumes transparency, but does not presume that how and what is transparent is not a matter for contention. Noting, as have others including authors above, how important transparency has become in many disciplines, Christiansen and Langer (2009) noted that the Internet has changed the way this concept plays out in society. However, these authors caution, transparency is not easy to achieve nor inherent to otherwise ethical discourse. Information can be viewed within an organization as being more or less transparent as it flows up or down. The same is true as it flows from and to the organization. So, merely finding flow does not or should not indicate transparency.

Many factors relate to transparency, including trust, strategic filtering, withholding for ethical reasons, and interpreting. How does one party know when to trust one or more others' information? In social media, for instance, presentation of some fact, a person caught doing something, can actually be subject to various interpretations. Leaks can distort matters rather than clarify them. Facts can be supplied without context. Can information, even as revealed, be strategically filtered so that the true nature of some matter may be hard to understand or construct? Scientific information can be strategically filtered to give a different impression than would occur, perhaps, if all of the information was readily available and at the same time. It can be strategically filtered because of efforts to avoid inconsistencies. Information, such as medical histories or security matters, can be withheld for ethical reasons. But such ethics can be abused. Finally, interpretation is never easy in matters of transparency. Is information fairly presented? Is it what it seems to be—and tell?

As Motion and Leitch (2002) have noted, information and transparency are key terms in the discussion of disciplinary intelligences. Organizations construct information packages or reports that become account technologies that are used to discipline internal audiences and keep external ones at bay. In both cases, what is offered up to publics in the name of transparency is actually a carefully constructed and narrated presentation that borders on legerdemain or trickery. Knowing these skills, individuals can easily use social media, as can organizations, to be seemingly transparent.

Power/knowledge

The second dimension of truth claims explored in this chapter is Foucault's (1980) concept of power/knowledge. According to Foucault (1980, p. 52): "The exercise of power perpetually creates knowledge and, conversely, knowledge constantly induces effects of power."

An example of power/knowledge in practice might be the publication of a new public relations theory in a leading academic journal by one of the field's most highly regarded professors. The powerful status of both the journal and the professor combine to increase the chances that the theory will come to be regarded as "knowledge." Once the theory is legitimated as knowledge, the power of the journal and the professor are further enhanced. In turn the application of this new "knowledge" may be seen as a power play by others, that is, as an action that displays or enhances an actor's power. Students may be assessed and graded by their professors on their ability to understand and apply the new theory. Public relations practitioners may use the theory to support and add legitimacy to their work. They may even develop their own proprietary public relations tools based on the theory. Eventually, another professor may seek to increase her power in the field by critiquing the theory and replacing it with an alternative theory of her own. Knowledge supports and enables the exercise of power while the exercise of power generates and legitimates knowledge. Conversely knowledge may also be deployed to undermine power by delegitimizing existing knowledge. It is the mutually reinforcing character and operation of power and knowledge within discourse that led Foucault to combine them into the single power/knowledge concept. In short, he saw the two concepts as inseparable.

From a Foucauldian perspective, public relations strategies and campaigns may be seen as attempts to establish, maintain, challenge or transform the power/knowledge configurations that underpin and legitimize truth claims (Motion and Leitch, 2007). As noted above, Goldberg (2010, p. 740) argues that participation in social media "embeds users within relations of power." We would go further and argue that social media embeds users within power/knowledge relations. We would also argue that distinctive characteristics of social media, which, in the main emanate from the sheer size and complexity of the Internet, bring a new dimension to our understanding of power/knowledge.

Foucault's work emphasizes the contingent and fluid nature of power/ knowledge relations. That is, such relations are not fixed but are constantly in a state of flux. One of the reasons for this fluidity is that the only way to demonstrate power/knowledge is to exercise or apply it. However, such exercises are risky endeavors that may result in challenges or failure. It is precisely this element of danger that lends fluidity to power/knowledge relations. Fluidity enables change, enables new sources of power to emerge and enables new knowledge to be accepted. Social media may therefore be seen as a context within which such fluid power/knowledge relations are played out. This context should, then, be understood as a constantly moving stream rather than as a place. The metaphor of social media as a stream occurs throughout this book and is purposely used to emphasize the dynamic character of social media.

Prior to the advent of the Internet, communication was marked by scarcity. For example, mass communication through newspapers, television or radio was constrained by time and space. Moreover, as with any market, scarcity drove price premiums making such mass communication very expensive. Social media and the Internet more generally are not bound by such constraints. Social media is not actually free (Internet connections cost money) and neither is it infinite (bandwidth and date storage constraints exist) but from a user perspective it may appear to be both of these things. Social media offers a constant stream of communication for individuals and organizations. The exercise of power/knowledge within such a stream has clear differences from its exercise in other contexts and eras. What then are the distinctive characteristics of power/knowledge in social media contexts?

The first characteristic of social media is the broader diffusion of communication power through networks that the Internet has engendered. Observing the diffusion of power engendered by new media, Meyers (2012, p. 1023) noted that:

> The advent of new interactive technological platforms like the internet did not create the active audience, but has made these practices visible and vital in ways that reconfigure audiences' role in media culture. In contrast to the traditional top-down hierarchy of commercial media in which professional producers or "cultural elites" create and circulate content (and cultural meaning) for mass consumption by (passive) audiences, new media technologies have made visible an "audience/producer" or what Bruns (2008) calls a "produser" that exists outside this traditional professional media producer class and threatens its commercial and cultural dominance.

Communication power within the "top-down hierarchy" means tight control over the timing, content, frequency, prominence, tone, authorship and other aspects of communication that determine what may or may not be said and by whom. In contrast, most social media streams have limited controls over some or all of these aspects of communication and they actively support the work of "produsers". For example, Twitter's content is entirely the work of its produsers. Twitter may be severely space limited in terms of length of communication (140 characters) but is both open to contributors and largely uncontrolled. Establishing truth claims on Twitter through the exercise of power/knowledge does mean adhering to what are known as the "Twitter rules." The preamble to the rules states:

> Our goal is to provide a service that allows you to discover and receive content from sources that interest you as well as to share your content with

others. We respect the ownership of the content that users share and each user is responsible for the content he or she provides. Because of these principles, we do not actively monitor and will not censor user content, except in limited circumstances described below.

(Retrieved 12 September 2015 from https://support.twitter.com/
articles/18311)

The Twitter rules prohibit: impersonation; trademark violations; unauthorized publication of private or confidential information; threats of violence; copyright infringements; posts that support illegal activities; and, finally, misuse of Twitter badges. Twitter is also concerned to reduce "abuse and spam" and any account that is found to have violated the rules or engaged in abuse or spam is shut down. Beyond this, Twitter does not pay attention to the various aspects of communication, such as timing, content, frequency, prominence, tone, or authorship of tweets, all of which were controlled by traditional media. Given the sheer volume of tweets—some 58 million per day in early 2014—the decentered approach is probably the only feasible one for Twitter to adopt. Moderating a stream in which over 9000 tweets are issued per second would be expensive and cumbersome, if not actually impossible, and it would reduce one of Twitter's key strengths, namely its immediacy.

Facebook has a similar philosophy to Twitter, as stated in the "Facebook Principles":

We are building Facebook to make the world more open and transparent, which we believe will create greater understanding and connection. Facebook promotes openness and transparency by giving individuals greater power to share and connect, and certain principles guide Facebook in pursuing these goals. Achieving these principles should be constrained only by limitations of law, technology, and evolving social norms. We therefore establish these Principles as the foundation of the rights and responsibilities of those within the Facebook Service.

(Retrieved 12 September 2015 from www.facebook.com/
principles.php)

The Facebook Principles include: the freedom to share information and connect with anyone who wants to connect with you or your organization; the right to own and control personal information; the free flow of information and access to tools that enable such a flow; the fundamental equality of all Facebook users; the right to have a Facebook page unless Facebook's Statement of Rights and Responsibilities is violated; the use of open platforms and standards; the fundamental services of Facebook should be free for individual users; alignment between the Facebook Statement of Rights and Responsibilities and the Facebook Principles; transparent processes on the part of Facebook in relation to its purpose, plans, policies, and operations; and, finally, a commitment to "one world" by providing a service that "should transcend geographic and national boundaries and be available to everyone in the world" (Retrieved 12 September 2015 from www.facebook.com/principles.php).

Both Twitter and Facebook, therefore, have a commitment to openness and place the rights and responsibilities for content primarily onto their "pro-dusers," rather than seeking to produce or control content centrally. Both of these social media platforms enable their Facebook page or Twitter stream creators to block posts and to reject unwanted "followers" or "friends." The Facebook page settings also enable page creators to block keywords and profanities. However, in practice the controls are somewhat weak because, although Facebook users have a degree of control over their own Facebook page, they do not have control over contributions to the platform more gener-ally. In such an open, decentered context, the exercise of power/knowledge for the establishment of truth claims is clearly a very different undertaking than it is in, for example, a newspaper. The page or stream "owner" can determine who is allowed to post comments and ban anyone they wish to exclude but they cannot prevent anyone from posting on other pages. Such posts are then potentially visible to anyone who searches. Moreover, searches may bring up old posts containing truth claims that have been long discredited from sources that may no longer even be active in a debate or who may have long since changed their views on the subject.

From a temporal perspective, then, social media appears to be immedi-ate and transient but may be surprisingly enduring. For example, posts that appear within the context of an informal, synchronous "chat" may also be available asynchronously and out of context to unknown others. These con-flicting and, sometimes, contradictory, temporal qualities constitute the second characteristic of the exercise of power/knowledge in social media contexts. One implication for public relations practice is that no subject is ever closed on social media. At best a subject may be said to be dormant, although it may spring to life at any time. There can be no last word in such ongoing streams of communication. Traditionally public relations practice has often taken the form of campaigns that have clearly defined lifespans. However, when such campaigns find their way into social media, they do not necessarily unfold in chronological order or cease even though a page or post has been removed. The defined campaign is, then, replaced by ongoing participation in streams of communication. As discussed above, power/knowledge has always been performative in the sense that it comes into being, is reinforced, or open to challenge only when it is demonstrated. However, the discrete performances of power/knowledge of the predigital age have been replaced by performances that are potentially never-ending.

The third characteristic of social media, context, was alluded to above. Communication is always highly contextual. In attempting to make sense of any communication act—be it written, spoken, or visual—we draw on broader contextual clues. When we encounter a red sign with the word "STOP" on it as we drive toward an intersection, we understand it to mean that we are required by law to stop our car. When we encounter the same sign in another context—broken in a field, hanging on a dorm room wall, reproduced in a painting—we understand that the sign has lost its legal force and has taken on new meanings. Changing the sign's context changes its meaning. Social media may itself be seen as a particular context within which meaning is created and interpreted. However, the slippery temporality of social media may also be seen to decontextualize and recontextualize communication, potentially, as part of an endless chain of "mash-ups."

The mash-up is not a new phenomenon but it has been massively enabled and amplified by digital technologies. A useful definition of the mash-up is offered by Jackson (2009, p. 730):

> Mash-ups are communicative forms whose essential character is that they are compositions, combinations, assimilations, and appropriations of things that already exist to create something—and this is crucial—that need show no allegiance or even connection to those original works. Mash-ups are not montages or summaries. They are forms of communication that depend—crucially—on unceasing transformation and accumulation of communication acts and interaction into data.

The digital mash-up has become ubiquitous in numerous spheres of activity and industry sectors, including music, software, photography, video, databases, blogs, and even traditional news media. A mash-up may be as simple as the combination of two previously disconnected things, such as the combination of two songs onto a single track. It may be as complex as the compilation of computer code from different sources to create new software.

Social media provide enabling platforms for the mash-up of words and images, granting individuals and organizations the ability to use and reuse content in ways unimagined or unapproved, much less intended, by the content creator. Under US copyright law, unauthorized, commercial music mash-ups are permitted provided a fee is paid to the original artist. However, in practice, many music mash-ups "sample" multiple artists without attribution or the payment of royalties. Potential negative implications of mash-ups for public relations practice include:

- loss of the original, contextual cues that guide the sensemaking activities of audiences;
- loss of authorship attributions and copyright violations;
- reappearance of outdated messages or images;
- juxtaposition of content with offensive or undesirable images or messages; and
- a myriad of unforeseen and unintended consequences that arise from the loss of control over context.

There are ways to mitigate or reduce the effects of these negative implications. For example, digital images may be configured to make it difficult for others to simply "cut and paste" them into other contexts. It is also possible to pursue legal redress for context shifts that violate copyright or libel laws. On the other hand there are also potentially positive implications of context-shifting, including the widespread sharing of organizational content at no cost to the organization. Indeed, "going viral" is an increasingly common strategy used by advertisers to drive millions of voluntary ad "views." The inclusion of organizational content, such as brand logos, in other contexts, may also be a sign of support or affection for the brand—even when these uses are irreverent. Enabling the recontextualization of content in order to build engagement with publics is, then, a potentially valuable addition to public relations strategy and practice.

The power/knowledge relations in which we are enmeshed through our participation in social media are, then, clearly shaped by the three characteristics of social media discussed above, namely:

1   the decentering of power and its *diffusion* through networks;
2   the complex and slippery *temporality* of social media content; and
3   the *decontextualization and recontextualization* of content.

In combination, these characteristics serve to render any organization-centric concept of public relations redundant. Such a concept, which places the organization firmly in charge of its communication, was always flawed (Leitch and Neilson, 2001). When applied to social media, organization-centric concepts have no remaining utility. Instead, power/relations in social media are better understood in terms of engagement with publics via streams of communication. Such publics comprise not passive message consumers but "prosumers" who may be actively involved in content creation (Meyers, 2012). We now turn to the third dimension of truth claims considered in this chapter, which is authenticity in communication.

Authenticity

Studies of social media participants have found that authenticity is a core value for many users of social media networks (Healey, 2010; Livingstone, 2008; Marwick and boyd, 2011). Healey (2010, p. 526) argues that there is an evident "bias towards issues of sincerity and authenticity in the networked public sphere." The reason for this bias, we suggest, is that because it is so easy to manufacture an online identity, fake friends abound. There have even been identity hoaxes on social media sites that have contributed to the suicide of site participants and such incidents have raised awareness of the ease of enacting deceit online (Ibrahim, 2008; Jordan, 2005). Authenticity must then be analyzed in terms of both identity and relationships. The former refers to the construction of the self—be it personal, celebrity, fictional or organizational. Taking an identity-based perspective on authenticity might lead you to ask— or angst—Who am I, really, at my core?

The relational perspective refers to the role of authenticity in the relationships between people or with organizations. It might lead you to ask: How am I to be in the world if I am being authentic i.e. true to myself? There are at least two main strands of relational authenticity. The first is about rejecting peer pressure to conform, which may take the form of active resistance to authority. In this case, inauthentic behavior may spring from fear of social rejection and may be seen as an act of cowardice. The second strand involves a moral imperative not to mislead and to be honest in one's dealings with others. In this case inauthentic behavior springs from a desire to manipulate others by appearing to be someone we are not—the modus operandi of the con artist. Before considering these two strands, however, we first need to consider what authenticity means in general and as it is played out in social media contexts.

Philosophers have long argued over the concept of authenticity. For the existentialists, authenticity involves being true to one's innermost self and resisting external pressures from society, work, religion or family to conform. In the existentialist fable of the frog and the scorpion, the two creatures meet at the side of a river. The scorpion begs the frog to carry him across the water but the frog declines, wary of the scorpion's lethal tail. The scorpion counters that the frog can trust him because their interests are intertwined. If the frog dies, the scorpion drowns. So, the frog relents and lets the scorpion climb on her back. But half way across the frog feels a sharp pain and cries out, "How could you? This is madness!" "I know," the scorpion replies sadly as they both sink beneath the water, "I had no choice—it is just my nature."

Like the scorpion—the existentialist would argue—we are driven to be true to our inner natures, even when this flies in the face of conventional wisdom and may lead to our destruction. But such essentialist formulations of authenticity, which are based on a belief in a single "true" self, run counter to the moral and legal codes of society. In this sense, they are antisociety and antimorality. Where, for example, is the possibility of redemption or change? If I have evil impulses, is it better that I resist my wicked true self and behave well or should I embrace my authentic badness? However, people are not born as fully formed beings, complete with knowledge, values and beliefs. Rather, the self to which we must be true is a constructed self—a self-forged from the many choices that we make as conscious beings, from our many lived experiences. If this true self is a construction of our thoughts, deeds, experiences and desires, then it stands to reason it is fluid rather than fixed. Change is not just possible but inevitable.

Just what it means to be true to a fluid rather than essential self, when that may mean different things at different times, is therefore unclear. Seen from a temporal perspective, authenticity becomes a very slippery and contingent concept. My five-year-old self and my 50-year-old self do not desire or believe in the same things. Being authentic may, then, simply translate into being whatever I want to be at this point in time. Even if we could make sense of a temporal flow of true selves, who or what is it, exactly, that is being true to the self? This dualistic framing implies yet another self who sits in a decision-making chair and determines which self we will be today—the authentic or the inauthentic. Or perhaps another self who sits in a judgment chair and decides whether or not we have measured up. So, in addition to our temporal flow of selves and our contextual range of selves—we now have these additional selves who are somehow in control of the whole task of "being authentic."

According to Larmore (2010, p. 4), philosophers regard authenticity as a rather misguided concept, arguing that:

> On a theoretical level, it has generally become an object of skepticism, if not flat-out rejection.... If the question even arises, it tends to be seen as no more than mirage or a mental confusion, which can also have unfortunate consequences.

The philosophical bases for rejecting the concept of authenticity are numerous. They include the view that "authenticity" implies a natural or essential self that is not influenced by others or bound by societal norms of behavior. Valery (1957, cited in Larmore and Bowman, 2010) argues that such an authentic self is neither possible nor desirable. It is not possible because the distinction between the conventional and the natural is itself a human construction. Thus, authenticity is another human construction and, as such, is no more or less "natural" than the others. Authenticity is viewed as undesirable because adherence to social conventions—at least to some extent—enables us to live together. A total disregard for the views of others would ultimately lead to the breakdown of societies. It runs counter to notions of "self-improvement" that might lead us to want to, for example, become kinder or more selfless in our relationships with others. It thus also runs counter to our dominant religious and moral codes, which tend to emphasize service to others or transcendence of what may be viewed as our baser, "natural" selves.

Philosophical critiques of the concept of authenticity provide strong grounds for rejection of the concept as an absolute ideal. However, authenticity is not generally understood or applied in such absolute terms within social media. Rather than alluding to the natural self that exists beyond/before societal conventions, authenticity may mean many different things. According to an old joke that has been retold in many different ways, the ability to fake authenticity or sincerity is the key to success. The joke is often told in relation to salespeople or politicians, two sets of professionals with a reputation for dishonesty and insincerity. The major implications of the joke would seem to be: first, that "sincerity" is a highly prized quality; second, that a fake version of sincerity can be manufactured and; third, that this is a dishonest practice which flourishes because of its value. In this conception, it is the *faking* of authenticity that requires work. It is the task to be accomplished and we must focus on this task to avoid our true, less valuable, selves, slipping out and ruining our clever schemes.

Within social media contexts, however, this formula is often reversed so that the hard work lies in being authentic rather than inauthentic. The true self is the hard choice and there are numerous advocates of the purposive use of authenticity. For example, blogger Scott Williams (2011) argues that authenticity is an "important interpersonal skill" that is increasingly rare but which can be learned. For Williams:

> The lack of authenticity does not only affect our daily face-to-face interactions, but it bleeds over into online interactions. We begin to develop the inauthentic Twitter and Facebook John or Nancy, which is a more courageous version of the In-Real-Life John or Nancy.
>
> The lack of authenticity boils down to insecurity, people are so insecure with who they are that they begin to mimic the likeness of others or put on a facade altogether [sic]. What is meant to come off as different, cool, real or strong comes across as "Jake The Fake." People can see inauthenticity from a mile away, a tweet away or a status update away… so go ahead and get real with yourself and others.

Authenticity is understood by Williams to mean resistance to external pressures to take on multiple personas "at home, work, church, online." An authentic person is, then, one who is not intentionally putting on a fake front and who maintains a seamless identity.

The equation of authenticity with a single identity resonates with research on the use of social media sites for self-presentation. Indeed, self-presentation may rank just below social networking as a primary driver of social media participation. For example, in her research on the similarities between scrapbooks and Facebook pages, Good (2013) found that both could be read as autobiographical texts, although the latter are more likely to be widely shared than were their paper-based predecessors. Indeed, "sharing" is a fundamental part of engaging with Facebook "friends." Good (2013) argues that the performative dimension of Facebook enables users to display their tastes and views—including personal affiliations and issue stances—which are signaled through the use of "Likes." ("Liking" a post on a friend's page indicates support for the posting, while "likes" also link personal pages with organizational pages.) However, the degree to which the self-presentation performances and displays enacted through social media may be judged "authentic" has itself been the subject of research. Back et al. (2010) found that contrary to expectations, people were not using social network sites to "promote an idealized self." They argue that the sites are an efficient way of communicating one's personality, which explains their popularity. Back et al.'s findings have been supported by a meta-analysis of other studies on this subject, which concludes that while enhancements may occur "profile owners are generally portraying a fairly accurate representation of their offline identity" (Wilson et al. 2012, p. 210).

However, the rider here is that accurate should not be equated with a deeper goal of authenticity. Rather, the personality portrayed through online postings appears to correlate with the personality displayed offline. Not intentionally putting on a false front or adopting a false persona is qualitatively different from seeking to live authentically. The "true self" in this research literature is equated with the self that an individual believes to be authentic but seldom shared with others. In this sense, the true self is the hidden self. Again, somewhat paradoxically, the lived self as expressed in our relationships with others becomes the inauthentic self, while the hidden self that we seldom share is the authentic us.

Bargh's (2002) early work on Internet sites, which deploys this definition of "true self" found

> (1) that by its very nature, [such sites] facilitate the expression and communication of one's true self to new acquaintances outside of one's established social network, which leads to forming relationships with them; and (2) that once these relationships are formed, features of Internet interaction facilitate the projection onto the partners of idealized qualities. In fact, these are precisely the features that previous research has determined to be critical for the formation of close intimate relationships: Internet communication enables self-disclosure because of its relatively anonymous nature, and it fosters idealization of the other in the absence of information to the contrary (e.g. Murray et al., 1996).
>
> (Bargh, 2002, p. 45)

Feelings of intimacy arise more rapidly online than in face to face settings and these intense feelings can cause havoc in our lives and existing relationships. This phenomenon underpins the rise of chat rooms and online dating. In order to gauge its significance as a potential force for change and disruption in our lives, we have to first consider the scale. In 2014, it was estimated that more than 40 million Americans had tried online dating and that 17 percent of new marriages in that country were occurring between people who had met online. In Australia, around a third of couples dating at the time of writing have met online and more than 80 percent of single Australians believe online dating sites are socially acceptable.

There are, of course many motivations for using online dating sites—not all of which involve sharing one's hidden true self in the hope of finding a soulmate. An earlier understanding of authenticity in social media concerned the ability of users to invent identities. This usage was summed up by the adage from a famous *New Yorker* cartoon that "on the internet, no one knows you're a dog." Second Life, with its elaborately constructed landscapes populated by avatars, is one the best known of these sites. However, for social media sites such as Facebook, the ability to relate to actual people is of prime importance. As blogger/journalist Aleks Krotoski (2012) argues:

> The pursuit of authenticity is creeping into the heart of most social media models and in the current internet landscape is playing an important role in how we engage with one another and with web content. For many people, Facebook and Google products are the sum total of their web

interaction, and the value in creating a platform that provides confidence that a person is who they say they are, rather than someone pretending to be them, is critical to a social network's success.

Authenticity is here seen as a countertrend to anonymity. The issue at the heart of this definition of authenticity is whether or not social media identities should be closely tied to the offline identities of the people who create them. To be an authentic social media user, then, is to be able to authenticate one's identity. As Krotoski (2012) puts it "if you want to be a dog on the internet in the future, you'll have to have papers to prove it."

In her research on blogging sites Meyers (2012) found that authenticity was primarily related to communication that at least appeared to occur outside of the control of communication professionals (including public relations). For example, posts made directly by celebrities, as opposed to by their publicists, were valued for their authenticity. This understanding of authenticity appears to signal public awareness of the extent to which social media is professionally managed. One of the reasons that celebrities engage professional help is the sheer scale of communication that occurs through social media. In January 2014 the "ten most followed on Twitter" were:

1   Katy Perry with 49,933,576 followers
2   Justin Bieber with 49,152,836 followers
3   President Barack Obama with 41,181,742 followers
4   The Goddess of Love (aka Lady Gaga) with 41,028,699 followers
5   YouTube with 38,836,366 followers
6   Taylor Swift with 38,650,509 followers
7   Britney Spears with 35,599,598 followers
8   Rihanna with 33,845,843 followers
9   Instagram with 30,463,527 followers
10   Justin Timberlake with 30,231,225 followers

(Source: http://twittercounter.com/pages/100 accessed
10:24am 29/01/2014)

This list includes seven singers, two social media sites and one president. Famous singers, the founders of burgeoning companies, and presidents all struggle to manage their own communications. Inevitably they employ professional assistance. The downside of using professionals, however, is that their use may serve to undermine what may be perceived as a direct, personal connection. Many of the tweets emanating from the accounts of the "top ten" are no more than advertising or promotion. The singers tweet about upcoming concerts or album releases. The Instagram and YouTube tweets direct followers to new or popular uploads of videos, blogs or images. President Obama's site makes it clear that the tweets are, for the most part, created and sent by professionals and not by the President himself, adding that "Tweets from the President are signed BO." At least in the terms understood by Meyer's (2012) research subjects, the "top ten" were not engaging in authentic communication. This lack of authenticity has clearly not been a barrier to popularity but it has reduced the perceived value of the tweets for users.

There are many reasons for faking a social media identity, some of them criminal. For example, fake Facebook pages may be used to "friend" other users, access their personal information and then commit identity theft. Online gamers cheat by creating false Facebook pages in order to gain access to virtual goods or points that are limited to gamers who play with their Facebook "friends." Comedians and actors, or their fans, create pages for the characters they play. At the time of writing, the Yoda character from Star Wars has over 110,000 followers on Twitter as well as his own Facebook page. The Easter Bunny is somewhat less popular, with just 916 followers, while Santa Claus has numerous Twitter handles. False or invented identities can then be created to serve a broad range of personal, commercial, criminal or entertainment purposes. Facebook itself estimated that its site contained more than 80 million fake Facebook accounts in 2014. In the past few years, there has been some speculation that social media sites such as Facebook are in decline—partly because younger people are moving to other sites such as Instagram (which, incidentally, is also owned by Facebook) but also due to privacy and security concerns, which are discussed in detail in later chapters.

The discussion above has highlighted the implicit complexity of authenticity as it is understood and played out within social media contexts. The concept has variously been understood as:

1 Being true to my unchanging, essential self
2 Being true to my current beliefs and values
3 Being honest and sincere with others
4 Being the same person in multiple contexts
5 Communicating as a real person, rather than an avatar
6 Revealing my hidden self to a trusted few
7 An important interpersonal skill that I can learn
8 Being nonymous rather than anonymous
9 A valuable quality I can fabricate for personal gain
10 A risky strategy due to security concerns
11 Engaging in direct rather than mediated communication

This final understanding of authenticity, which is a direct outcome of the deinstitutionalization of communication by social media, is likely to be of most concern for public relations. Public relations, as a practice, involves a mediating role between organizations (or high profile individuals) and their publics. In enacting this role, public relations practice facilitates communication but such engagements may not be seen as authentic and may, therefore, struggle for credibility. There is a clear tension between the efficiency of mediated communication and the greater credibility of personal communication.

Transparency, power/knowledge, authenticity and truth claims

Legitimating ideas by establishing the truth of certain facts or perspectives arguably lies at the heart of effective public relations practice. In this chapter we have analyzed the three core dimensions of truth claims—transparency, power/knowledge and authenticity—in terms of the subtle and not-so-subtle changes for public relations practice associated with the advent of social media. In light of this analysis, it is clear that many of our established understandings of effective or ethical practice have been challenged or turned on their heads. For example, in the age of information overload, simply releasing large volumes of information does not equate with transparent communication. Indeed, such releases may be seen as unethical if there is suspicion that potentially embarrassing information has been buried within a mountain of undifferentiated data. Similarly, the diffusion of power/knowledge through networks of communication means rethinking public relations as engagement within streams of communication rather than as a centralized, controlled activity. Indeed, the temporal shifts engendered by social media have put an end to the time-limited campaign. The third dimension of truth claims, authenticity, is perhaps the most challenging for public relations. Authenticity in social media contexts has multiple meanings but inevitably involves some form of self-presentation. The involvement of communication professionals in social media therefore both enables popular social media sites to function while at the same time, devaluing these same sites by reducing their authenticity.

References

Back, M., Stopfer, J., Vazire, S., Gaddis, S. Schmukle, S., Egloff, B., and Gosling, S. (2010). Facebook profiles reflect actual personality, not self-idealization. *Psychological Science*, 21(3), 372–374.

Bargh, J., McKenna, K., and Fitzsimons, G. (2002). Can you see the real me? Activation and expression of the "True Self" on the Internet. *Journal of Social Issues*, 58(1), 33–48.

Christianson, L.T. and Langer, R. (2009). Public relations and the strategic use of transparency: Consistency, hypocrisy, and corporate change. In R.L. Heath, E.L. Toth, and D. Waymer (eds.), *Rhetorical and Critical Approaches to Public Relations II*, pp. 129–153. New York: Routledge.

Coombs, T. and Holladay, S. (2011). The pseudo-panopticon: The illusion created by CSR-related transparency and the internet. *Corporate Communication: An International Journal*, 18(2), 212–227.

DiStaso, M. and Bortree, D. (2012). Multi-method analysis of transparency in social media practices: Survey, interview and content analysis. *Public Relations Review*, 38, 511–514.

Fitzpatrick, K.R. and Palenchar, M.J. (2006). Disclosing special interests: Constitutional restrictions on front groups. *Journal of Public Relations Research*, 18(3), 203–224.

Foucault, M. (1977). *Discipline and Punish: The Birth of the Prison* (trans. A. Sheridan). New York: Pantheon Books.

Foucault, M. (1980). *Power/Knowledge: Selected Interviews and Other Writings, 1972–1977*. London: Vintage.

Goldberg, G. (2010). Rethinking the public/virtual sphere: The problem with participation. *New Media & Society*, 13(5), 739–754.

Healey, K. (2010). The pastor in the basement: Discourses of authenticity in the networked public sphere. Symbolic Interaction, 33(4), 526–551.

Good, K.D. (2013). From scrapbook to Facebook: A history of personal media assemblage and archives. *New Media & Society*, 15(4), 557–573.

Ibrahim, Y. (2008). The new risk communities: Social networking sites and risk. *International Journal of Media and Cultural Politics*, 4(2), 245–253.

Jackson, M. (2009). The mash-up: A new archetype for communication. *Journal of Computer-Mediated Communication*, 14(3), 730–734.

Jordan, J. (2005). A virtual death and a real dilemma: Identity, trust, and community in cyberspace. *Southern Communication Journal*, 70(3), 200–218.

Krotoski, A. (2012)Online identity: Is authenticity or anonymity more important? Retrieved on 29 January 2014 from www.theguardian.com/technology/2012/apr/19/online-identity-authenticity-anonymity

Larmore, C. (2010). *The Practices of the Self.* (trans. S. Bowman). Chicago, IL: The University of Chicago Press.

Leitch, S. and Davenport, S. (2011). Corporate identity as an enabler and constraint on the pursuit of corporate objectives. *European Journal of Marketing*, 45 (9/10), 1501–1520.

Leitch, S. and Motion, J. (2010). Publics and public relations: Effecting change. In R. Heath (ed.). *The Sage Handbook of Public Relations*, pp. 99–110. Thousand Oaks, CA: Sage.

Leitch, S. and Neilson, D. (2001). Bringing publics into public relations: New theoretical frameworks for practice. In R. Heath (ed.) *Handbook of Public Relations*, pp. 127–138. Thousand Oaks, CA: Sage.

Livingstone, S. (2008). Taking risky opportunities in youthful content creation: Teenagers' use of social networking sites for intimacy, privacy and self-expression. *New Media & Society*, 10(3), 393–411.

McGongale, J. and Vella, C. (2007). I spy your company secrets. *Security Management*, February, 64–70.

Marwick, A. and boyd, d. (2011). I tweet honestly, I tweet passionately: Twitter users, context collapse and the imagined audience. *New Media & Society*, 13(1), 114–133.

Meyers, E. (2012). "Blogs give regular people the chance to talk back": Rethinking "professional" media hierarchies in new media. *New Media & Society*, 14(6, 1022–1038.

Motion, J. and Leitch, S. (2002). The technologies of corporate identity. *International Studies of Management and Organization*, 32(3), 45–64.

Motion, J. and Leitch, S. (2007). A toolbox for public relations: The oeuvre of Michal Foucault. *Public Relations Review*, 33, 263–268.

Rawlins, B. (2009). Give the emperor a mirror: Toward developing a stakeholder measurement of organizational transparency. *Journal of Public Relations Research*, 21(1), 71–99.

Stauber, J. and Rampton, S. (1995), *Toxic Sludge Is Good for You: Lies, Damn Lies and the Public Relations Industry*. Monroe, ME: Common Courage Press.

Trilling, L. (1971). *Sincerity and Authenticity*. Cambridge, MA: Harvard University Press.

Williams, S. (2011). The authenticity of Facebook and Twitter. Retrieved 29 January 2014 from www.bigisthenewsmall.com/2011/02/16/the-authenticity-of-facebook-and-twitter/

Wilson, R., Gosling, S., and Graham, L. (2012). A review of Facebook research in the social sciences. *Perspectives on Psychological Science*, 7(3), 203–220.

5 Engage

One-way, two-way, and every-way

Social media has managed to gain such a hold over many of our lives. It can be populist, compelling and addictive, yet at the same time provoke concern and action to address serious issues. Some of that action is proactive, but it may also be reactive. Reactions might be repressive, which is moral or immoral depending on circumstances.

Although we are able to have some control over the social media landscapes we participate in, significant public relations effort is expended trying to encourage us to engage with and connect to various platforms, sites and networks. The production of discourse through storytelling and conversational techniques is a vital part of public relations in social media. However, participants must perceive the stories and conversations as meaningful. Within this chapter we explore how popularity and meaningfulness play out within a range of social media stories and conversations. We focus first on notions of one-way, two-way and "every-way" communication to argue that it is not the direction of communication that matters—it is the intent and meaning. We then discuss the concept of engagement, which allows us to examine governance issues where organizational initiatives and responses either align with or diverge from public expectations. In doing so, we consider how organizational communication may move from the pseudopersonal to a more authentic or playful mode. The aim of the chapter is to provide insights into how some organizations have driven social change or engaged with "difficult" publics through social media platforms.

Two-way, one-way, and every-way

Consideration of direction, one-way and two-way modes of thinking about communication, is perhaps a somewhat traditional, but possibly even controversial, approach when theorizing for social media. As interpretive/critical scholars we have always been more concerned with meaning, engagement and the social impact of communication, than advocating the use of directional modes of conceptualizing public relations. Yet, we also acknowledge that it is useful to think through how one-way, two-way and "every-way" communication patterns play out in social media platforms and the types of problems that directional approaches mask. Whether leading or following, US public relations icon, Scot Cutlip added the notion of two-way to the definition of public relations that he codified with Allen Center. That line of thinking became even more codified in the descriptive and normative approach to excellent public relations by James Grunig. One-way communication was positioned as inferior to the two-way communication model both normatively and in impact. One-way communication was associated with press agentry and propaganda, and even "scientific persuasion." In contrast, two-way communication was positioned as superior because, even when "asymmetrical," it was a kind of engagement.

Normatively, the best model of public relations was the two-way symmetrical approach, so the argument went. The later concept of two-way symmetrical communication in the functionalist intellectual tradition was used as the centerpiece and foundational principle of excellent public relations. The excellence research and behavioral science driven paradigm served as the gold standard for public relations practice and, in some circles, still does. As the notion of dialogue emerged and gained currency, two-way symmetrists said that is what we believe and champion. And, social media was believed to be the latest, best evidence that two-way was superior to one-way approaches, and realizable through social media. Thus, social media was seen as a major step toward the reality and actualization of two-way symmetrical excellent public relations.

As a foundation for understanding social media—and its connections to public relations, it is time to revisit the directional paradigm in both the large and specific senses. First, close examination suggests a contextual virtue of one-way, and its prevalence, in social media contexts, to two-way. Second, social media can be used ethically and effectively for one-way communication. Third, it is possible, probable, and even certain that social media does not inherently achieve or predict a time when two-way symmetry emerges as the enduring paradigm of reasonable, responsible, and reflective public relations.

In several important contexts, social media provides strategic opportunities for supplying targeted information to willing audiences. One is the use of social media by news organizations to provide news alerts, weather updates especially during storm warnings, bush fire alerts, and traffic monitoring to advise about congested roads and streets. News alerts can come to social media users without their having to be tied to a television. Even print media use such alerts to notify readers of breaking stories. If a storm approaches and poses a threat to the social media user, targeted information can be provided in an as-desired timeframe.

Links can provide additional emergency response information ranging for instance from shelter in place to evacuation. Schools, universities, and myriad workplaces now have the capability of real time communication providing emergency alerts and response information. Industrial and governmental organizations now have the capability of warning workers and near neighbors of crisis circumstances. Such warnings can be followed by users, and users can obtain real-time emergency response information. Nongovernmental organizations can use social media to deliver newsletters to followers. Such alerts also have interactive options and are even used to raise funds and coordinate volunteer efforts. In fact, one can imagine that a great deal of the communication in social media is actually one-way, but nevertheless socially redeeming.

One of the problems with the conceptualization of two-way communication is that interaction is not really communication. For instance, politicians use social media to notify citizens of the noteworthy actions and policy positions that have consumed each politician's busy time. This "I'm-working-for-you" announcement is often slanted for political advantage. Most recipients merely note what is said and give it passing judgement. Some recipients voice approval, while others react negatively. Statements get made by those who support and oppose what the politician has done or said, but it is unlikely that the communication is dialogic. Dialogic communication presumes that through interactive discourse decisions can be made and influences exerted. Change can happen and be co-managed by many parties. But rather than seeking collaboration, dialogue, and change, the vast number of political messages are merely designed to stir the pot, reinforcing what is assumed to be the positions favored by 50 percent of the voters, plus one.

Within the following political exchange we examine our assertion that interaction is not really communication. In February 2015 speculation about a potential leadership challenge for the Australian Prime Minister's position escalated. A Twitter exchange between two potential challengers, the deputy leader of the Liberal Party, Julie Bishop, and the Minister of Communications, Malcolm Turnbull, attracted significant media attention. A Sydney-based journalist, Ben Fordham, tweeted the following message: "Interesting fact—@JulieBishopMP and @TurnbullMalcolm have arranged to meet at his Sydney home today. #auspol—BenFordham (@BenFordham) February 5, 2015" (Knott, 2015).

In response, a spokesperson for Malcolm Turnbull explained that the minister was actually on his way out of town to an event and had no plans to meet with Ms. Bishop.

The journalist countered with the following tweet: "Don't know why office of @TurnbullMalcolm is denying meeting with @JulieBishopMP at his Sydney home today. He won't. She won't. #auspol—BenFordham (@BenFordham) February 5, 2015" (Knott, 2015)

Malcolm Turnbull then tweeted the following message accompanied by a photo of himself on a train: "You need to improve yr surveillance! I am on train to Tuggerah. PoliticsinPub Nth Wyong 2nite." (Knott, 2015). Photos of scenery from the train journey were then tweeted.

Julie Bishop also took to Twitter to correct the journalist's tweet: "@BenFordham @TurnbullMalcolm Wrong information! In Canberra this morning flew to Sydney filmed by @channel9 now with @FionaScottMP." She then followed up that tweet with this message: "@BenFordham I did not meet @TurnbullMalcolm at his home—I even told you @Qantas flight I was on! So what is the point you're (not) making?" (Knott, 2015).

In a further tweet Turnbull posted a photo of himself at his destination under the Tuggerah train station signpost to prove he had arrived at his destination. Next, he tweeted that he would not be meeting Bishop unless she turned up at the same venue out of Sydney. Bishop responded directly to Turnbull and said she would not be meeting him.

Clearly this interchange directed at the journalist had many intended audiences and meanings—and would be difficult to characterize as one-way or two-way—perhaps the notion of "every-way" best sums up the flow.

Focusing on direction as a mechanism for understanding communication in a social media instance such as this example does not provide insights into the political strategies at play. We actually learn very little from the exchange. It is possible to assume, however, after a number of highly contentious leadership challenges and changes experienced by the opposition Labor Party when they were in power, that it is likely neither Bishop nor Turnbull wanted to publicly damage their Liberal Party's stability, or to be seen openly undermining the Prime Minister and plotting to overthrow him. Social media, in this instance, was used to maintain the reputational capital of the Liberal Party, Julie Bishop and Malcolm Turnbull. What really stands out in this political interchange is the playful way that the politicians engaged with the speculation about their whereabouts and potential involvement in a leadership challenge. This is an insight into how social media can enable politicians to project personality—but it is an entertaining diversion from politics, rather than particularly meaningful communication.

Dave Carroll's protest song about unacceptable customer service is a striking example of the impact of one-way communication and how social media storytelling may change the power relations between organizations and customers. In 2008, on a United Airlines flight from Halifax, Nova Scotia to Omaha, Nebraska, Carroll, a Canadian musician, overheard another passenger, say "My god, they're throwing guitars out there." On arrival at Omaha, Nebraska, Carroll discovered that it was actually his US$3500 Taylor-made guitar that was broken. Carroll raised the matter with United Airlines and filed a claim. However, because the claim was not filed within 24 hours of the incident, he was deemed ineligible for compensation. Carroll tried, unsuccessfully, for 9 months to get compensation. As a result, he wrote a song about his experience of United Airlines' inflexible policies titled "United breaks guitars" and uploaded a video of the song to YouTube on July 6 2009. The video went viral on YouTube receiving 150,000 views on the first day, 1 million views in three days, and by mid-August it had 5 million views (see www.youtube.com/watch?v=5YGc4zOqozo). In addition the video became a number one hit on iTunes.

For United Airline this was a global public relations disaster. The video issue attracted international media coverage and, according to the BBC, United Airlines shares dropped by US$180 million (Singers' airline tune takes off,

2009). What we see in this primarily one-way social media interaction is an example of how popular culture may be mobilized to express dissatisfaction with corporate performance and force organizational engagement. The "United Breaks guitars" issue captured the public imagination because the flying public can identify with the too-common occurrence of damaged luggage. More broadly, a global audience could identify with the inflexible application of organizational policy and a seemingly unwavering lack of response to complaints. The song voiced the feelings of frustration and powerlessness that publics experience when organizations behave badly.

At the same time, it opened up a platform for social media criticism of the airline. It offers a model for voicing authentic complaints and points to how social media may be effectively mobilized via one way communication to protest unacceptable organizational behavior, destabilize power relations and drive demands for change. Assessments of the effectiveness of such protests need to consider what has changed as a result of this protest? Have company policy or practices changed or was the protest a random, but very effective, one-off instance? Equally significant is the way in which social media may be leveraged to influence sense-making about United Airline and its corporate identity. The key to protest-oriented, storytelling success is building upon moments of localized resistance that tap into or create identification with popular fantasies about defeating corporate power and thus give expressive shape to hopes of changing our condition.

One-way communication can be a very powerful agent for addressing serious issues and driving social change. The #LikeAGirl campaign was designed to provoke serious questions about the way that gendered criticisms are normalized and naturalized and to specifically interrogate the notion that doing something "like a girl" is a negative thing. The Procter and Gamble feminine protection brand, Always, launched the #LikeAGirl campaign as part of their puberty education program. A video developed by the documentarian, Lauren Grenfield, sought to challenge the negative connotations of the phrase "like a girl." Although societal norms may be shifting, it is difficult for public relations to develop campaigns for products that are not openly spoken about and that many would perceive as private and even distasteful.

Selection of a salient social cause—the social construction of gender inequity—has made this campaign a striking example of how a public relations approach may target social change. The #LikeAGirl campaign video opens with a television studio stage with a young woman who appears to be auditioning and then cuts to the following text onscreen asking the question, "When did doing something like a girl become an insult?" The director then says to the young woman, "Okay, so I'm going to give you some actions to do. Just do the first thing that comes to mind. Show me what it means to run like a girl." A series of people are asked to enact certain actions "like a girl"—"show me what it means to run like a girl;" "show me what it means to fight like a girl;" "now throw like a girl" and invariably running, fighting and throwing are portrayed as weak and even comical.

The following statement then appears in text on the screen: "We asked young girls the same question." A series of young girls are then asked to run, fight and throw like a girl and they put all of their energy and effort into it. A young girl is then asked, "What does it mean to you when I say 'run like a girl'"? She replies. "It means run as fast as you can." Text on screen asks, "When did doing something like a girl become an insult?" The video cuts back to a boy in the earlier scene who had negatively performed like a girl and he is asked "So do you think you just insulted your sister?" He replies, "No, I mean, yeah, insulted girls but not my sister." A young girl is asked, "Is like a girl a bad thing?" She responds, "Actually I don't know what, if it is a bad thing or a good thing. Sounds like a bad thing. Sounds like you are trying to humiliate someone." The text on screen reads, "A girl's confidence plummets during puberty." Several young women comment and offer advice on what to do when told to run like a girl and reinterpret and reenact the phrase "like a girl" in a more positive way. The campaign concludes with the following text "Let's make 'like a girl' mean amazing things." The final screen shot invites social media participation by asking people to "rewrite the rules" and "SHARE to inspire girls everywhere," "TWEET the amazing things you do #LIKEAGIRL," and to "STAND UP for girls' confidence at ALWAYS.COM."

The campaign video, published on YouTube on 26 June 2014, also went viral via Facebook, Twitter and Instagram and it is estimated that it may have over 80 million views (Griner and Ciambriello, 2015). This campaign is an excellent example of one-way communication that seems designed to motivate social change by reclaiming a discursive position and modifying societal perceptions—although it may be argued that the invitation to engage in social media conversations modified the one-way video medium into a more interactive process. Transforming #LikeAGirl into an expression of strength offers a positive storyline that has empowering, confidence-building possibilities for young women to identify with cognitively and affectively.

Brown et al. (2009, p. 325) suggest that "stories are always replete with meaning, often contain moral judgments and frequently elicit strong emotional reactions." The #LikeAGirl video functioned as a moral tale that invited reflection and reflexivity on gender relations and equity issues. Through a series of critical questions, ways of thinking about and talking about gender were challenged. This generative campaign will, at the very least, make it less acceptable to use the phrase "like a girl" as an insult. This story constitutes a politics of change about how we value girls and women in society: "Whether stories are interpreted as constituting, mapping, encouraging, managing, upsetting, preventing or inviting change, they are an ever present feature of patterns of becoming, always evocative of actual futures and possible worlds" (Brown et al. 2009, p. 325). The brand associated with the campaign, Always, chose a topic relevant to its target market and, as a consequence, has accrued positive brand recognition and associations in terms of gender relations and social justice through one-way communication.

The two-way paradigm can play out in many contexts, whether reputational, identity based, product/service marketing, or public policy debate. Even though two-way options are provided by the mechanisms of the social media design, the intent of the parties "engaged" plays an important role in the enactment of the medium. It is also likely that the organization that employs the social media venue and content does so with a "linear" intent. Much of the content tends to be ranted commentary. Such discourse style is likely to reduce the likelihood of dialogue simply because it is so fraught with acrimony.

Organizations that attempt to force conversations with customers who may not wish to engage in conversation will also face criticism. The Starbucks campaign, #RaceTogether, was intended to encourage discussions about race issues. Baristas were expected to write #RaceTogether on customers' coffee cups. A company spokesperson explained that the initiative was intended "spark the conversation, because we believe that is the first step in a complicated issue" (Somaiya, 2015). The campaign did not attract a favorable response. Criticism of the campaign accused Starbucks of "trying to reduce an incendiary issue to a marketing tagline" (Helmore, 2015).

The objectives seemed too general and poorly focused. It seemed that the inclusion of a hashtag in the title, #RaceTogether, meant that there may have been expectations that the campaign would take place in Starbucks cafés and in social media. From a practical perspective it was unrealistic—although considerable time may be spent in the queue to get coffee, the actual conversational exchanges with Starbucks employees are brief. The campaign "was mocked with such vengeance on social media that the company's senior vice president for global communications deleted his Twitter account because, as he wrote on Medium, he felt 'personally attacked in a cascade of negativity'" (Somaiya, 2015). The two-way nature of Twitter conversations was not something that Starbucks was prepared for nor was it prepared for the type of negativity that such a campaign may spark.

Although the account was restored the following day (Helmore, 2015), it may be argued that the campaign was predicated on a model of understanding social media as a "hybrid element of the promotion mix" (Mangold and Faulds, 2009, p. 357). From this promotional perspective, organizations talk *to* customers, "shape" customer conversations and enable "customers to talk directly to one another" (Mangold and Faulds, 2009, p. 357). Understanding social media in this way is deeply problematic. It is a model in which organizations attempt to control the conversation—and demonstrates a fundamental lack of understanding of the norms of everyday conversations and how they play out in social media. More broadly, it reflects a misunderstanding of social media cultural norms. Organizations that seek to spark conversations about controversial topics need to listen and engage with customers—not just attempt to set or shape the agenda. Conversations need to be "every way." The response to the social media onslaught appears to be removal of the hashtag—Starbucks' discussions of the campaign no longer mention the hashtag.

Criticism of the campaign has focused on a number of issues, in particular the distinctive lack of diversity evident in the senior management hiring policies at Starbuck. The campaign may be interpreted as a denial of Starbuck's own indifference to racism and a lack of any sense of obligation. Rather than addressing the problems within their own organization, racism is positioned as something done by others. This generalization and abstraction of racism into an issue for a promotional campaign suggests a lack of sensitivity about the complexities of racism and a disconnection from their own practices.

Ironically, the campaign actually served to draw attention to a lack of communication about what exactly Starbucks is doing internally to advance diversity at senior levels. Images of the predominantly white male senior management of Starbucks circulated via Facebook, Twitter and Instagram. Although Starbucks may attempt to position itself as "sparking" the conversation, there are already numerous conversations about racism. It was noted in social media conversations about the campaign that many others, especially people of color, were already very engaged in issues of race (Helmore, 2015). In response to these criticisms, the CEO of Starbucks, Howard Schultz, stated, "he is leading Starbucks to try to redefine the role and responsibility of a public company" (Helmore, 2015). A fundamental reason why many social campaigns fail is that the issue selected is perceived as an unnatural fit for that particular organization or business. As a consequence, the organization lacks credibility in relation to the social cause selected and suspicion and cynicism are expressed about the motive. For example, Twitter conversations suggested that the #RaceTogether campaign may be part of a marketing push to establish Starbucks in lower socioeconomic districts/regions. The absence of Starbucks in such districts was noted but potential attempts to expand into these markets were criticized: "Starbucks is too white, and they charge too much damn money" (Helmore, 2015).

What Starbucks also failed to do was consider who could take part in the conversations—and whether such conversations make a difference. This insensitive colonization of such a controversial and foundational issue is likely to be perceived as just another marginalizing promotional strategy by an American global corporation. Starbucks has unintentionally positioned itself as a type of fake friend—insensitive to the needs of others and impervious to the difficulties that such conversations may create for those who experience racism. Further, Starbucks lacks the credibility and legitimacy to lead such a contentious conversation.

Although Starbucks has indeed sparked a conversation, the problem is that the conversation is about Starbucks rather than racism. For Starbucks, the conversation about racism and associated changes in practice had to happen within the organization before it attempted to tackle the issues externally. Yes, it is important to open up expressive possibilities in relation to contentious issues but the question that needs to be explored is whether Starbucks is an appropriate organization that could authentically and justifiably do that? Drawing on Hawkins (2004) a counterargument about the value of a "politics of disturbance" could be presented that makes the case that Starbucks has indeed opened up expressive possibilities and troubled expectations of the role of corporations in contemporary capitalist societies. What is less clear is whether that disturbance will result in any positive change, within Starbucks or society.

But, two-way communication can also be positive and productive. Individuals can seek information, for instance, about a vacation spot and even obtain reviews of persons who have traveled there, used various hotels, visited various attractions, and dined in one place or another. Reports can even be made in real time (leading some in travel public relations to monitor such conversations to claim the good news and blunt the bad comments). The content of comments can be better than merely seeing a score, such as the number of stars for a hotel or restaurant, but even then does that predict how well the user of the site will agree with the comments based on his or her actual experience?

City governments, for instance, can offer a comment option regarding items that come forward for deliberation and action. The siting of a park, or the changing of the hours of a park's operation, for instance, could be an item of business that provoked commentary. Such comments are a bit like a dialogue, although they do not necessarily respond to one another in the spirit of collaboration. But, there is interaction and politicians and other voices, such as the city parks director and an expert on park design and safety, can weigh in on the discussion. Such social media town hall meetings allow for two-way communication, however dialogic, which can lead communities to be better places to live and work—one of the broad, socially redeeming goals of public relations. In sum, directional modes of thinking about social media have value.

In sum, one-way communication can be extremely effective and is neither inherently inferior nor (ethically) inadequate by comparison to the "two-way option." However, there are limitations within the directional modes of conceptualizing public relations that become evident when thinking about social media. Rather than directionality, should not the emphasis be placed in discourse, meanings, and the potentially enriching insights that can result, regardless of attempts to privilege or denigrate directionality? Such attempts can also have elitist underpinnings, even when such is not the intention.

We now explore how the notion of engagement opens up possibilities for expanding our understanding of the relationship between public relations and social media.

The turn to engagement

The term "engagement" generally signals some sort of personal connection, productive involvement or interactive exchange—a useful starting point for any analysis of how public relations practices play out in social media. Modes for thinking about social media cultures and how social media participants connect relationally, how particular encounters and actions signal involvement and the meanings of those interactions (and the interactions of meanings) are essential for a progressive public relations that not only advances clients' priorities but also those of society. The cultural transformations that are being shaped within social media call for new modes of operating that include sharing and reciprocity and involve publics in decision-making. Within this section we discuss how contemporary studies of public engagement may inform such a change. We focus, in particular, on how those charged with self-governance responsibilities may open up possibilities for productive explorations of societal concerns and preferences.

Disrupting institutional determinism

Studies of public engagement processes offer insights into the ways in which organizations such as government or science formally organize interactions with civil society. Engagement based on true public participation is defined "as the practice of consultation and involving members of the public in the agenda-setting, decision-making, and political forming activities of organizations or institutions responsible for policy development" (Rowe et al., 2004, p. 512). The essence of engagement would seem to be the reaching of opinion, conclusions, judgements, issue preferences, and even reputations that are not predetermined or even preferred by one part. The centering notion of engagement is joint, or joined. Similarly, as a participatory culture, social media has sharing as its "constitutive activity" (John, 2013, p. 179). Engagement, then, is fundamentally aligned to social media practices.

Alternative terms used to refer to engagement include "deliberative democracy," "community engagement," "outreach," "deliberative decision-making," "public participation," "stakeholder participation" and "deliberative participatory engagement." Engagement interactions may be driven by institutional determinism that privileges organizational interests and imperatives or a broader governance orientation that seeks to advance the interests of civil society. Thus, public engagement may be just a perfunctory exercise in compliance designed to meet legislated obligations or form part of a broader movement towards participatory deliberation and democracy (Powell and Colin, 2008).

Engagement processes that are primarily compliance exercises tend to carefully manage citizen power and to regulate influence on decision-making. This approach is predicated upon institutional determinism—the organization pursues its own managerially driven interests and imperatives. In contrast, a key tenet of democratic-oriented public engagement is that deliberation and decision-making should be on "citizens' terms and towards goals they value" (Powell et al., 2011, p. 66). Social media operates in a similar way—except that citizen publics generally have more agency to dictate the terms of engagement within social media.

Organizationally driven engagement practices that seek to open up citizen choices and drive positive societal change disrupt patterns of determinism and are more likely to be welcome in the social media spaces that citizen publics inhabit. Expressive cultures and networks within social media moderate organizational intrusions and establish boundaries in line with their own agendas. Deterministic engagement practices that do not align with the things that matter to citizen publics—that have a conflicting starting point—are unlikely to connect with or be meaningful to publics. From a governance perspective, democratic principles of openness, adaptability, choice, and change need to be forefront rather than organizational goals. There are, of course, hybrid forms of engagement that may privilege governance priorities but also allow publics choices and open possibilities for change. Central to the success of these types of engagements that pursue multiple goals are a sense of trust, an expectation of fairness and an assurance of good intentions.

Disrupting organizational power relations

Issues of power relations are entangled in engagement and participation processes. Arnstein (1969) developed a laddered model of citizen participation that delineated between varying levels of participation and identified citizen power to determine their own and their collective social future. The eight levels of participation begin with nonparticipation and progress to degrees of tokenism and increased degrees of citizen participation.

The first level is manipulation, followed by therapy, informing, consultation, placation, partnership, delegated power and at the top is citizen control. This model is useful for analyzing public relations levels of engagement in social media, although Arnstein (1969) acknowledges that the model is a "simplification" of the engagement process and points out further limitations in that both the "have-nots" and the "powerholders" do not all share the same views and interests; and that "roadblocks" such as paternalism need to also be taken into account (p. 217).

However, her model of levels of participation provides explicit recognition that participation and engagement involve relations of power. For Foucault (1980) power was relational—"a more or less organized, hierarchical, coordinated cluster of relations" (Foucault, 1980, p. 198). Discussions about communication direction or flow often provide a very narrowly circumscribed set of approaches for considering the power relationships between public relations and social media participants. Public engagement theories and processes, in contrast, draw attention to and open up a diverse range of possibilities for thinking about how public relations may and does operate within social media spaces. In particular, studies of engagement focus our attention on a range of democratic issues associated with the production of social meanings and complexities of power relations. Power relations are embedded within public relations efforts to politicize or popularize particular sociocultural, technical and political factors in governance processes (Macnaghten et al., 2005), yet considerations of these political dimensions of public relations are typically absent from discussions of one-way and two-communication.

Critical questions about how power relations are configured within various forms of engagement challenge traditional modes of public relations and governance practices. Democratic principles are increasingly promoted and regulated by social media publics and commentators. Situating considerations of public relations engagement in social media within a broader governance framework shifts attention from individual relations of power to considerations of how expressive cultures and networks interact with organizational public relations efforts. Engagement efforts in social media require that organizations understand the changing power relations, listen to citizens and then embed citizens' concerns into agenda setting or policy changes.

That is not to say that social media is essentially a democratic space—however, publics do have an apparent sense of choice about who they engage with and what they engage about. The problematic for public relations professionals is reconciling democratic expectations of social media with client stipulations and conditions.

Disrupting organizational intentionality

Stirling (2008) suggests that participatory activities are implemented for three key reasons: instrumental, substantive and normative. An instrumental rationale is when there is a "predefined end"; a substantive rationale is predicated on the understanding that "the best result will emerge through the process"; and a normative rationale implies that the process is paramount, instead of the outcome—it is seen as "right thing to do" (Stirling, 2008, p. 268–269). For public relations, clarity and transparency about the rationale and purpose of engagement with publics is essential in social media platforms. Stirling (2008) differentiates between engagement-oriented communication that is intended to seek appraisal or evaluation (open-ended) and communication that seeks approval or commitment (a predefined end).

From a public relations perspective, if the task is to advance an organization or client's objectives then approval and commitment are likely to be the desired goal of engagement. This type of engagement may be represented as consultative, but in practice it is also instrumental and one-sided. Public engagement programs that seek early deliberation, collaboration and participation in project planning, agenda setting, policy formation and decision-making phases are referred to as upstream engagement. Programs that occur later in the decision-making process, that do not allow publics to set the agenda, are referred to as downstream. Involving publics in upstream engagement means that issues of power need to be resolved in order to embark on the codesign and co-organization of the engagement process (Powell and Colin, 2008) and potentially the co-production of solutions (Bovaird, 2007).

Ideally, engagement processes should inform organizational policy and have the potential to influence decisions (Rayner, 2003) in order to avoid engagement fatigue and cynicism. This shift to thinking about the starting point rather than the end point of public relations draws attention to democratic potential of engagement that one way and two-way approaches ignore. Entering social media spaces requires a willingness to genuinely engage—to be changed as well as to change. It suggests that public relations may learn much from the key principles of democratically oriented public engagement studies and practices. We should also pay attention to how public relations inserts itself into our everyday lives through social media—and critically examine whether it is for positive, productive purposes.

Public relations professionals need to consider how the empowerment and/ or power-sharing principles of engagement process are transferable to social media spaces—there are expectations that goals are transparent, institutionally sponsored projects are openly declared, and engagement attempts are meaningful and related to the values and interests of social media publics. In the following case study we examine how a public utility organization sought to engage with its constituents in an integrated promotional campaign.

TAP™ campaign: Engaging with citizen concerns.

Sydney Water, the largest public water utility in Australia, is responsible for protecting public health and the environment, along with being tasked to be a successful business (Sydney Water, nd). In 2011, Sydney Water introduced the tap™ campaign that was designed to position Sydney Water as a sustainable, progressive brand and reintroduce the public to the benefits of tap water. Water from the tap was promoted as if it were a brand itself, in direct competition with bottled water. The branded "tap" water was launched in hundreds of cafés and bars in Sydney by supplying almost 2000 specially designed and branded bottles for tap water to be served in. Sydney Water invited cafés to take part in the campaign and become "a registered tap™ destination." Cafés that opted to sign up to serve tap™ could choose to display "tap™ served here" window decals and/or tap™ stickers on café water bottles. Cafés that signed up were promoted on the tap™ web site via the "find a tap™ cafe" feature—users could enter their suburb or postcode and find a registered café.

The brand strategy was simple and memorable. Sustainability, cost effectiveness and high quality brand values increased the likelihood of connecting with multiple publics with environmental, economic, or health concerns. Bottled water was positioned as unsustainable and drinking tap™ water was positioned as sustainable and trendy. The brand values were echoed in communication messages such as "it's better for the planet, your pocket, and your health" that linked back to environmental, economic and health concerns.

Embedding citizen concerns into the campaign increased the likelihood of meaningful public engagement and identification with the messages. The messages were also designed to target people's identity aspirations—such as being perceived as environmentally conscious: "Get sustainable, drink tap" or "tap™ is the original eco water." The tone of the messages was noteworthy— the social media messages were conversational and engaging. There was an absence of scientific jargon. Rather than attempting to present facts or translate complex science, the communication efforts were framed in line with public concerns (Latour, 2004), focused instead on people's everyday actions and empowered publics by providing a sense that they could take control of the issue and influence change.

An online campaign was also launched featuring images of people drinking directly from their own taps and a series of short films that could be shared across social media platforms. Within their web site and a mobile app, interactive and locative media such as Google maps showed Sydney residents where tap™ was served. The campaign offered a number of online interactive opportunities. People were encouraged to take a "pledge," drink sustainable tap™ water and share the pledge through social media networks.

The campaign was integrated into everyday life through locative media—an interactive Google map and a mobile app were provided to identify the cafés where tap™ could be located. Another interactive opportunity available via the Facebook page was "Flashback Friday" which profiled a series of historical photos relating to water. Flashback Friday involved people in understanding the history of water in an engaging way by asking them to comment or speculate on aspects of the photo. Competitions were often used by Sydney Water to engage their customers via social media. An excellent example of this is the competition in which they invited artists to create designs for a refillable tap™ water bottle.

Further community interaction was generated by giving away the refillable tap™ water bottles and family passes to the Powerhouse Museum via the Sydney Water Twitter #tappyhour competition. Sydney Water's weekly #tappyhour competition was not only used to connect with their Twitter community but to also demonstrate support for organizations and events that shared their eco values. A blogger outreach program was developed by Sydney Water to encourage bloggers to run competitions to give away campaign-related prizes. Through these initiatives, a network of online supporters or a coalition of advocates could potentially be formed.

All online text was accompanied by images and embedded videos. The images were linked to popular culture, social meanings and everyday life and provided talking points about Sydney Water sponsored events that were happening in Sydney, as well as images demonstrating their campaign in action and water related spaces in Sydney. The story of tap™ was described in an animated video featured on the Sydney Water tap™ web site. Throughout the video, the link between the brand name, tap™, and sustainability was reinforced through the imagery of taps and pipes. The animated images and narrative voiceover appealed to social concerns and eco identity aspirations.

The social component of this campaign conducted on Facebook and Twitter reached almost one million people. People began to customize their own bottles and started taking a "tap pledge" to use tap water rather than bottled water.

Insights for public relations

Although this campaign was driven by a policy agenda developed by Sydney Water, we suggest that it was not an instance of institutional determinism because it was a governance-oriented proposal to promote social change rather than just advance Sydney Water. Power relations were reconfigured by the shift from interacting with publics as customers to engaging with concerned citizens. Café owners and citizens were empowered by a sense of agency that offered them some control of the issue. Sydney Water established multiple spaces where conversations about the value of tap water could take place.

Appeal to multiple values

A campaign that targets multiple values is more likely to resonate with publics because they do not have to prioritize or select from potentially conflicting values. In this instance the campaign brand values linked to three potential matters of concern—environmental sustainability, health and safety and economic issues. The campaign reach could be extended because the selection of a number of brand values made it possible to create multiple messages and target diverse publics.

Connect with everyday meanings and practices—address things that matter

Campaigns and communicative efforts that focus on everyday experiences and popular culture are more likely to connect with the ordinary ways we experience the world and have meaning for us. The creative idea, to re-establish tap water as the preferred drink of choice was linked to popular culture—tap™ was available in cafés, associated with art and promoted at popular Sydney events. Sydney Water created opportunities to connect and engage with people and their concerns about water—campaigns need to provide a starting point for conversations and educational initiatives. The online efforts provided spaces for conversations to take place but publics could set the agenda.

Develop a network of advocates

Key stakeholders need to be positioned as partners and trusting relationships developed. Cafés were invited to become part of a coalition of advocates, educating and helping customers to act sustainably and save money. By targeting eco-conscious bloggers, with a particular emphasis on eco-conscious art bloggers and family/parenting bloggers, Sydney Water was able to extend their audience for the tap™ campaign and communicate with target audiences that they may struggle to reach directly.

Inspire change

Sydney water adopted an interactive approach to meet its objectives of pro-tecting public health and the environment. Governance, practiced in this way, has the potential to drive social change. In their communication with cafés Sydney Water adopted a conversational tone that did not focus on unsustain-able choices, rather they aspired to help people—and invited cafés to help—by making the sustainable choice easier, cheaper and fun.

Indirectly "seed" online conversations

Social media is a space where people share their everyday lives. Conversational approaches and use of visual imagery rather than just factual messaging and lan-guage resonate with digitally literate publics. Sydney water engaged in online conversations, demonstrating that it does listen to and respond to negative com-ments that are raised in social media forums in a timely, positive and helpful way.

Conceptualized as true engagement, the voice of dialogue shifts from I/me and they/them, to we/us. The agency of engagement is not organization-centric but community-centric. Often it is hard for public relations practitioners to truly think in terms of we, but social media as a message, as McLuhan argued, is likely to shift organizational grammar.

Conclusion

The aim of this chapter was to examine how public relations may interact, engage and respond in social media by critiquing notions of one-way, two-way and every-way communication. We have argued that directional approaches have value for theorizing public relations interactions within social media but that such theory should not boilerplate the ethics of one direction but rather the dynamics of engagement. To appreciate the dynamics of one-way and two-way, rather than theorizing with a bias for or against a paradigm, the best way to proceed is to look at the dynamics of each context, the motives and roles of the participants, and the information acquisition, dialogue, and interaction needs of the various participants. This requires a shift from an organization-centric, to a community-centric approach to public relations that integrates considerations of public interest.

Implementation of one-way social media campaigns can mediate or lead change through meaningful discursive strategies that provoke identification and align with citizen values or concerns. Despite the tendency to valorize two-way communication efforts for their dialogic potential, if public and organizational starting points are not aligned, effective engagement is unlikely. Naivety or ignorance about how conversations play out in everyday life and the centrality of listening also undermines the dialogic potential of two-way communication. Alternatively, communication that connects meaningfully with publics has the potential to drive change, regardless of the communication direction.

Engagement theories, we suggest, are valuable for addressing the shortcomings of directional models, particularly in relation to governance activities via social media. Drawing upon public engagement theory, we have suggested that communication with and between publics in social media needs to be on terms that are agreed upon or accepted by all participants. This explicitly democratic expectation of public relations supersedes considerations of direction and flow and disrupts institutional determinism.

At the heart of this engagement approach is the notion that public relations must in some way connect with social media publics, engage their interest and respond to concerns. Organizations charged with governance responsibilities need to consider how they may connect with and mobilize publics through social media to achieve social change or justice. If public relations wishes to insert itself within everyday social media networks, it must be able to demonstrate positive, productive effects and impact. Expressive cultures and networks within social media have implicit expectations about how engagement should work.

Our discussion of engagement raises not just issues of power relations but points to the value of empowerment and/or power sharing as a way of working through social justice and change issues. Empowerment and/or power sharing, we suggest, are potential modes for disrupting organizationally dominated forms of power relations and moving beyond polarized positions and interests to a collaborative politics of change.

References

Arnstein, S. R. (1969). Ladder of citizen participation. *Journal of the American Institute of Planners*, 35(4), 216–224.

Bovaird, T. (2007). Beyond engagement and participation: User and community coproduction of public services. *Public Administration Review*, 67(5), 846–860.

Brown, A.D., Gabriel, Y., and Gherardi, S. (2009). Storytelling and change: An unfolding story. *Organization*, 16(3), 323–333.

Foucault, M. (1980). *Power/Knowledge*. New York: Pantheon.

Griner, D. and Ciambrello, R. (2015). Hugely popular "Like a Girl" campaign from Always will return as a superbowl ad. *Adweek*, 29 January. Retrieved from 7 April 2015 from www.adweek.com/news/advertising-branding/hugely-popular-girl-campaign-always-will-return-sunday-super-bowl-ad-162619

Hawkins, G. (2004). Shit in public. *Australian Humanities Review*, April (31–32).

Helmore, E. (2015). How Starbucks wants to be the face of "conscious capitalism." *Guardian*, 22 March. Retrieved 23 March 2015 from www.theguardian.com/business/2015/mar/21/starbucks-face-conscious-capitalism.

John, N.A. (2013). Sharing and web 2.0: The emergence of a keyword. *New Media & Society*, 15(2), 167–182.

Knott, M. (2015). As leadership speculation reaches fever pitch, Malcolm Bishop and Julie Bishop take to Twitter. *Sydney Morning Herald*, 5 February. Retrieved 20 March, 2015 from www.smh.com.au/federal-politics/political-news/as-leadership-speculation-reaches-fever-pitch-malcolm-turnbull-and-julie-bishop-take-to-twitter-20150205-136y7f.html

Latour, B. (2004). Why has critique run out of steam? From matters of fact to matters of concern. *Critical Inquiry*, 30(2), 225–248.

Macnaghten, P., Kearnes, M.B., and Wynne, B. (2005). Nanotechnology, governance and public deliberation: What role for social sciences? *Science Communication*, 27(2), 268–291.

Mangold, W.G. and Faulds, D.J. (2009). Social media: The new hybrid element of the promotion mix. *Business Horizons*, 52(4), 357–365.

Powell, M.C., and Colin, M. (2008). Meaningful citizen engagement in science and technology: What would it really take? *Science Communication*, 30(1), 126–136.

Powell, M., Colin, M., Lee Kleinman, D., Delborne, J., and Anderson, A. (2011). Imagining ordinary citizens? Conceptualized and actual participants for deliberations on emerging technologies. *Science as Culture*, 20(1), 37–70.

Rayner, S. (2003). Democracy in the age of assessment: reflections on the roles of expertise and democracy in public-sector decision making. *Science and Public Policy*, 30(3), 163–170.

Rowe, G., Marsh, R., and Frewer, L.J. (2004). Evaluation of a deliberative conference. *Science, Technology & Human Values*, 29(1), 88–121.

Somaiya, R. (2015). Starbucks ends conversation starters on race. *New York Times*. Retrieved 23 March 2015 from www.nytimes.com/2015/03/23/business/media/starbucks-ends-tempestuous-initiative-on-race.html

Stirling, A. (2008). "Opening Up" and "Closing Down": Power, Participation and Pluralism in the Social Appraisal of Technology. *Science, Technology and Human Values*, 33(2), 262–294.

Sydney Water (nd). Retrieved 2 April 2014 from www.sydneywater.com.au/SW/about-us/our-organisation/who-we-are/index.htm

6 Connect creatively

Worlds, identities, and publics as content production and co-production

Many years ago, legend had it that the Internet was being kept alive with scientific papers and pornography. Today, a new version of that legend for social media might ask, is there life for social media after cats (especially grumpy ones), selfies, and cryptic statements: "I'm here, where are you?" "See my cat leap into and out of a basket."

Each of these instances has implications for the discourse participants' sense of identity and the relational costs calculated as social exchange: identity projected into the Internet as people used to project family vacation photos onto a white screen set up in the living room. Sharing identities is both a rationale for and the outcome of communication, a ripe launching point for the analysis of social media. But, is the reward of engagement worth the cost? Thus, these paradoxes cry out for logics, theories, methodologies, and strategies to systematically study this socially mediated moment in the human condition. Such examination offers important implications for both interactions among individuals, and as a means by which organizations can successfully and ethically seek access to the discourse spaces of those individuals.

One of the enduring issues of sociology and interpersonal communication is knowing how and why people connect (or do not, even disconnect) with one another. Years ago, sociologists crafted sociograms to track and calculate who (for instance, school children) are the most/least popular and most/least interacted with as a social scientific means for charting relationships. Such tools can calculate the frequency of interactions, the networks of interactions, the power structures of interaction webs, and so forth. Teachers have been advised to use such charts to create a positive learning environment. And interpersonal communication tools and strategies have been developed over time to regulate and reward, even disincentivize, such interactions.

By extrapolation, such interaction patterns enacted through social media suggest insights for understanding the enactment of the human condition. These patterns appear to offer keys to unlock the mysteries of how and why social media is important for individuals' identities and interconnections. Or is the equation the other way around: identities and interconnections are the energy and lubrication that drive social media?

In addition to these streams of analysis, media usage and its relationship to identity, identification, and interaction seem important. Marshall McLuhan (1964; McLuhan and Powers, 1989) reasoned that global villages exist because of people's media utilization. On a given evening, some families around a nation (and world) watch a cultural event/program. Others watch a sports event (and by subdivisions, many watching many such individual events). Some watch the news, and news entertainment networks. Viewers select (assuming programming availability) the news presentation they prefer.

Because of the dynamics of viewer self-selection, each group of people engaged in each unique viewing pattern is part of the coconstruction of a "village" that is in various ways unique from other "villages." Shared experience with its cocreated meaning coupled with the attitudinal/belief (personality) incentives of each village lead to a reflexive and self-identifying use of media. Such media utilization is not only, therefore, an enacted expression of "village" identity and identification but also a means by which those identities were shared, developed, maintained, and reinforced.

Conversations the next day become tests of individuals' identification patterns. "What did you think of the bad call in the last seconds of the game?" "Did you ever suspect that Milly was the murderer?" "Did you see the comments by Senator Blowhard on global warming?" These conversational moments are crucial to individuals' mediated and nonmediated interactions and identifications. (Ironically, with tweets, viewers can share comments in "real" time.) Viewing patterns prepare individuals for interpersonal experiences that co-define the knowledge norms and values of group membership and identification. They cocreate the group's identity and those of the individuals who cocreate the group and use the group to cocreate their individual identities. These patterns are driven by factors of social exchange, the cost/reward ratios of relational/group membership.

Each "village" is what it is because of the self-selective inclusions which, by function and structure, create group membership in good standing. This process includes exclusions for being an outlier. People simply do not, and do not want to, watch all of the same media content. But what drives general mass media utilization, and social media utilization as well? Identities, identifications, and content co-production: Those seem to be central to the answer to that question. Thus, the identities and identifications of each village are crafted through shared mediated experiences and the content and meaning of those experiences. What is the reward of identity, as well as the cost of demonstrating identification with others?

For decades, the standard lore of marketing communication, advertising, publicity and promotion was that mass media (newspapers, magazines, and radio/television programming) gathered markets for the targeting of marketing messages. Thus, advertisers were willing to fund programming as a return on investment for gaining access to consumers' eyes and ears. Then, some marketers believed that pop-up ads would not damage relationships and fail to sell products. They were like an intruder seeking access to individuals' life spaces.

Shared experiences are vital to the human condition. Humans seem quite interested in not only being connected with one another, but also in making sure that others know about such interactions and connections. Gossip, over the backyard fence, was traditionally a means for gaining and giving information relevant to neighborhoods. Today social media has become the backyard fence—or the porch or living room, bar, or coffee shop. Where do people gather to "reveal" themselves, demonstrate their identifications, connect with one another, and coproduce the content by which societal norms are constructed, implemented, and rewarded?

Themes such a romance, friendship, workplace relationships, after work relationships, academic and professional collegiality presume the identification and understanding of interaction patterns. ("Join LinkedIn to stay in touch with other professionals." "Do you want to see who of your graduation class remembers you?") Such fascinations continue as a logic that motivates and guides the study and use of social media. Thus, here, we investigate worlds, identities, and publics as relationship and content production and co-production. The assumption is that in various ways and with different motives and commitments, people craft relationships through social media, or use social media as tools for crafting relationships. Thus, by extension, public relations practitioners working for clients become called on to strive to figure out and implement relationship building strategies and tools for the benefit of organizations—and even for publics.

Such mediated villaging is not new, but the potentiality of achieving a better quality of dialogue is still more illusive than routine (McCallister-Spooner, 2009). For instance, decades of magazine designs both followed and led publics' tastes. A visitor to someone's home could attribute volumes about that person, for instance, by noting which magazines provided evidence of reading preferences—and the associated opinions and tastes. Today, persons with various tastes are invited to "follow" some individual or organization with similar interests. Such patterns now are shaped and reshaped by the design and interwoven meanings of myriad social media. Those topics will be examined in more detail in the sections that follow.

Identity and interaction (rituals) and spirals

Narratively, the star of a dramatic or comedic production is the focal point of the plot, action and dialogue. That person's identity is key to the identities of other characters. Other characters' identities not only feed off that of the central character, but also add to it generically as protagonists and antagonists. And, as described by network analysis, the star is a person through which and because of whom information flows and is disseminated to others: That is true, for instance in *The Great Gatsby*, although there is a narrator who focalizes information, but all information ultimately is focused on the character of Jay Gatsby. So, we know that the star is also the focal point of what others' say and do. Narratives, by convention, drive such enactments.

In this way, networks interconnect zones of meaning. Networks become the functionalities and structures of interaction, whereas the meanings necessary for social life become interconnected, overlapping, competing, and conflicting zones of meaning. Such networks tend to be quite invisible. They are there for participants to join (or there for others to join). Through myriad links they seem, and often functionally are, seamless. The functionality, however, is manifested through the perils and processes of identity management (Giddens, 1991; Mazzarella, 2005).

Identities, whether individual or organizational, drive social media. Social media facilitates identities. Years ago, a grandmother could regale her rest home colleagues with books and stacks of the latest pictures, often of children, grandchildren, and even more precious, great grandchildren. For the moment, her stories and pictures were center stage in the old folks' drama. But that narrative focal point would change as others got their latest picture updates. Today's star is tomorrow's supporting actress in the drama of grandmotherhood.

Jump to today! Now, with a tablet or laptop, a grandmother can connect her colleagues with one or more family networks on Facebook, or even FaceTime or Skype. A grandmother can babysit a continent away. She can tweet her feelings about government policy on elder care—or other matters of public policy. She has video so her colleagues can marvel at the accomplishments of her family and friends. For that moment, she is the star. Then, she has to become a supporting actress as another friend goes center stage. She brings the world to her, but also can join the world from the confines of the rest home. And, today, is one of the requirements of a proper eldercare facility the quality of its Wi-Fi?

As does grandmother, teenagers know the price and power (social exchange rituals) of inclusion and exclusion. That is a serious socialization waltz played with various motives, scripts, and skills. These young people realize that conversation units about some matter can be enhanced by conversation units during some event. They don't have to tell their friends about the concert or trip. They can share, involve, their friends in the concert or trip. Smartphones become the eyes and ears of friends. They can tweet each other about the "progress of a date." Imagine a young couple on a date interacting face to face while each is connected to others wanting an update commentary about the date on Facebook or texting. Imagine its potential similarity to "Cyrano de Bergerac" during which one character whispers (tweets or texts) romantic lines (scripts) to another.

By clever use of social media, two young women, for instance, can vet the quality of a potential relational partner for one of the interviewers. Using Skype or FaceTime, the candidate can engage with the interrogators who can interact with the "victim" and share glances and muted affirming or negating comments about the interviewee. In organizational contexts, telephone interviews with a potential employee can now become a Skyped interview with members of the team watching a candidate's reactions to questions and comments. Oh, what a tangled web people weave, and now with social media?

Reflection has been replaced, or at least reshaped, by electronic participation. Teens can reassure their parents about their openness and inclusion by sharing their participation in the "family's" Facebook. But, they also know where to go to text and engage with various friends on social media sites out of the view of parents. They can, as has always been the case, be "public" while being "private." And, employing loosely a theme of Rudyard Kipling, "never the twain shall meet."

Companies spend millions seeking to get people to join their villages ("Follow us"), and now spend millions seeking to join the villages created by individuals (customers) through social media. Rare is the web site, for instance, that does not include invitations for "customers" or "supporters" to become "friends." The assumption, using the birds-of-a-feather logic, is that people silo themselves into interest groups. In conversation, one person might say to another, "We were just talking about a trip to Tuscany," and the newcomer to the conversation might say, "Really, and I was just talking to friends about my latest luggage purchase." Now, two topic fields are on the floor. Where will the conversation go from there?

What if that same conversation occurs in social media? Companies and countries working to foster tourism can "find" such conversations and seek to join them. Since they can't monitor all of the phone conversations and computer-assisted communication (searches, chats, tweets, links as likes, and such), they pay a "conversation facilitator" to help them gain access to the structures, functions, and content of such conversations. "Here is our latest bargain on suitcases." "Tuscany is lovely this time of year. There are some real bargains on hotels."

In conversation, such comments are called demand tickets, those conversational snippets that conversationalists use to decide (by accepting or not) which topic next to pursue. In social media, they might not have a "name" but they nevertheless serve as a demand ticket inviting "conversation" on a topic relevant to the interests of the entity(ies) seeking admission to the "conversation."

Communication patterns, here perhaps best understood as interaction rituals, have long perplexed communication scholars. They ask various broad questions. Is communication "one-way"? Is it "two-way"? Is the process dialogue, or merely interaction? What is the nature of interaction? Is it something that is statically cybernetic or spiraling? If spiraling, does communicative interaction and content coconstruction improve or devolve? And, is communication an end or a means to some other concept, such as relationship quality—or purchase intention?

However unsettled researchers are on these paradigms, lack of consensus as to the nature of communication merely mounts when social media is discussed. For instance, one of the foundations of this discussion is systems theory and its subtext of network theory, along with another subtext, network analysis. At its foundation, this line of research emphasizes how interaction consists of structured and functional flows of information among members (formal and informal) of networks.

This analysis offers some insights into how and why information flows (or fails to do so) cybernetically among the members of a network. Such insights can help participants and researchers understand the quality of network functionality. But such analysis is limited insofar as network theory does not readily predict the coconstruction of meaning as a function of the network and as both a product of and guidance system for the rituals of interaction. It also is limited because it cannot explain how individuals interact with one another as means for fostering, maintaining, and repairing a system to serve those who are its members.

Although information is a touchstone, larger issues of layers of textuality, meanings coconstructed, are not well explained and even trivialized by network analysis. Network analysis, for instance, might suggest that one of the power moves in a network is to include or exclude participants from the information flow—or even to presume that their interests can be harmed by providing misinformation or disinformation into the parts of the system to which they have access. Power, thus enacted, involves inclusion or exclusion. Power moves are enacted by allowing or preventing individuals from achieving access to specific networks.

But, is that the extent of the power and identity that seem to be the key aspects of networks enacted through social media? That theme is central to the discussion of this chapter. As a launching point for expanding that theme, it is important to speculate on how and why interaction rituals, identity and impression management, and tangles of coconstructions are the defining aspects of social media.

To foster insights into social media and public relations, Kent (2014) noted how such study often focuses on interfaces such as Facebook or Twitter, but does not address in detail how those engaged (including those who want to be engaged, as in the case of public relations for an organization) actually "engage." A starting point in such matters, he argued, must begin with this realization: "Social media tools represent only a medium, or channel, through which public relations is practiced" (p. 1). Likewise, he could have contended that interpersonal communication (friendship, romance, or workplace) must likewise start with the acknowledged principle that social media tools are channels.

Consequently, scholarship and professional practice, Kent warned, must build on an understanding of the technology as consisting of complexes of technologies that facilitate and/or hinder interaction functionally and structurally. Secondly, he reasoned that each discipline, public relations in this case, must entail theories central to the discipline to understand how the practice can engage, interact, and cocreate enactable meaning with network participants. That also must presume that no entity can control the flow of information or socially construct important meanings independent of the other participants who are variously active, and self-interested.

Media scholars emphasize how media selection and use also are purposeful. The selection and use of media are goal directed and purposeful, however elusive and complex. Although Slater's (2007) specific focus is on "mass" media, his insights into the nature of the processes of mass media engagement and enactment are relevant to the discussion of social media. Thus, it is tantalizing to adopt the logics of what he refers "to as reinforcing spirals framework for understanding media selectivity and effects as dynamic, mutually influencing processes" (pp. 281–282).

Particularly relevant to this line of analysis is a medium's (the media's) ability to help explain how people use mediated communication for socialization and the development, as well as enactment, of subcultures—such as political, religious—and lifestyles that are essential to the complex of norms, beliefs, and meanings needed for a functional society. Such analysis is keenly aware of media and media programming choices and uses that are relevant to demographic factors such as age, gender, prior experiences, moods, needs, identities, sociopolitical influences, socioeconomics, and all of the other narrative factors of human existence. As such, media use, including social media, is real and important as a means by which individuals mediate their interconnections.

Such factors and processes are shaped by individuals' enacted narratives, especially as is relevant to their identities. The guiding model of this process, Slater (2007) reasoned, is a spiral which is coenacted as a means for creating, refining, maintaining, and repairing the beliefs, attitudes, and behaviors that are necessary for the individual and collective management of identities and identifications. Through iterative interactions people seek and share information relevant to their operant beliefs. They create, test, refine, and abandon attitudes as they are found to be variously functional and purposeful. They similarly propose, invoke, test, refine, and abandon behaviors, both through media use and for "real-life" purposes.

Each programming exposure, for this reason, offers content by which the individual self-examines her or his identity. "I'm the sort of person who likes this content and/or believes what is being said or dramatized." Each exposure, as a spiral allows for other information which is variously enriching and confirming. It is a reality check for the person's operant beliefs and attitudes on some matter.

Such interaction rituals are knowable and comanaged, especially through social media. To offer additional insights, Slater (2007) called on the work by Tajfel and Turner (1986) on social identity theory and by Hecht (1993) on communicative identity. Tajfel and Turner suggested that personal identity is idiosyncratically individual (Who am I?) whereas social identity results from various kinds and degrees of identifications with "groups" of others (Who are we?). Such social identities, and the groups that share them and confirm or disconfirm them, can be identified as religious, ideological, or lifestyle groups, but can also be co-defined by demographics.

Although Hecht (1993) appreciated interpersonal relationships' impact on communicative identities, he emphasized how important media selection and utilization are to these communal identities. Given this foundation based on identity, Slater (2007) proposed the nexus of media use and identity management this way: "Identification with a given social group is in part maintained by the dynamic mutual reinforcement patterns of media selection and influence as well as by associated patterns of choice in interpersonal association and communication" (p. 291). Individuals, for instance, identify through the use of media for news/entertainment. So, access to (utilization) of the network is motivated by identity and identification needs that are self-confirming and informing—and therefore fodder for conversation. "Could you stand to watch the entire game as our team lost?" "Wasn't she brilliantly evil?" "The commentator really blistered the opponents to that bill." Such normative content is the fodder of "villages," cocreated zones of meaning.

That theme, seen as spirals, is ready made for the discussion of identity, identification, and social media, a topic that is expanded in the next section.

Identities, identifications, and narratives

Identities and identifications are narratively created, maintained, and enacted, even overlapping and interconnecting. This is not only possible but required since individuals have not one but many, or multiple identities (Cheney, 1991). Both as individuals and group members, persons work to "manage" these multiple identities, such as (1) working, (2) moms, (3) who are responsible for care of elderly parents, and (4) gardening enthusiasts. That's a lot of "identities" to balance.

Also, other entities, such as organizations, seek or at least should attempt to shape, control, and help individual and group management of identities. Such identities not only are shaped by individuals' knowledge of the collective identities of people with whom they identify, but also the value (emotional, connection, support, etc.) of such identity, and identification (Cheney, 1991).

But the challenge is to not manage these identities to the interest of the organization, especially against the real interest of the individuals. Commercials have for generations tended to "manage" the identities and lifestyles of targeted markets. But, the challenge is to avoid an inherently elitist function by helping individual to achieve self-realization. Even the notion of "follow us on" is an elitist move that can presume that individuals yearn to be led and compensate leaders accordingly.

Narrative theory suggests that humans enact their identities and identifications (persona) through plots, as characters (roles), with voices, as themes leading to morals (as in the moral of the story), in places/locations/sets, and as collectivities, relationships. Such dynamic enactments also call for individuals to variously be narrators, voices, and auditors/listeners (Heath, 1994). Narrative theory explains how in each "scene" individuals take on competing, conflicting, and complementary roles with unique scripts. "I have to complete this report, but should be at our child's soccer game which starts shortly. Dad would like to attend, but he moves so slowly and then will want to treat to supper. When can I get this report done?" Then, our star character thinks, "Can Dad enjoy bits of the game posted on Facebook?"

Social media is inherently relational, and therefore can be explained as the product of as well as the means for relationship development and identity management. As such, relationships require that people make themselves known to one another by using verbal and nonverbal relational messages and interaction styles, those that acknowledge and define relationships (Burgoon and Hale, 1984). As they spiral, such enactments of relationships are episodic. They are shaped by dramatic forms (Gergen, 2000; Gergen and Gergen, 1988). Ironically, the role of harried worker serves as rationale that may help Dad be satisfied by watching bits of a game posted on Facebook. "Since I did not have time to get you to the game, I wanted you to see the 'star' player."

The nature of social media is such that narratives of identity not only become part of what each individual can use to manage—or seek to—the impressions others have about this person, but they also give organizations—especially businesses—the opportunity to tailor messages to individuals based on the identity each posts and enacts through social media use. (Is it wise, therefore, to include a clip of the "star" player with the email transmitting the report which was sent two hours late, but still not out of "deadline"?) Even watching and participating in tweet trends (as spirals between self and mediated others) can give individuals a sense of how they, their identities, interests, and those with whom they identify fit into some matter. This can be true for tweets about celebrities, issues of public policy, news reports and commentary, activities such as celebrations of collegiate athletics, or clothing styles.

Use trends can be identified for those employing social media as part of their involvement in and interest about social movement activism. Vraga et al. (2014) examined how two social movements (Occupy Wall Street and California's Proposition 8's initiative on same sex marriage) varied in the use of YouTube. Supporters of Occupy tended to feature less engagement but contained more content using video of live events. In contrast, Prop 8 content revealed more engagement and more content formats. The authors of this study suggested that the identities of the participants were revealed in the amount and kind of engagement as well as the content. Occupy seemingly had less to engage with or about, and tended to rely more on amateur content. Prop 8 discourse contained lots of monologue, persons affected by the proposition talking to the camera about how it affected them, as well as live footage about the protest and protestors.

By design, social media is identity centered, which can be good—and bad. The good impact arises from individuals' abilities to let others know who they are and as a means for staying in close contact. Families and friends can share personal information that allows them to identify with one another based on the social constructions of friendship and familyship. Wang (2013) discovered a direct path based on extraversion to Facebook check in through disclosure and sharing. Patterns for check in were related to life expectations in ways that differed for extraverts and introverts. Such patterns (as discussed as spirals above) suggest that individuals variously see social media as a means for checking on their self-presentation that necessarily requires monitoring, including frequent check in, as a means for assessing the feedback regarding favorable responses to the self-presentation strategies.

Such analysis assumes that individuals monitor their identities by how they act, how others act toward them, and how such actions and reactions define, confirm, or disconfirm the senses of identities individuals are seeking to form, manage, and repair. By that reasoning, it becomes important to some (more for extraverts, perhaps) to have lots of followers/likes. That pattern might also indicate why those who want to be extroverts are more sensitive to how others react to them—favorably or unfavorably—as such. Is check-in frequency a way to monitor how well messaging is accomplishing that goal and therefore requiring more or less disclosure as reason for others to react? Such factors may also account for the importance of check-in frequency? Check-in, links, likes, tweets, and such become a kind of thermometer or barometer for measuring relational success and response competence. Just like some students, social media users can hardly wait to "get the exam results" regarding how well they manage their identities vis a vis others.

Patterns of identity motivation may differ by age and role, but those established through adolescence may predict continued use and/or use by older populations. Barker (2009) analyzed the connections between social network site (SNS) use, group belonging/identification, collective self-esteem, and gender. In this investigation, collective self-esteem was treated as "the aspect of identity that has to do with the value placed on group membership" (p. 210).

Collective self-esteem appears to be a motivator for adolescents, especially females, to use SNSs to interact with peers. High collective self-esteem predicted the use of SNSs to maintain in-group contact, pass time, and be entertained. Adolescents with lower collective self-esteem exhibit a pattern of using SNSs as an alternative to communicating to other members. Males in particular demonstrated lower collective self-esteem and more likely use of SNS as a substitute for social compensation and social identity gratifications. For those individuals, ones who feel more social isolation, SNS use seems to be a form of virtual companionship—social compensation. For those with lower collective self-esteem, SNSs appear to be a substitute for rather than positive means of group involvement. As such, those with higher collective self-esteem use SNSs actively to participate with others. For those with lower collective self-esteem, their use of SNSs may be motivated by information seeking to learn the skills and strategies of in-group engagement.

Identity, by these means, begins by allowing/requiring users to present their profile. Who am I and who are you are routine scripts of initial interaction that supplies fodder for attributions imposed by relational partners on one another. Individuals do that every day in conversation, and therefore it is easy to see social media utilization as a tool for "virtual" conversation. Those profiles may be quite false. If deception is prevalent in interpersonal communication (even organizational communication) why would we think it was not also the fodder of social media?

Such disclosure/self-presentation also can be dangerous. Adolescents are especially vulnerable to predation and bullying if they are not quite strategic in how and when they present details about themselves. As much as self-disclosure is a currency for social media inclusion, it is also problematic and requires a lot of trust testing. Such details can also be used for targeted marketing, as are factors of trust testing. Is the organization what its profile suggests?

Parents seem to variously be concerned and therefore monitor social media use by their children for several reasons. One is protective information seeking by which parents strive to know what content their children might encounter that is not age appropriate or is otherwise harmful—such as hate speech. Another is problem solving, the efforts of parents to help children to understand and deal with complications that arise from the technologies themselves as well as the content, such as threats, exploitations, and bullying. The third method is attentive learning, a means parents use to understand the nature of social media systems that can lead children into trouble of various kinds. Such profiles suggest how parents are not passive, but still are not completely able to exert as much protection for their children as they desire (Davis, 2012). One of parents' identities is that of gatekeeper and message decoder as an identity buffer.

Identity, as a concept, seems to be a primary predictor of how, why, and when individuals use social media. Their use, variously unique by demographic identity, leads observers to conclude that social media is a tool by which individuals navigate social circumstances, especially identity management and group belonging. As noted above, those who use social media to communicate with in-group members can and probably should acknowledge the multidimensional, multilayered, and multitextual nature of identities. Such insights would seem particularly important for professional communicators who seek to engage with employees and followers, as well as organizations such as companies who want to interact, even dialogue, with external publics, such as customers and special interest issue advocates.

Internal to organizations, those persons (such as experts in human resources and development departments) who use social media as tools are advised to realize the multiple identities of users as a driver for how they access and process messages, as well as behave based on the information provided. Beyond "merely" being employees, some have children of various ages and health. Others have parents of various ages and health. Employees vary by age, degree of identification with the company, industry, and employment (job status, profession, job satisfaction, etc.). It's interesting, for instance, to imagine the damage to some employees whose lives are strained by conflicting identities when they see others rewarded for attendance and performance—especially if they are known to have less identity conflict.

If one of the challenges of human resources is to build a coherent and dedicated work place of individuals, what insights are needed to appreciate the role of social media as a communication tool? Institutional theory, for instance, might predict (and prescribe) that such communication is intended to help the individual know how and why to fit into the organization, a combination of individual and corporate agency. Advocates of neoinstitutional theory might, in contrast, argue that social media, especially to the extent that they are interactive even if not dialogic, can be used by the organization's leaders and members to cocreate an effective organization because it is a good place to work.

If, for instance, a company is making a strong commitment to operate in ways that are more integrative and sensitive to the multiple identities of employees/members how then can they use social media? To what extent is the answer to that question inherent in the (multiple) identity uses of social media? Similarly, taking the focal point of management, the related topic of social media suggests identity challenges, for organizations and people. Those are themes addressed in the next section.

Worlds (as villages) and strangers (as participants)

Worlds are discourse arenas, or perhaps it is best phrased this way: Discourse arenas are worlds coconstructed for various personal, social, political, and economic reasons. Grandkids, moms/dads, and grandparents, employers or employees: However connected through social media, these types coconstruct their identities and relationships, but also occupy worlds that never meet.

Avid foodies, for instance, take pictures of their meal and share it in real time with those in their social media nets. But experience cannot readily be transmitted to (shared with) those who do not live that experience. For instance, vacationers might send postcards with messages, "Wish you were here!" Social media, however, gives some alternative tools that allow for "lived" experience, such as a selfie shared on Facebook. "It's almost as though you really were there!" Thus, people try with degrees of success to share experience. But they can only partially overcome distance, and never really bridge times: "When I was young" is a statement that has immediate but not actual long-term meaning.

All ages, but especially young people, opt for worlds that only they share with one another. Such privacy (which really is public) allows them to bond and create the sorts of zones of meanings, communication skills and patterns, and relationships by which they will replace previous generations and become the "next one." Consequently, they are selectively present in the worlds of their parents and grandparents, but also in worlds of their own making. As well as global villages, we have global living rooms where families and other units of analysis negotiate time, distance, space, cocreated meaning, and geography in varying degrees of geographic separation (Merolla, 2010). That, however, is nothing new, just different or unique to today because of the functionality of social media.

By this logic, which added to by Venn diagrams, suggests, that the "world" is a myriad of overlapping zones of meaning that are variously interconnected (and in conflict and competition). Each world, however large or small, is an identifiable discourse arena. Given the nature of social media, individuals—rather than organizations—are the inherent interaction and messaging fabric from which these arenas are interwoven. Social media are tools individuals (and organizational managements) use to connect one another as they enact various identities.

Traditionally, relationship development, maintenance, and continuity tended to ignore key variables, one of which is distance which can also include separation by time. For instance, time zone differences create problems for continuity by time for which even international calling and Skype can only partially compensate. Merolla (2010) suggested, therefore, that relationship continuity must include conceptualization of experienced noncopresence. People cannot be in physical contact, copresent, at times that may be vital to relationship continuity. Copresence, or its absence, is important for full understanding of how people act before, during, and after noncopresence. Such factors are relevant to the expectations of rational patterns and the cost/reward ratios of social exchange. (What faculty member has not gone online to read a message from an irate student who had in a previous email at 2:34 AM asked a question about an assignment? "Please get back to me as soon as possible.")

For that reason, concepts such as interaction length, frequency, perceived pace, emotional intensity, and overall rhythm are worth consideration. Such inquiry is important because what was for centuries a tightly bonded and geographically bounded enactment of family and friends has become distanced. People who are rule-expected to live "together" now are increasingly living apart from one another. Such matters, including the moving away phenomenon, have created noticeable communication patterns (and their changes). For instance, students leaving home for college often have exhibited patterns of frequent letter writing to less frequent and frequent long-distance calling to less frequent contact of all kinds. Letters from home (and the military front) were golden in times of military service separation. Work migration has added to such patterns. Apropos to such conditions are the variables of self, relational system, network, and culture (Dainton, 2003). Workplaces and battlefields often allow for and provide social media contact with employees' and military personnel's friends and families.

To understand such patterns, Merolla (2010) suggested the dimensions of amplitude, scale, pace, sequence, and rhythm. Amplitude refers to emotional intensity. Scale is a matter of duration (long or short), temporally measurable as months, days, hours or seconds. Pace is a variation of scale, more subjective than scale and related to personality and individual expectation/want/need. Sequence refers to orderliness and routine. It can include other factors such as turn-taking, self-disclosure, and predictability. Rhythm is the product of the other factors. It is exhibited, for instance, as reliable continuity of engagement. What factors affect rhythm (such as military deployment) and do they excuse changes and violations of rhythm expectations. (Likewise, corporations' response to stakeholders' rhythm expectations becomes a sign of the organization's responsiveness, transparency, and participation.)

Facebook has relational value since it is a way to compensate for distance and noncopresence by giving the "illusion" of copresence. But, how individuals use

Facebook for relationship maintenance is subject to the patterns of amplitude, scale, pace, sequence, and rhythm. Can users achieve appropriate amplitude without going overboard or seeming indifferent? (First children always end up with more pictures and latter ones "evaporate." How many variations of cat behavior are there?) Scale requires messages that are just long enough, and, for instance, video, that is not too long. It also suggests that messages require variety, renewal, and continuity. Is grandma excused if she fails to respond to something relevant to a grandchild? Are parents similarly excused? What about siblings? How do the "family narratives" define appropriate interaction? Such matters are indicators of users' pace. Sequence is a matter of decorum, among other factors. Is the birthday child expected to post a selfie wearing the shirt received as a gift? How long can a person take in complimenting a friend's wedding pictures? Does that vary by gender? Rhythm: as patterns develop, how do they change and what is the relationship impact of such changes? For instance, does an increase by one or both romantic partners require changes in rhythm? Should those changes become part of what is discussed? How do these factors vary by age and other relationship factors—such as school friendships? (Is that why smartphone companies charge by each individual text? Is that the appeal of "unlimited text"?)

How and why do people of all ages use media of all types as important and even incidental aspects of their lives? Have social media changed for the better or worse such patterns? In the instance of children's development and safety, how involved are parents and others? Processes of *parental mediation* have been studied to understand how parents can guide children's use of media/content as well as their access to it. Parents and older siblings can affect how younger members of a family view advertising and judge the merits of its appeals. A toy, by that logic, can be more appealing through "third-party endorsement." The opposite can also happen: "That's a really dumb toy; it will not do what you see on TV and will break easily."

Parental mediation often is employed to explain how parents can and do mitigate the effects of media content on children. It can, however, also be used through "third-party endorsement" to augment a child's curiosity and knowledge on some matter. This topic in general has become more important as digital and mobile media can offer more opportunities for entertainment, advertising, and information. Thus, social media is creating a need to rethink the landscape of how families, segmented and interconnected, use media. The theory has focused attention on media access/content vulnerability (Clark, 2011). But, not only children, but also other family members are variously "vulnerable," and focus on the negative aspects of media access/content ignores positive aspects of mediation.

Scholars such as Clark (2011) warn parents not to overassume how much control they can exert over access by using Internet filters and GPS-enabled cell phones. But also, they should be encouraged to explore how media use can foster intergenerational connections, for instance, as grandparents play games or even only observe such games being played by grandchildren. As is true of other "conversational forms," parents are advised to regulate how and how much children are using texting. "No texting during meals." Such are the challenges of helping children become socialized in multidimensional, multilayered, and multitextual ways. Thus, at minimum, factors such as active and restrictive mediation, as well as coviewing, become important concepts. As in interpersonal and organizational communication, conversational rules become important tools for helping communicants to be more constructive than destructive. Scholars, such as Clark, reason that media utilization and mediation should be conceptualized, especially with younger family members, as experiential learning opportunities. She advised: "future research into parental mediation should consider how parents and children engage media in processes of participatory learning so as to better understand how parents and children negotiate interpersonal relationships in and through digital and mobile media" (p. 335).

As individuals, people tend to navigate social media, or use social media to navigate, the implications of their identities, identifications, and issues. But, into such worlds, organizations try by various means to enter and/or have a copresence. One of the ways to address that from an organizational point of view is by focusing on social media and human resources (HR), topics relevant to organizational communication.

Interviewing: over the years, hiring practices have developed to assure/increase the likelihood that a good fit occurs between organization and employee. Job candidates present themselves to organizations. Organizations take a look, and make a decision. One decision is whether or not to consider the person more closely. In such circumstances, what tools are available to HR professionals? Is one of them social media? Should potential employers feel ethically privileged to seek and examine an applicant's social media profile? What about that profile is relevant, or not, to such decision-making? Should users of social media guard against such eventuality by not having a profile there? What are the identity consequences of not having a profile? How true is the profile that emerges from an individual's self-presentation of social media? Should individuals create and manage an identity with an eye to future employment, or is an individual's personal life exactly that? How is such detail relevant to decisions to hire—or not?

Such questions are hard to document empirically. Should a prospective employer notify a candidate that such an inquiry is going to be conducted—or could be? If the organization wants a copresence with the employee after employment, what are the necessary conditions of such a relationship? These important issues are explored further in Chapter 8. Does unauthorized accessing of profiles threaten employer-employee relationships?

Organizations for about as long as they have had homepages began to use an intranet as an electronic means for internal communication. Employee communication (often a cotask of HR and PR) has long used the traditional and then the latest media. That was true of the era of the intranet. But, the intranet was considered one-way, and not dialogic. That one-way characteristic often hurt the fuller impact of employee communication.

Copresence can provide HR a door into the lives of employees but seems to be well advised to understand that employees strategically access and manage as a spiral of interaction between the organization's communication content (including rumors) and the individual's identities and identifications. All of this necessarily asks whether the dialogic/interactive nature of individuals use of social media is prevented or muted by the use and design of social media by HR?

Consider something as simple as this. The company wants to foster a culture of safety. To do so, it often acknowledges a safety accomplishment. It could be X years of driving a truck for the company without an accident. As the HR department announces its pleasure over such an accomplishment, should that presentation, with a smiling employee, be open to comments by fellow employees? Is there risk? Might an employee out the person saying that he/she actually is not considered by peers to be that safe? Should that kind of event be minimized, even prevented, by having the nominations trickle up through the organization's social media? Should employees nominate those believed to be safe drivers (or whatever)? If the company is large enough is there a return on investment (ROI) break point at which the effort to make such positive attention becomes counterproductive? What goals should such an HR campaign achieve and what is the cost/reward benefit? The selection process is a power move fraught with the dynamics and perils of power resource management.

HR and other internal disciplines seek to help the organization be orderly and efficient. At what point does that effort become sufficiently rigid to ignore the role complexity plays in monitoring, planning, implementing, and assessing management policy. Can employees be empowered, through social media for instance, to bring matters to the attention of management? Can the complexity inherent in organizational culture be fostered and amplified by the copresence of employee voices?

For instance, if the company uses social events to help employees and management bond, is the reporting of such events managed from the top down? Or, is the culture such, flexible enough—richly complex—to allow and even encourage employees to post pictures and videos of such social events. Should the postings be edited, and censured? Surely social media allows employees to know what we posted on the intranet—and what was not. Such selective posting necessarily says something about the management—and the employees? Is the culture such that it embraces complexity, or "edits" it out of the world of the organization? That question necessarily makes evident the productive and collision possibilities of the worlds of an organization—internally and externally. (Recall how pictures of employee hazing affected the public reputation of Blackwater XE—as did other images obtained from social media.)

Such outed communication often has intrinsic credibility because it seems authentic and unfiltered/managed. Mitt Romney was caught on video in a candid (and therefore "honest and truthful" moment) in which he marginalized the "47 percent" who favored Obama because they were dependent on government.

Consider how organizations, often through marketing communication, seek to connect their worlds with those of customers. Studies on such topics seem to focus on which keys unlock "closed" doors to gain access to others' worlds. Addressing that theme from the point of view of activists, Sommerfeldt (2011) discovered that activists tend to use interest alignment as a key, bridge, between their "world" and those of targets. To seek to create/connect with and build on identification, activists can be found to use three identification strategies: Sympathy, antithesis, and unawareness. In the case of activists, identification by sympathy and unawareness appear to be rhetorical facilitators of relational cohesion. These strategies seem most effective for connecting the organization to persons the organization seeks to help and from those the organization seeks resources. Shared loyalties, zones of meanings, and the strategies and products of identification appear to be keys for gaining entrance into others worlds and for inviting the targeted individuals into the world of the organization.

If one assumes a more complex model than is implied by an OPR (organization–public relationship), the potential is that some existing link occurs between the target and an organization which with another organization can connect, conceptualized as OsSsRs (Heath, 2013). Frandsen and Johansen (2014) building on this more complex model of OPRs tout the role of the intermediary as a resource an organization(s) can use to link with a stakeholder(s). Access to one party in the equation becomes a means by which access can be gained to the worlds of others. Such access is a resource, and therefore resource exchange becomes the paradigm for entry and maintenance. Such links are functional, but inherently subject to the coconstructions that the participants in the network use to define the relationships and resource management (see also, Sommerfeldt, 2011).

A variation of the paradigm features social media influencers. As noted in the brief discussion of networks and sociograms above, an influencer is a member (individual, group, or organization—even institution) of a network that can help parts of that network to connect with, build and maintain a relationship with others. Freburg et al. (2011) offer insights into this complexity. They note, as is widely discussed, how organizations (such as Google or Facebook) that provide social media monitor the connections (linkages) and coconstructions (topics discussed as well as relationships defined). Such information has financial value to companies and other organizations desiring entry to others worlds. These researchers find as well that certain persons/organizations in a network take pleasure in linking entities. Related factors include spokesperson credibility and willingness as well as interest to share advice.

Without addressing the "key" challenges, research often focuses on the positive outcomes to be achieved through the dialogue between an organization and those who it serves, and who support it, as in the case of the Red Cross. Research, and counseling based on it, tends to feature the strategies of dialogue and engagement, as well as the pitfalls of time and staff limitations—both of which are effects of leadership decisions (Briones et al., 2011).

In social media, merely having a profile may not be the lure that attracts others or the key that unlocks their worlds. Many factors serve the interest of nonprofits, including disclosure, information dissemination, and functions that involve persons attracted to sites. Disclosure includes information about the organization's persona: description, history, mission statement, logo, and administrators. Information includes news links, photos, video and audio files, posted items, discussion walls, press releases and campaign summaries. Behaviors of involvement include email options, phone numbers, usable message board, calendars of events, volunteer opportunities, as well as calls for donation and stores at which related material can be purchased. Such options become increasingly available and are enriched by the social media used, but nonprofits continue in a learning and use curve (Waters et al., 2009).

Authors such as Yang and Kang (2009) have discovered that blogs, in their research, provide access and credibility because of the conversational and authentic communication style and content employed. Such communication features increase the likelihood of engagement that fits the standard assumptions of the cognitive/knowledge, attitudinal, and behavior paradigm. Their work featured the role and impact of four conversational or engagement dimensions: Contingency interactivity, existing self-company connections including coconstructed and aligned identities and identifications, company attitudes, and "word of mouth" intentions the functionality and propensity to pass information and recommendations to others.

By that logic, scholars of social media can come to realize the central principle of corporate social responsibility and environmentalism: The environment is not something "outside" of people, there to serve them, but people are "inside" the environment and therefore inherently challenged to act constructively. The challenge is not to separate from social media or become totally immersed, but to bend the media to ones interests rather than become bent through media to others' interests.

Such use of social media presumes various kinds of returns on investments, whether they are relationship strength, customer satisfaction, or marketing effectiveness. That paradigm is the centerpiece of the next section.

Social media enactment as return on investment: Organizations as social media partners

Do organizations seek to engage with individuals for purely altruistic reasons, or are they motivated by return on investment? Does that engagement purpose necessarily influence the attributions that are made about the identity, role, voice, and motive of the organization as it seeks to cocreate meaning with key publics/stakeholders? Do people enact their identities as a means for gaining various rewards? Do organizations, as individuals, have multiple identities or communicate in various ways that given users of different channels different perspectives on organizations?

Addressing the last of these questions, Gilpin (2010) reported how organizational image construction can become fragmented because of the various messaging that occurs in different online, social media. The paper presumes the need for organizations, Whole Foods in this case, to use the same terms in various media to craft a coherent, not-fragmented image. She observed how similar words were used to frame the organization's self-identity in some media, but were not well coordinated across all of the media the company used to communicate with customers and other stakeholders. The concern is that different narratives emerge across different media which ultimately fragment the organization's image/identity.

That question becomes even more important as the role of organizations, through public relations, are discussed as part of the use of social media. Public relations traditionally had as a key element of its structure and function the use of other peoples' media for the gain of the organization. Thus, media relations is a means to obtain favorable reporting on an organization. During crisis, the organization's response is made through reporters who served as gatekeepers and conduits between the organization and the "world." (The organization also tends to use media, social media and home pages, to communicate "directly" with stakeholders.) Because of this paradigm, public relations researchers have examined the relational variables that seem to make an organization capable of stronger and more beneficial relationships through media, others' and the organization's.

Enter social media. To some extent organizations have adapted media relations to social media. Their public statements can be accessed through social media. They are conveyed and vetted through blogs. But, they can potentially be seen as interlopers and intruders into individuals' discourse arenas. This phenomenon is a variation of media relations where a reader, listener, or viewer would necessarily "encounter" comments by organizational spokespersons on some matter important to the organization, and ostensibly important to the individual. And, stakeholders who use different channels can get different information and messaging.

Media relations was one of several keys public relations professionals used to unlock and gain entry to individuals' discourse space. And, reporters could provide, with varying degrees of intentionality, third-party confirmation or disconfirmation for the position taken by the organization. Along the way, different reporters, however, were likely to frame an organization's messages in different ways. Thus, fragmentation and incoherence is an eternal problematic.

Similarly, and quite differently, organizations seek through professional public relations to gain access to the discourse spheres of individuals. As such they are like, but also dissimilar, to other individuals. How similar they are determines the extent to which their purpose and message aligns with that of the discussants. Because of the different predispositions of stakeholders, media selection can also add to the fragmentation.

Strategic consensus and strategic interest alignment appear to be relevant predictors of how well organizations become part of individuals' discourse space. Walter et al. (2013) are among the several discussants who are working to help practitioners and scholars understand the nature and impact of these concepts. Strategic alignment is reflected in the degree of fit between an organization's strategic priorities and those salient in the organization's environment. Strategic consensus is a factor of the degree of fit between what the organization "believes" and what key stakeholders "believe." The hypothesis of such work reasons that successful organizations are such because they are in consensus and shared alignment with their stakeholders. By this logic, it can be reasoned that not only success, but also access to discourse arenas, depends on the extent to which organizations and stakeholders share consensus and aligned interests.

If organizations are perceived to be out of sync (or even disingenuous) with stakeholder preferences they lack the means for access to them as well as a successful relationship with them. Ravasi and Phillips (2011) reasoned that strategies of alignment are particularly crucial during those times when organizations are engaged in change management. The ability to project an identity that is congruent with change and aligned with the interests of stakeholders is vital to successful change management.

Social media, sensitive to the standard assessments of fake friendships, suggests that the power publics are able to exert results from their ability as a social network to allow admittance and share a world view with organizations. The identities of organizations must align with those of each social network. So, too the interests need to be in consensus. As much as these conditions are vital to normal activities they become paramount to efforts to engage in change management.

Reprising the concept of community (one that lingers in the wings but often is not central to the drama of public relations), Valentini et al. (2012) work to shift the focus of practitioners and theorists. The motive of the shift is multifold, but directs attention to the reality that social media give organizational opportunities to units of people, often only linked by a social media platform and an interest. For this reason, these authors revise that community qualitatively defined be the focal point of public relations practice and research. Social media are turning old notions and equations on their heads because publics can self-form and therefore grassroots is a real term, and relationships are driven by forces outside of organizations, and probably beyond their control. Social media are creating a "public" centric approach to public relations rather than one that is organization-centric.

Conclusions

Connections: As much as connections seem to be facilitated by social media, they encounter numerous stumbling blocks. By their very nature, social mediated networks are fluid, contingent on many factors that predict access, relationship development, consensus, shared identity, and aligned interests. As much as alignment is often conceptualized as a public relations outcome, it may well be a vital predictor of access to strategic publics. It is the currency of admission to the social media show.

Such relational conditions are influenced by the communication styles of those who seek to gain access to and participation in discourse arenas. But more important than relationship management styles alone, discourse conditions supply the power publics use to determine the conditions of social media engagement. Often very subtle, but nevertheless powerful, socially constructed meanings govern the consensus, alignment, and fit between participants seeking access to and influence from social media membership.

As is the case for individuals, organizations encounter the ROI challenge of calculating and addressing the return on investment for working to gain access to social media. What is the cost of access? What is the gain? What is the cost of not accessing? The irony of looking at that quandary from an organization's point of view, the same metrics are foundational to individual access to and inclusion/exclusion in such networks. Individuals quickly realize the cost, the ROI, of membership/participationship in social media nets. The same is true for organizations, including the need to be responsive, authentic, and aligned.

References

Barker, V. (2009). Older adolescents' motivations for social network site use: The influence of gender, group identity, and collective self-esteem. *CyberPsychology & Behavior*, 12(2), 209–214.

Briones, R.L., Kuch, B., Liu, B.F., and Jin, Y. (2011). Keeping up with the digital age: How the American Red Cross uses social media to build relationships. *Public Relations Review*, 37, 37–43.

Burgoon, J.K., and Hale, J.L. (1984). The fundamental topoi of relational communication. *Communication Monographs*, 51, 193–214.

Cheney, G. (1991). *Rhetoric in an Organizational Society: Managing Multiple Identities*. Columbia, SC: University of South Carolina Press.

Clark, L.S. (2011). Parental mediation theory for the digital age. *Communication Theory*, 21, 323–343.

Dainton, M. (2003). Erecting a framework for understanding relational maintenance: An epilogue. In D.J. Canary and M. Dainton (eds.), *Maintaining Relationships through Communication: Relational, Contextual, and Cultural Variations*, pp. 299–321. Hillsdale, NJ: Lawrence Erlbaum.

Davis, V. (2012). Interconnected but underprotected: Parents' methods and motivations for information seeking on digital safety issues. *CyberPsychology, Behavior, & Social Networking*, 15(12), 669–674.

Frandsen, F. and Johansen, W. (2014). Outline of a general theory of intermediaries in strategic communication. Paper presented at the 17th Annual International Public Relations Conference, Miami, FL.

Freburg, K., Graham, K., McGaughey, K., and Freburg, L. (2011). Who are the social media influencers? A study of public perceptions of personality. *Public Relations Review*, 37, 90–92.

Gergen, K.J. (2000). *An Invitation to Social Construction*. London: Sage.

Gergen, K.J., and Gergen, M.M. (1988). Narrative and the self as relationship. In L. Berkowitz (ed.), *Advances in Experimental Social Psychology*, vol. 21; pp. 17–56. New York: Academic Press.

Giddens, A. (1991). *Modernity and Self-Identity: Self and Society in the Late Modern Age*. Cambridge, UK: Polity Press.

Gilpin, D. (2010). Organizational image construction in a fragmented online media environment. *Journal of Public Relations Research*, 22, 265–287.

Heath, R.L. (1994). *Management of Corporate Communication: From Interpersonal Contacts to External Affairs*. Hillsdale, NJ: Lawrence Erlbaum.

Heath, R.L. (2013). The journey to understand and champion OPR takes many roads, some not yet well traveled. *Public Relations Review*, 39, 426–431.

Hecht, M.L. (1993). 2002: A research odyssey: Toward the development of a communication theory of identity. *Communication Monographs*, 60, 76–82.

Kent, M.L. (2014). Rethinking technology research and social media. *Public Relations Review*, 40, 1–2.

Mazzarela, S. (ed.) (2005). *Girl Wide Web: Girls, the Internet, and the Negotiation of Identity*. New York: Peter Lang.

McAllister-Spooner, S.M. (2009). Fulfilling the dialogic promise: A ten-year reflective survey on dialogic Internet principles. *Public Relations Review*, 35, 320–322.

McLuhan, M. (1964). *Understanding Media: The Expressions of Man*. New York: McGraw Hill.

McLuhan, M. and Powers, B.R. (1989). *The Global Village: Transformations in World Life and Media in the 21st Century*. New York: Oxford University Press.

Merolla, A.J. (2010). Relational maintenance and noncopresence reconsidered: Conceptualizing geographic separation in close relationships. *Communication Theory*, 20, 169–193.

Ravasi, D. and Phillips, N. (2011). Strategies of alignment: Organizational identity management and strategic change at Bang & Olufsen. *Strategic Organization*, 9, 103–135.

Slater, M.D. (2007). Reinforcing spirals: The mutual influence of media selectivity and media effects and their impact on individual behavior and social identity. *Communication Theory*, 17, 281–303.

Tajfel, H. and Turner, J.C. (1986). The social identity theory of intergroup behavior. In S. Worchel and W.G. Austin (eds.), *Psychology of Intergroup Relation*, pp. 7–24. Chicago: Nelson-Hall.

Yang, S.U. and Kang, M. (2009). Measuring blog engagement: Testing a four-dimensional scale. *Public Relations Review*, 35, 323–324.

Vraga, E.K., Bode, L., Wells, C., Driscoll, K., and Thorson, K. (2014). The rules of engagement: Comparing two social protest movements on YouTube. *CyberPsychology, Behavior, & Social*, 17(3), 133–140.

Valentini, C., Kruckeberg, D., and Starck, K. (2012). Public relations and community: A persistent covenant. *Public Relations Review*, 38, 873–879.

Walter, J., Kellermanns, F.W., Floyd, S.W., Veiga, J.F., and Matherne, C. (2013). Strategic alignment: A missing link in the relationship between strategic consensus and organizational performance. *Strategic Organization*, 11, 304–328.

Waters, R D., Burnett, E., Lamm, A., and Lucas, J. (2009). Engaging stakeholders through social networking: How nonprofit organizations are using Facebook. *Public Relations Review*, 35, 102–106.

7 Engage critically

Activist power

Debates about the power of social media to facilitate change often focus upon a "big bang" conceptualization of instantaneous and momentous transformation—the notion that change may actually occur at an often imperceptible and infinitesimal pace is less likely to attract attention and be interesting. Demetrious (2013) suggests that the "claim that the internet has facilitated enduring social and economic change as well as greater agency, after consideration of undesirable effects, is contestable" (p. 143). If a big bang theory approach is applied then the efficacy of social media activism, and the Internet more generally, is indeed contestable. However, within this chapter, we focus on how civil society leverages social media to achieve a gradual erosion of public confidence and how the accumulative effects of multiple civil society campaigns may undermine the social license that legitimates and safeguards organizations. In doing so, we seek to construct an alternative approach to understanding how social media discursively empowers activists by examining how critical public engagement processes problematize and gradually reshape societal understandings, at least among an important segment of each society.

As well as offering key channels for activist change management, social media also offers organizations alternative communication networks that provide considerable control over corporate identities, brands and messages. The shift from the traditional broadcast model of communicating through journalist intermediaries to the social media model of independent posting allows organizations to bypass media filters and circumvent many of the public relations challenges associated with traditional media. Most significantly, it offers organizations avenues to speak directly to audiences, build discourse connections and relationships, share information and engage in conversations.

The risk for organizations of every type, however, is that social media may also give free reign for participants to say whatever they want, and to post and share their own content. For civil society, social media has opened up possibilities for organizing and popularizing protest that may escalate from seemingly minor complaints to critical public engagement, direct action and even sabotage and terrorism. Thus, organizations that ignore societal expectations may very rapidly experience public criticism that is expressed as protest through social media.

Challenges to corporate power that escalate into issues-based and reputational-based controversy are generally defined as activist when they emphasize contestation, advocacy, conflict, transgression, and more broadly, social transformation (Ganesh and Zoller, 2012). However, conceptualizing civil society criticism and protest as "activism" is problematic. Organizations may label such challenges as "activism" in an attempt to marginalize and delegitimize opposition, yet efforts to oppose particular power relations are part of a broader democratic landscape. The goal of activists is political; activists seek to engage with, challenge or redistribute decision-making power by "opening up" (Stirling, 2008, p. 262) public conversations and mobilizing publics to express dissent. Thus, we suggest that activism is better understood as a form of critical public engagement—a segment of the general public is quite literally engaging critically.

Contemporary scholarly interrogations of the relationship between public relations and activism also point to the need to reconceive how we understand activism. Holtzhausen (2014) situates her work within an organizational context and argues for public relations to adopt a postmodern activist perspective, and thereby to address discrimination and drive critical change. For Holtzhausen, "activism is resistance in the small things and the big things" (p. xv). Central to the conceptualization of resistance is an understanding of how power relations play out in organization and the notion that the organization is "a site of political struggle" (Holtzhausen, 2014, p. 107). For these reasons, Holtzhausen compellingly argues that public relations professionals need to inspire social action that identifies and ends discriminatory or dehumanizing practices.

In contrast, Demetrious (2013) situates her work within a social context, focusing on a grassroots activist orientation. Her work innovatively tracks the complex intersections between professional organizational public relations, governance processes and activist efforts to affect those governance processes. Although Demetrious subtitles her final chapter "Not public relations: Sustainable communication," she advocates use of the term "public communication" as an alternative to public relations. The approach she advocates is very much a form of sustainable communication for organizations that draws upon activist principles integrated with Habermasian lifeworld priorities of outward focus and openness. The aim is to generate an alternative mode of ethical communication for driving ecological and social change.

Both Holtzhausen (2014) and Demetrious (2013) critique the ways that power plays out in organizational communication and advocate a systemic change to the norms that drive organizational public relations. Ideally, activists and organizations would work together, collaborating for the betterment of society. Such thoughts call for a reorientation of public relations theory from a corporate orientation to a fully functional societal perspective that sees coordinated change management as a collective benefit. Such change is slowed by the hegemony of an organization-centric model of communication; as it prevails it advocates that modes of communication that are not public or societally oriented are deemed somehow less ethical. This may indeed be so.

However, it is important to note that conflict, adversarial communication and advocacy are not inherently unethical—they are a feature of a representational democratic process (Mouffe, 1993; Ganesh and Zoller, 2012; Motion et al., 2015). Both civil society and their professional communication counterparts mobilize similar discursive strategies and practices in their attempts to influence politics, policy and public opinion. A typical limitation of organization-centric communication is that when organizations attempt to advocate and persuade rather than engage collaboratively, activist publics also tend to deploy adversarial modes of communication. Power relations tend to favour organizations in a contest of legitimacy.

As a consequence, civil society draws upon a set of restricted, often confrontational, communicative possibilities in order to critically engage with organizations and popularize their cause. Thinking about activism as a form of critical public engagement focuses attention on the discursive interplay between organizations and publics and the complicated expectations, interests and desired outcomes that motivate such interactions. Clegg, Courpasson and Phillips (2006: 319) argue that resistance is "largely done discursively," which suggests that we need to understand the discourse context and how alternative sense-making practices are established to challenge or resist dominant hegemonic discourses. Resistance becomes a process of critically engaging with and reinterpreting organizational discourses.

Thomas and Davies (2005) characterized resistance in dualistic terms as both oppositional and negative and as a critical and generative reflexive process (p. 727). Their view of resistance as both oppositional and generative highlights the complicated nature of this type of critical public engagement. Foucault (1980) stated that "there are no relations of power without resistance" (p. 142). Citizen publics are therefore not powerless—resistance is the power they mobilize to engage with organizations and activate change. Organizations that favour advocacy models of communication may expect resistance—activism is often the only option that civil society has for various advocates to publicly engage with such organizations. From this perspective, "resistance may be thought of as a component of engagement—resistance is an attempt to create a conversation or communicate" (Leitch and Motion, 2010, p. 108).

In relation to these communicative challenges, we therefore argue for an understanding of activist communication as an alternative form of citizen-driven public relations in which civilian publics critically engage with organizations to provoke and achieve social change. From this perspective, critical public engagement may be characterized as a form of political public relations. Critical public engagement is thus concerned with furthering societal priorities through the expression and performance of societal sensibilities, sensitivities and concerns. Social media opens up spaces for civil society voices and understandings. At the heart of our critique in this chapter is an interest in theorizing this form of critical public engagement and what that means for the discursive expression and performance of societal concerns.

Discourse and change

Discourse theory offers a range of conceptual and analytical frameworks that generate insights into how to advance critical public engagement in political decision-making and the power of social media to transform social conditions, government policy or organizational practices. Although there are a variety of approaches to discourse theory, the work of Michel Foucault and Norman Fairclough is particularly salient for analyzing critical public engagement because of the focus on power, meaning and change (Leitch and Motion, 2010; Motion and Leitch, 1996). Discourses, the systems of meanings that frame and shape how we understand the world, establish ideological systems and political practices that are grounded in particular power relations. Attempts at societal transformation often start with discussions of the most appropriate persuasive strategies to influence public opinion. However, discourse theory draws attention to power relationships and the legitimation of truth claims (Leitch and Motion, 2010). Attempts to transform sense-making or material practices target underlying assumptions that maintain and protect particular societal power dynamics. What this means for citizen publics is that the relationships between particular power relations and associated political and ideological practices need to be identified, destabilized and reoriented.

To challenge existing power dynamics, certainties have to be weakened, meanings contested and alternative possibilities proposed. Fairclough (1992) referred to those who engineer social and cultural change as "professional technologists who research, redesign and provide training in discourse practices" (p. 8). Professional public relations practitioners and their so-called role as "thought leaders" fit with Fairclough's characterization of discourse technologists (Motion and Leitch, 1996). Civil society publics, too, act as discourse technologists attempting to intervene in discourse formations in order to reconfigure governance, organizational and social structures and practices. Discourse formation and modification processes establish and transform the criteria for the sets of rules about all the objects, operations, concepts, and theoretical options (Foucault, 1991). Citizens who seek to challenge or undo particular regimes of discourse need to concern themselves with discourse formations and how to transform them.

Foucault (1991) offered insights into and "content" for what he referred to as "the monotonous and empty concept of change" (p. 58) by identifying the conditions of discourse formation, constant transformation and the multiple intersections between discourses. Critical public engagement strategies that are designed to stake a claim for discursive power need to take into account political practices that create the conditions for the emergence, insertion and functioning of a particular discourse. Foucault (1988) described four major types of "technologies," that act as mechanisms for the emergence, insertion and functioning of discourse:

1   technologies of production, which permit us to produce, transform, or manipulate things;
2   technologies of sign systems, which permit us to use signs, meanings, symbols, or signification;

3   technologies of power, which determine the conduct of individuals and submit them to certain ends or domination, an objectivizing of the subject;
4   technologies of the self, which permit individuals to effect by their own means or with the help of others a certain number of operations on their own bodies and souls, thoughts, conduct, and way of being, so as to transform themselves in order to attain a certain state of happiness, purity, wisdom, perfection, or immortality.

These technologies influence the ways in which discourses may function as a "regime of truth" (Foucault, 1980, p. 133) that influence sense-making processes.

Discourses function according to a particular set of rules that delimit what is included and excluded in that sense-making domain, the types of identities or individuals that have access to and power within the discourse, "the limits and forms of what is sayable" (Foucault, 1991, p. 59) and where and how a particular discourse circulates within society. Changes in discourses, Foucault (1991, p. 56–57) explained, are marked by:

1   a shift in the boundaries which define and map out what is included in a discourse;
2   new subject positions and roles for those acting within the discourse;
3   different modes of language; and/or
4   altered forms and ways of circulating the discourse within society.

Appreciation of these dimensions of discourse transformation provides insights for critical engagement with the strategic design or modification of discourse formations. A shift or expansion of the boundaries of a discourse opens up or closes down the possibilities for what may be included within the discourse and introduces alternative sense-making options. The development of new subject positions or identities and roles establishes alternative power relations and changes what may be said and by whom. Language design is a key dimension of discourse technologization, according to Fairclough (1992). Attempts to challenge and transform discourse through the introduction of new or alternative modes of language influences knowledge production and reconfigures the sense-making processes that govern how something may be understood and spoken about. A key task in effecting a discourse transformation is to determine how a new or modified discourse circulates within society. Social media provides citizen activists with an alternative means (a nonestablishment channel) of circulating discourse in ways that are affordable and somewhat less regulated or controlled by the owners/influencers of the established media.

Critical public engagement may be conceived as a political struggle to establish an alternative "regime of truth" (Foucault, 1980, p. 133) through discursive contestation. The contexts, conditions and complexities that determine the possibilities for transformation and the types of discourses which are accepted and function as true need to be taken into account. From this perspective, then, citizen-driven critical public engagement functions as a series of discursive interventions that articulate and shape a constellation of concerns and sensitivities into a discursive formation/modification to challenge the rules that determine "the status of truth and the economic and political role it plays" (Foucault, 1980, p. 132).

Citizens and civil society groups mobilize social media as a critical public engagement technology for negotiating sociocultural, political and economic concerns and challenging inequitable power relations. The concept of popularization is useful for considering how social media may be mobilized for critical public engagement purposes because it integrates notions of popularity and politicization with considerations of social relevance (Motion et al. 2015). Key challenges for those who seek to popularize opposition to particular, strategic organizational practices include determining how to open up issues for public consideration and debate and how to successfully stage a series of interventions that galvanize broader support for their cause. Such approaches are deliberately popularist and adversarial in order to marshal interest and gain support.

Ganesh and Zoller (2012) suggest that although consensual approaches have been idealized as the ethical mode for problem resolution, such collaborative, dialogical approaches ignore the unequal power relations that influence situations and limit potential outcomes. For controversial initiatives, consensual approaches are less likely to open up broader public consideration, mobilize public opinion or provoke political action. Mouffe's (1999) notion of "agonistic pluralism" underpins this insight into why and how activists engage in confrontation. In agonistic, pluralist approaches, advocated by Mouffe (2002), competition and conflict are considered a necessary part of democratic procedures and decision-making. Rather than view opponents as enemies, they are understood as competitors in a struggle to occupy positions of power and articulate "any possible alternative to the current hegemonic order" (Mouffe, 2002, p. 61).

Resistance, therefore, is a necessary, resistance is a necessary discursive strategy for addressing sets of problems within democratic societies and opening up possibilities for critical public engagement. For organizations, resistance and dissent operate as a type of fault line that signals potential controversy and public concern. Opposition, resistance and activism, then, are not acts of transgression, but rather form part of the complex landscape of critical public engagement in democratic processes.

A typical organizational response to expressions of dissent is to assume that if the public knew more of the corporate position they would accept or at least acquiesce to an organization's proposals and practices. This approach is grounded in the deficit model (Irwin and Wynne, 1996)—the assumption is that public ignorance, rather than public concern, is the problem. Information or sophisticated persuasive strategies are seen as the solution. However, the real issue is that organizations are not listening to their stakeholders and taking their perspectives into account. Public controversies often begin as attempts to open up an issue and express concerns but escalate into controversial interventions in organizational processes—the aim of such interventions is to publicly engage with the organization, challenge inequitable power relations and reassert or reconfigure societal priorities. Strategies that citizens and civil society groups marshal to provoke engagement emphasize social, political, economic or democratic concerns and align those concerns with deeply held public concerns and attachments (Marres, 2012). At the same time, efforts to attract attention to and popularize an issue or cause may deliberately reposition issues within citizens' everyday lives, language and popular culture (Motion et al., 2015). These popularization strategies are intended to foster connections with publics, establish social relevance and develop a sense of meaningfulness that creates identification with the cause (Motion et al., 2015).

Social media plays a number of roles in the popularization of activist efforts to instigate critical public engagement. At a material level, social media offers activists a series of technological platforms to express concern and dissent. The instantaneous and "spreadable" (Jenkins et al., 2013) nature of online activist campaigns is generally understood to increase audience reach and awareness. However, at a more fundamental level, the value of social media is not about reach or awareness—it is the potential to affect change. Social media offers access to multiple networked communities who may share similar cultural worldviews, values, and sense-making practices. Networked communities may be understood as a discursive domain for circulating alternative ideas, a place to voice concerns and a site for provoking and organizing action. Within the next section we discuss how civil society groups use social media as a discursive domain to campaign against oil companies by highlighting and criticizing practices that are perceived to contravene societal expectations.

Lego-Shell cobranded partnership: A social media avalanche

Organizations may seek to redefine their brand identity, discursively reposition their brand and build brand equity (Motion et al., 2003, p. 1080) by engaging in cobranding partnerships that offer opportunities to augment positive brand values or undermine negative reputational associations. Successful cobranding should significantly enhance brand reputation, increase customer loyalty and differentiate a cobrand from its competitors (Blackett and Boad, 1999). Since the 1960s, Lego and Shell engaged in various promotional and cobranded arrangements for mutual benefits (Starr, 2014). For Lego, the long-standing, cobranding partnership is valued at £68 million with Shell petrol stations in 26 countries distributing Shell-branded Lego toy sets (Vaughan, 2014b).

For Shell, the cobranding relationship has offered significant promotional opportunities that not only provide positive brand associations but that, we argue, may also more implicitly seek to legitimize the oil industry. However, the benefits for Lego and Shell were undermined in July 2014 when Greenpeace launched a global campaign to pressure Lego to cease its cobranded partnership with Shell. The aim of the campaign was to highlight the role of Shell in the exploitation of Arctic oil reserves and to protest the normalization of the Shell brand to children (Polisano, 2014). Greenpeace explained the rationale for the campaign by stating,

> We love LEGO. You love LEGO. Everyone loves LEGO. But when LEGO's halo effect is being used to sell propaganda to children, especially by an unethical corporation who are busy destroying the natural world our children will

inherit, we have to do something.... Help us stop Shell polluting them by telling LEGO to stop selling Shell-branded bricks and kits today.

(Starr, 2014)

Strategic decisions on how to frame an activist campaign typically seek to renegotiate power relations by expressing political ideologies (Lakoff, 2010) and representing particular moral matters of concern (Latour, 2004). In the instance of Lego and Shell, Greenpeace's efforts to frame the activist campaign as moral concerns about propaganda directed at children may be interpreted as an attempt to mobilize socio-ontological associations about the innocence of childhood and provoke condemnation of indirect marketing to children. Capturing the public imagination is vital to the success of critical public engagement campaigns that seek to intensify concerns, mobilize public opinion and exert appropriate pressure to destabilize an organization's social license.

Greenpeace campaign strategies included an online petition, direct action protests and a video that went viral. The campaign launched with the generation and delivery of a petition to the Lego headquarters. When Lego refused to receive the petition, the campaign communication then critiqued Lego for not listening to its customers. Greenpeace invited a journalist, creative agencies and supporters to participate in the protest and shape the campaign. Opening up the campaign in this way ensured creative, expert support.

Professional involvement adds inclusivity and assists in transforming publics into citizens by facilitating a distinctively creative articulation of issues as matters of public concern. Professional involvement in critical public engagement campaigns may also intensify the process of how civil society groups target social concerns and attachments (Marres, 2012). Numerous creative direct action protests were initiated, including a demonstration by 50 children outside the London Shell office that featured arctic animals made of oversize Lego bricks. When Shell announced their plan to resume drilling in the Arctic at the same time as cobranded Lego toy collections were promoted at Shell petrol stations, the petition was reinstated online and escalated to 1 million signatures.

However, it was the Greenpeace video posted to YouTube that accompanied the petition that garnered the most public support. The video opens with the song, "Everything is Awesome," that was "borrowed" from the Lego movie, and featured an idyllic Arctic Lego-built snowscape featuring polar bears and huskies from the Lego Arctic range. The video scene then cuts to a Lego-built Shell drilling scene and shows oil leaking and drowning everything in the Arctic landscape. The video closes with oil covering all of the Lego set except for a Lego flag with the Shell logo. The final text shots read, "Shell is polluting our kids imagination. Tell LEGO to end its partnership with Shell." The video attracted over 6 million views and, as a consequence, on 9 October 2014 Lego announced that it would not renew its contract with Shell. The CEO of the Lego Group, Jørgen Vig Knudstorp, stated,

> The Greenpeace campaign uses the LEGO brand to target Shell. As we have stated before, we firmly believe Greenpeace ought to have a direct conversation with Shell. The LEGO brand, and everyone who enjoys creative play, should never become part of this dispute between Greenpeace and Shell.
>
> (Vaughan, 2014b)

Clearly, Lego's CEO did not perceive that Lego was at fault by partnering with Shell. An issue for social media monitoring is how to determine when an issue that is trending has gained traction. In this instance, 6 million global views is certainly evidence of traction and rapidly escalating popularity. The other factor that may determine whether an intervention is needed in social media is to consider whether an issue is politicizing publics and attracting the attention of government (Motion et al., 2015). For Shell, restrictive precautionary regulation about drilling the Arctic would not be a welcome outcome from the cobranding partnership.

The management of corporate cobranding requires that brand values are aligned and common starting points for the establishment of a viable cobranded identity are identified. Those common starting points may then form the foundation for the marketing communications campaign, providing the basis for all advertising and media statements. Within corporate cobranding communication, the process of articulation may serve to link particular associations at an ideological, strategic, tactical and emotional level. A critical question to be asked is "what beneficial associations did Lego gain from its relationship with Shell?" Could Lego support oil drilling in the Arctic? Value, or cobrand equity is established through a strategic alignment process, but emerges from the marketing communications efforts. In the case of the Lego–Shell cobrand, the key source of corporate cobrand equity was the marketing communications relationship (see Motion et al., 2003, pp. 1091–1092).

Discursively, the campaign was not so much about narrowing boundaries as closing down the articulation process that established particular relational connections and symbolic associations. The aim was to denaturalize any connections between Lego and Shell and to replace that with a connection between Shell and environmental damage. For Lego, there was a potential connection that they would not want emphasized—Lego bricks are made of plastic—and therefore oil (Turner, 2014). However, Lego now espouses a sustainability discourse and aims to adopt practices in alignment with renewable energy practices and find alternative nonfossil based alternative materials for its bricks.

Positioning itself in this way has meant that Shell was the target of the campaign and Lego was able to continue to position itself as a positive feature in children's lives. Disentangling the Shell–Lego cobranded relationship has meant that Shell cannot borrow positive brand associations; its marketing options are therefore more constrained and it cannot target children. Discursive possibilities for Shell have been restricted and the power of Shell to influence global debates and decision-making has potentially been weakened. Shell is positioned as the villain and Lego continues to evade scrutiny for its own unsustainable practices. The role of social media seems primarily about extending awareness of the campaign and audience reach. However, growing global online communities are participating in campaign sharing, signing petitions and participating in direct action. The development of online communities that are more knowledgeable about environmental issues, concerned about the power relations and discursive strategies of controversial industries marks a significant escalation of critical public engagement in environmental issues. It also marks a shift in cultural responses to ecological issues and the types of meanings that organizations may circulate about themselves.

BP and the Tate sponsorship: Erosion of possibilities

Strategic sponsorship is generally perceived as a useful public relations practice designed to offer sponsoring organizations promotional and publicity opportunities, but perhaps more significantly, it offers sponsored organizations economic development opportunities. Organizations leverage sponsorship to develop positive brand associations, meanings and experiences (De Chernatony and Dall'Olmo Riley, 1998, Cliffe and Motion, 2005). Sponsorship strategies are designed to maximize brand objectives, manage stakeholder relations, achieve brand awareness, project brand image/personality, create brand experiences and create brand loyalty (Cliffe and Motion, 2005). Selection of organizations to sponsor may be intended to offer implicit endorsement for the sponsoring organization.

The endorsement strategy relies upon a type of halo effect in which positive associations are transferred to the sponsoring organization and positive reputational capital is accrued through the relationship. Outcomes of sponsorship may include enhanced reputations, complementary brand personalities, stakeholder experiences that deliver on brand meanings and promises, loyal relational and emotional connections and added value (Cliffe and Motion, 2005). Sponsorship deals are not without controversy; lending credibility to organizations we distrust has the potential to damage both partner organizations' reputations.

In 1990, British Petroleum (BP) became a sponsor of a new initiative at the Tate Gallery named "New Displays." BP's logo appeared on banners outside the building, on gallery walls, in publications and in advertising (Liberate Tate, 2014). The stated justification for the sponsorship was that it increased opportunities to display and expand the Tate's art collection (Liberate Tate, 2014). Corporate sponsorship of art galleries and museums by organizations with problematic social and environmental track records has attracted considerable criticism. These types of sponsorship relationships are critiqued as attempts by controversial organizations to represent themselves as socially responsible (Ihlen and Roper, 2014). The use of sponsorship as a corporate social responsibility (CSR) mechanism may be variously interpreted as a rhetorical, aspirational focus that guides organizations to do the right thing or as a form of "greenwashing" that seeks to distract attention from any damaging practices and provide organizations with green legitimation—without necessarily addressing contentious issues (Beder, 2002).

"Greenwashing," according to Stauber and Rampton (1995, p. 127), is a pejorative term "commonly used to describe the ways that polluters employ deceptive PR to falsely paint themselves an environmentally responsible public image, while covering up their abuses of the biosphere and public health."

Sponsorship relationships are promoted and justified by the Tate in the following statement: "As our sponsor you can build an engagement with art and education to fit your corporate social responsibility (CSR) agenda... We will work with you to ensure your social responsibilities are met" (Tate, 2014).

From this perspective, the role of the Tate in the sponsorship relationship is presented as an ethical guide and mentor for sponsoring organizations. However, questions remain about whether art sponsorship influences the governance of art institutions and the political and social change agendas of artists. The following statement on the Tate web site, for example, suggests that commercial imperatives may drive the partnership: "We provide a platform from which you can speak to an audience of millions—opinion formers, industry leaders and consumers alike. Choose a Tate exhibition and together we can build a package to mirror your brand, ethos and style" (Tate, 2014). In this statement, the Tate is clearly privileging promotion of the sponsoring organization's brand strategy. Although it would be naive to suggest that using corporate speak is unacceptable, it is possible to ask whether corporate sponsorship creates a form of colonization and enculturation that undermines the political and social agendas of art.

Protests against BP arts sponsorship are led by a number of activist groups. Liberate Tate, a network of activist artists, was founded in 2010 to highlight environmental damage caused by oil companies and, more specifically, to end the BP sponsorship of the Tate Modern (Rustin, 2013; 2014). Ironically, the network was established during a Tate workshop on art and activism. When Tate curators tried to prevent the workshop from developing interventions against Tate sponsors, workshop participants decided to set up the Liberate Tate network. Liberate Tate explain their objection to BP sponsorship in this way:

> Many of those wanting an end to the sponsorship argue that Tate is being used by BP as a way to help it create a "social license to operate"—to gain the support of society to continue a business model which explicitly involves the destruction of a safe, liveable environment and climate.
>
> (Liberate Tate, 2014)

Liberate Tate interventions include art installations and performances for the Tate galleries that are designed to attract "international headlines on the issue and inspire other artists to add their voice and art to end Tate's promotion of fossil fuels through its BP sponsorship" (Liberate Tate, 2014). Here, the Tate is explicitly positioned as complicit in the promotion of fossil fuels. The accusation continues:

> Tate's vision states that it will "demonstrate leadership in response to climate change" yet it promotes a company in BP that creates dangerous climate change. Climate-conscious gallery visitors are forced into an uncomfortable position if they want to enjoy art at Tate. Artists are also objecting in greater numbers to the support of BP. As are communities negatively affected by BP operations around the world.
>
> (Liberate Tate, 2014)

Liberate Tate interventions creatively integrate activist politics and artistic practice to popularize resistance to the BP sponsorship of the Tate. For example, on 7 July 2012 over a hundred members of Liberate Tate arrived at the Tate Modern with a new, uninvited installation for the gallery titled "the gift": a 54-foot, one-and-a-half tonne wind turbine blade. Although security guards attempted to prevent the installation, the activists installed the blade in the Tate. Liberate Tate submitted documentation designating the artwork as an official "gift to the nation", a status that meant the gallery must officially process the artwork and consider it for entry to the Tate's permanent collection (see www.vice.com/en_uk/vice-news/liberate-tates-the-gift-tate-modern-art-prank-bp). Other performances include "Parts per million" that involved 50 people dressed in black with veils performing rising carbon levels; "Human Cost" a performance that involved pouring an oil like substance over a naked group; "License to spill," an oil spill at the Tate Summer party in 2010 that was intended to celebrate 10 years of BP support; and "Dead in the water" another contribution to the ten-year celebrations that involved hanging dead fish and birds from helium balloons (Liberate Tate, 2015). These performances are then shared online to reach a broader audience.

"Art not Oil," an activist group, staged an intervention at the National Portrait gallery before the celebration of 25 years of BP sponsorship. The video clip available on YouTube documents the performance of "Portraits in oil" in which participants are daubed with black oil. The last screen shot of the video has the following text: "25 years is enough. It's time for the National Portrait Gallery to cut its ties with BP. @artnotoil. #BPPortrait" (see www.youtube.com/watch?v=SSAlxCqz_Ac).

The online representations of these interventions play a key role in reaching wider publics. The groups use a range of online platforms including both commercial and alternative online media: blogs, YouTube, Vimeo, Facebook, Twitter and Indymedia. Uldam (2014, p. 8) suggests that

> online platforms serve two main purposes when drawing attention to the discrepancies between oil companies' operations and their image as caring companies that generously sponsor cultural activities: (1) to facilitate the virtual circulation of visual and multimodal documentation of actions after the event has taken place, and (2) to access traditional mass media.

Social media played a key role in enabling footage and photos from the interventions to go viral, both in terms of numbers and reach. Without online mediation—and its uptake in traditional mass media—the interventions would remain largely unnoticed beyond the spectators present at the events and limit possibilities for criticizing oil companies' claims to benevolent corporate citizenship.

Questions about the transparency of the sponsorship deals, the government role, and the contractual obligations and expectations have recently been raised. A freedom of information request was made in April 2012 by the campaign group, Request Initiative (Brown, 2015). Although the museum consistently evaded such an undertaking, in March 2014 the Information Commissioner ruled that the Tate must reveal some of the information from its sponsorship meeting with BP. The museum subsequently appealed and requested exemption from the Freedom of Information Act but has now revealed that BP has donated a total of £3.8 million in 17 years, donated in varying sums averaging £224,000 a year (Brown, 2015). The Tate describes it as "considerable sum" whereas protestors have described it as "an embarrassingly small figure" (Brown, 2015).

In response, on 31 January 2015, the art collective, Liberate Tate, staged a performance titled "The reveal" that involved throwing £240,000 of specially designed BP/Tate money down into the main entrance of the Tate galleries (Liberate Tate, 2015). Has knowing the amount made a difference? Those who support the sponsorship arrangement argue that the Tate has benefitted greatly from the arrangement and helped the Tate "develop access to the Tate collection and to present changing displays of work by a wide range of artists in the national collection of British art" (Brown, 2015). Those who oppose the arrangement argue that BP's environmental record overshadows what are now perceived as minimal financial benefits. When money is the only advantage from a sponsorship relationship, and that financial advantage is perceived as insignificant, is it justifiable for the Tate to continue the sponsorship arrangement?

Analysis of the campaign suggests multiple motivations for the critical public engagement interventions. Clearly, the campaign is designed to interrogate the value of the Tate—BP sponsorship relationship and close it down. More generally, the campaign offers a criticism of the fossil fuel industry and its role in climate change. In this instance, the approach to motivating change in the campaigns directed at the BP–Tate sponsorship relationship by various groups is both discursive and performative.

The discursive strategies reflect a philosophical conflict about truth and transparency—calls for the Tate to reveal the financial figures raise ethical questions about funding of public spaces and accountability to society. The Liberate Tate campaigns, in particular, are predominantly performances that enact concern, conflict and resistance. Within this chapter we use and reclaim the more literal interpretation of notions of performance and draw upon Spicer et al. (2009) who propose that "critical performativity involves the active and subversive intervention into managerial discourses and practices" (p. 544). "Performativity" is thus used here to signal a move beyond discursive notions of talk to action. For Spicer et al. (2009) performativity is the political process through which discourses are "actively used, parodied and changed" (p. 544). Entangled in these philosophical issues are political tensions about art sovereignty and the potential for commercial objectives to override artistic considerations. It may also be understood a territorial dispute—the protest performances reclaim the gallery space for artistic endeavors rather than visibility of sponsors.

What this means in practice is that the art of activism may be conceived as both "cultural resistance and political action" (Duncombe, 2002, p. 8) that results in social media acting as an ideological space for "new language, meanings and visions of the future" and a material space "to build community, networks and organizational models." Within the performative aspects of the resistance and action, digital cultural artefacts are created to document and interpret the cultural implications of the colonization of the Tate. From a social media perspective, the Liberate Tate performances are a type of "ethical spectacle" (Duncombe, 2007, p. 9) that is highly suitable for social media circulation and draw attention to issues of cultural identity, ownership and transgressions. This strategy is intended to open up the Tate as a space for artistic rather than commercial expression and reconfigure the boundaries of what is acceptable in publicly owned art spaces. The power relations within the sponsorship arrangements are interrogated and a shift in the cultural terrain asserted. The performances thus "thematize, draw and operate upon endangered attachments" (Marres, 2007, p. 776) in order to resonate with and mobilize public concern. At the same time, a shared culture of resistance as a form of critical public engagement is popularized.

A significant generative feature of the ongoing critical engagement is that it results in the production of activist art. Activist art is thus a contingent act and, the sponsorship actually serves as a resource for art. The modes of protest in this instance successfully raise awareness through widespread social media circulation. However, it is not yet apparent whether the interventions will result in change. It may be argued that while the campaign is discursively weakening the case of BP sponsorship of the Tate and contesting the truth about the value of the relationship—the short term goal of overturning the sponsorship arrangements may not succeed because of a failure to propose funding alternatives.

Could, for example, an innovative social media crowdsourcing campaign raise sufficient funds that the Tate would find it difficult to defend the sponsorship? The risk of the recursive intervention patterns that have been established is that they will lose the potential to create an impact and drive change. This observation is not intended to suggest that the campaign is self-serving, but rather to acknowledge the contradictions and complications of critical public engagement. However, Foucault's suggestion that "the work of deep transformation can be done in the open and always turbulent atmosphere of a continuous criticism" (Foucault, 1994, p. 457) implies that the impact of these cultural interventions will need a long-term commitment to weakening certainty about the value and contribution of questionable sponsorship arrangements and the role of fossil fuel.

We suggest that the power of social media resides in the continual, persistent creation of political and cultural possibilities not only for destabilizing the corporate rhetoric attached to sponsorship arrangements that offer the BP brand positive associations and reputational capital, but more generally for the cultural ways in which dissent and resistance plays out. Such campaigns build and empower communities, and networks, and result in a collective, shared understanding of cultural manipulation.

Divestment

The divestment campaign is driven by an international network of campaigners who challenge institutions to avoid new investment in fossil fuel companies and divest from funds that include fossil fuel equities and bonds. Internationally, campaigns are independently run and have diverse messages. The origins of the divestment campaigns are attributed to American university campuses. The campaigns have challenged individuals and institutions to divest their financial investments as a way of tackling climate change and resulted in "a total of $50bn divested so far, according to the US Fossil Free campaign" (Vaughan, 2014a). Critical public engagement, here, is designed to move beyond targeting individual citizen endeavors to get organizations to also take a stand against fossil fuels and more broadly, climate change. The discursive strategies of divestment campaigns focus on visibility and connectivity: the impact of investment patterns is rendered visible, and individuals and institutions are challenged to make connections between investing in fossil industry practices and climate change. Universities and churches have led the divestment campaigns. Although it may be argued that at this stage the activists' campaign's success is primarily symbolic, the campaigns have gained momentum.

Within Australia, a striking example of a divestment campaign that attracted international attention was the Australian National University (ANU) decision to divest $16 million from seven resource companies linked to fossil fuel industry (Young, 2014). The decision attracted considerable political criticism. The Australian Prime Minister, Tony Abbott, who is on record as stating "coal is good for humanity" (Young, 2014), described the ANU divestment as "a stupid decision" (Cox, 2014). The Australian Government Treasurer, Joe Hockey stated, "I would suggest they're removed from the reality of what is helping to drive the Australian economy and create more employment. Sometimes the view looks different from the lofty rooms of a university" (Milman, 2014).

Political intervention in the internal investment decision-making processes of an Australian university is extraordinary, and, perhaps for that reason, these comments were labeled "bullying." They may also be interpreted as a governmental denial of climate change and an attempt to defend policies that are out of step with contemporary thinking. In response, in an article titled "Time to move to a post-carbon world," Professor Ian Young, the Vice Chancellor of ANU, contextualized the decision as part of a broader debate about carbon and carbon pricing and described the ANU initiative as "another domino in the divestment movement effect" (Young, 2014). He outlined the rationale in terms of "betterment" of the university community, explained the complexities of the divestment decision-making process and emphasized that within a "carbon constrained world" Australia would need to produce alternative energy that generated employment. Professor Young explained that his own views were that "the world must eventually move away from the use of fossil fuels" (Young, 2014).

The ANU decision attracted widespread international media attention and served to popularize (and politicize) the divestment movement. When a campaign gains momentum and institutions as well as individuals participate, a shift in public sentiment is discernible and may be labeled a movement. Clearly, the ANU divestment initiative unsettled and disturbed the government—a leading national university speaking out and acting in direct contrast to its policies is a cause for concern.

The ANU decision may be interpreted as a form of critical public engagement with the fossil fuel industry that opened up the issue for broader public consideration and debate. ANU gained first mover advantage in opening up and leading the conversation, but more importantly, it seized the high moral ground and promoted itself as both a critic for society and an innovative institution. Adopting such a critical stance was risky but positioned ANU as a key player in the energy debate. The ANU divestment marked a significant discursive shift, in which the status quo, the investment in and commitment to fossil fuel in Australia was openly challenged. ANU, it may be argued, is leading a discourse transformation. For critical public engagement to take place, the discourse boundaries of the energy discourse have to be destabilized. By opening up and normalizing divestment, the boundaries of fossil fuel energy discourse are less stable, making it possible to contest their hegemonic position and popularize renewable energy options and innovations.

Potential new subject positions—workers in a postcarbon world—were suggested that directly undermine the employment rhetoric that is used to justify and legitimate fossil fuel industries. Equally important is the introduction of language that provides ways of imagining the future—the term "postcarbon," for example, provides ways of talking about the significant shifts that will occur within the economy. Popularization of divestment by ANU has established a common discourse for critical public engagement with the fossil fuel industry both online and in direct action protests. The political interventions served to highlight the potential power of divestment and lent it credibility as a technique for critical public engagement that is both discursive and performative—it is a sense-making process that directly impacts on behavior.

In perhaps the most significant divestment campaign to date, the *Guardian*, a British newspaper group, has partnered with 350.org, a global climate change movement with networks in 188 countries focused on the growing fossil fuel divestment movement. The campaign, titled "Keep it in the ground," calls for the majority of fossil fuels to remain in the ground. For online readers, the first experience of the campaign was an image that took over the screen of black oil running down the homepage. Clicking on the screen led to a series of articles and an online petition that called on the world's two largest charitable funds, the Bill and Melinda Gates Foundation and the Wellcome Trust, to divest funds from fossil fuel industries. The rationale for and development of the campaign is outlined in a podcast series (see Howard, 2015). The *Guardian* campaign is evolving—each Friday climate change related articles are profiled. A series of podcasts are broadcast that explain the progress to date. On 1 April 2015, the Guardian Media Group divested its £800m fund from fossil fuels (Henn, 2015). Most recently, *The Guardian* has called upon supporters who signed the petition to write letters to members of the Wellcome Trust Board expressing their concerns. The letters have been published online in a special *Guardian* "Dear Wellcome Trust" interactive and in the print version. This initiative represents a radical departure from the notion of an objective, neutral media and has significant implications for public relations. When media outlets partner with social movements, adopt principled standpoints and campaign against elite interests, it is increasingly difficult for public relations to insert elite discourses into media discourse. The participatory politics at play in this campaign are aimed at achieving significant social change. This shift means that public relations is facing an ever-decreasing selection of outlets for promoting elite discourses that work against the public interest.

Naomi Klein, the Canadian author and activist, considered that the fossil fuel divestment campaign was a key step forward in tackling climate change:

> I think this is part of a process of delegitimising this sector and saying these are odious profits, this is not a legitimate business model... This is the beginning of the kind of model that we need, and the first step is saying these profits are not acceptable and once we collectively say that and believe that and express that in our universities, in our faith institutions, at city council level, then we're one step away from where we need to be, which is polluter pays.
>
> (cited in Vaughan, 2014a)

Conclusion

Critical public engagement is participatory politics in action. Civil society groups may challenge, question or open up conversations within social media in order to reconfigure organizational agendas and drive social change. Organizations and civil society have very different starting points. The tendency for organizations to present their offerings as the solution to a problem that civil society may not prioritize or possibly even recognize has the potential to provoke adversarial forms of critical public engagement. By not inviting civil society to engage in agenda setting and problem definition activities, organizations make assumptions about what is best for society. As a result, civil society groups seek alternative discursive spaces, such as social media, to challenge those assumptions, question organizational priorities and stage interventions in organizational strategies. Critical public engagement interventions destabilize or delegitimize organizational meaning production, often by seeking to re-establish connections between organizations and undesirable practices. Social media offers an open space for alternative voices to challenge hegemonic discourses and contest organizational power. Within the first two cases examined in this chapter, the Lego-Shell cobranded partnership and the Tate-BP sponsorship partnership, the commercial relationships were established to create favorable associations for Shell and BP by linking them to popular, socially acceptable organizations in an attempt to gain legitimacy and to appropriate or borrow the social license of their partner. An implicit aim of such relationships is also to minimize or negate unfavorable associations with environmental damage. Critical public engagement seeks to re-establish such associations and to also connect publics with the consequences of their own practices. Undoing the Lego-Shell cobranding relationship potentially reminds consumers that using fossil fuels has an impact on the environment. What was perhaps strategically ignored, was the potential to connect the composition of Lego bricks with their fossil fuel origins. This type of strategic contradiction, the deliberate pursuit of one goal while ignoring an equally important issue, is often interpreted as a values conflict. Strategic contradiction is a technique that civil society brings into play when focused on achieving a short-term goal. It would seem that immediate wins are considered more influential and valuable that a consistent message. Although the campaign to undo the Tate-BP sponsorship partnership has not yet succeeded, small victories are evident. Disclosure of the financial value of the arrangement makes it increasingly difficult to justify continuation of the sponsorship and is evidence of momentum building against such partnerships.

The Lego-Shell cobranded partnership and the Tate-BP sponsorship partnership, along with the divestment case, all take place within a broader context of climate change concern. Although each campaign, studied in isolation, may suggest that the outcomes of critical public engagement are minimal, it may be argued that the combined efforts of these campaigns are weakening the legitimation and acceptance of fossil fuel organizations.

Social media is an ideal vehicle for critical public engagement. Although the campaigns selected here showcase integrated traditional, digital and social media, they provide useful insights into the role of social media in critical public engagement. Audience awareness and reach is significantly extended—discursive and performative challenges may be generated, enacted and shared globally. The potential and real reach of social media offers a form of power—fear of such immeasurable exposure may force organizations to engage and even change policies and practices. As some forms of protests such as petitions have moved online and been taken up via social media their influence has increased. Awareness of multiple critical public engagement campaigns that social media affords means that although each campaign may not result in the "big bang" in terms of change, a gradual erosion of public confidence has the potential to build into an avalanche of public disapproval.

References

Beder, S. and Beder. (2002). *Global Spin: The Corporate Assault on Environmentalism*. Devon, UK: Green Books.

Blackett, T. and Boad, B. (1999). *Co-Branding: The Science of Alliance*. London, Macmillan.

Brown, M. (2015). Tate's BP sponsorship was £150,00 to £330,000 a year, figures show. *Guardian*, 26 January. Retrieved 21 February, 2015 from www.theguardian.com/artanddesign/2015/jan/26/tate-reveal-bp-sponsorship-150000-330000-platform-information-tribunal

Clegg, C. Phillips (2006). Clegg, S.R., Courpasson, D., and Phillips, N.(2006). *Power and Organizations*. London: Sage.

Cliffe, S.J. and Motion, J. (2005). Building contemporary brands: a sponsorship-based strategy. *Journal of Business Research*, 58(8), 1068–1077.

Cox, L. (2014, October 15). Tony Abbott attacks ANU's 'stupid decision' to dump fossil fuel investments. *The Guardian*. Retrieved 26 September 2015 from: www.smh.com.au/federal-politics/political-news/tony-abbott-attacks-anus-stupid-decision-to-dump-fossil-fuel-investments-20141015-116a0y.html

De Chernatony, L. and Dall'Olmo Riley, F. (1998). Defining a "brand": Beyond the literature with experts' interpretations. *Journal of Marketing Management*, 14(5), 417–443.

Demetrious, K. (2013). *Public Relations, Activism, and Social Change: Speaking Up*. New York: Routledge.

Duncombe, S. (ed.). (2002). *Cultural Resistance Reader*. London: Verso.

Duncombe, S. (2007). *Dream: Re-imagining Progressive Politics in an Age of Fantasy*. New York: New Press.

Fairclough, N. (1992). *Discourse and Social Change*. Cambridge: Polity Press.

Foucault, M. (1980). *Power/Knowledge: Selected Interviews and Other Writings 1972–1977*. New York: Pantheon.

Foucault, M. (1988). Technologies of the self. In L. Martin, H. Gutman, and P. Hutton (eds), *Technologies of the Self: A Seminar with Michel Foucault* (pp. 16–48). Amherst: University of Massachusetts.

Foucault, M. (1991). Politics and the study of discourse. In G. Burchell, C.Gordon, and P. Miller (eds), *The Foucault Effect: Studies in Governmentality with Two Lectures and an interview with Michel Foucault* (pp. 53–72). Chicago: University of Chicago.

Foucault, M. (1994). *Power*. In J.D. Faubion (ed.), *Essential Works of Foucault 1954–1984*, vol. 3, trans. R. Hurley and others. London: Penguin.

Ganesh, S. and Zoller, H.M. (2012). Dialogue, activism and democratic social change. *Communication Theory*, 22(1), 66-91.

Henn, J. (2015). Our media partnership with the Guardian. 350.org, 1 April. Retrieved 6 April, 2015 from https://350.org/our-media-partnership-with-the-guardian/

Holtzhausen, D.R. (2014). *Public Relations as Activism: Postmodern Approaches to Theory and Practice*. New York, NY: Routledge.

Howard, E. (2015). The biggest story in the world: Inside the Guardian's Climate Change campaign. *Guardian*, 27 March. Retrieved 6 April, 2015 from www.theguardian.com/environment/keep-it-in-the-ground-blog/2015/mar/20/the-biggest-story-in-the-world-inside-the-guardians-climate-change-campaign

Ihlen, Ø. and Roper, J. (2014). Corporate reports on sustainability and sustainable development: 'we have arrived'. *Sustainable Development*, 22(1), 42–51.

Irwin, A. and Wynne, B. (1996). *Misunderstanding Science: The Public Reconstruction of Science and Technology*. Cambridge: Cambridge University Press.

Jenkins, H., Ford, S., and Green, J. (2013). *Spreadable Media: Creating Value and Meaning in a Networked World*. New York: New York University Press.

Lakoff, G. (2010). Why it matters how we frame the environment. *Environmental Communication*, 4(1), 70-81.

Latour, B. (2004). Why has critique run out of steam? From matters of fact to matters of concern. *Critical Inquiry*, 30(2), 225–248.

Leitch, S. and Motion, J. (2010). Publics and public relations: Effecting change. In R. Heath (ed.). *The Sage Handbook of Public Relations*, pp. 99–110. Thousand Oaks, CA: Sage.

Liberate Tate (2014) Tate & BP: Background. Retrieved 13 February 2014 from https://liberatetate.wordpress.com/tate-and-bp/

Liberate Tate. (2015). £240,000 of "BP money" thrown from the top of Tate Britain into its oil company sponsored galleries. https://liberatetate.wordpress.com/

Marres, N. (2007). The issues deserve more credit pragmatist contributions to the study of public involvement in controversy. *Social Studies of Science*, 37(5), 759–780.

Marres, N. (2012). *Material Participation: Technology, The Environment and Everyday Publics*. London: Palgrave Macmillan.

Milman, O. (2014). Coalition accused of "bullying" ANU after criticism of fossil fuel divestment. Guardian, 13 October. Retrieved 10 March 2015 from www.theguardian.com/

australia-news/2014/oct/13/coalition-accused-of-bullying-anu-after-criticism-of-fossil-fuel-divestment

Motion, J., Leitch, S., and Brodie, R.J. (2003). Equity in corporate co-branding: the case of Adidas and the All Blacks. *European Journal of Marketing*, 37(7/8), 1080–1094.

Motion, J., Leitch, S., and Weaver, C.K. (2015). Popularizing dissent: A civil society perspective. *Public Understanding of Science*, 24(4), 496–510.

Mouffe, C. (1993). *The Return of the Political*. London: Verso.

Mouffe, C. (1999). Deliberative democracy or agonistic pluralism? *Social Research*, 66(3), 745–758.

Polisano, E. (2014). Greenpeace: How our campaign ended the Lego-Shell partnership. *Guardian*, 10 October. Retrieved 2 August 2014 from www.theguardian.com/voluntary-sector-network/2014/oct/10/greenpeace- lego-shell-climate-change-arctic-oil

Rustin, S. (2013, 25 April). Can Liberate Tate free the arts from BP? *The Guardian*. Retrieved 1 September 2015 from www.theguardian.com/artanddesign/2013/apr/24/liberate-tate-arts-bp

Spicer, A., Alvesson, M., and Kärreman, D. (2009). Critical performativity: The unfinished business of critical management studies. *Human Relations*, 62(4), 537–560.

Starr, M. (2014). Lego ends partnership with Shell over Greenpeace campaign. *CNET*, 10 October. Retrieved 2 August 2015 from www.cnet.com/au/news/LEGO-ends-partnership-with-shell-over-greenpeace-campaign/

Stauber, J. and Rampton, S. (1995). *Toxic Sludge is Good for You*. Monroe, ME: Common Courage Press.

Stirling, A. (2008). 'Opening up' and 'Closing down': Power, participation and pluralism in the social appraisal of technology. *Science, Technology and Human Values*, 33(2), 262–294.

Tate (2014). Corporate social responsibility. Retrieved 12 February 2015 from www.tate.org.uk/join-support/corporate-support/sponsorship/corporate-social-responsibility

Taylor, L. (2014). Tony's [sic] Abbott's "coal is good" line is familiar and troubling. *The Guardian*, 14 October. Retrieved 10 March 2015 from www.theguardian.com/australia-news/2014/oct/14/tonys-abbotts-coal-is-good-line-is-familiar-and-troubling

Thomas, R. and Davies, A. (2005). Theorizing the micro-politics of resistance: New public management and managerial identities in the UK public services. *Organization studies*, 26(5), 683–706.

Turner, J. (2014). Today Lego dumped Shell—Here's why it matters to us all. Greenpeace [web log]. Retrieved 23 February 2015 from www.greenpeace.org/international/en/news/Blogs/makingwaves/save-the-arctic-lego-dumps-shell/blog/50926/

Uldam, J. (2014). Corporate management of visibility and the fantasy of the post-political: Social media and surveillance. New Media & Society. Retrieved 1 September from http://nms.sagepub.com.wwwproxy0.library.unsw.edu.au/content/early/2014/06/30/1461444814541526.full.pdf+html

Vaughan, A. (2014a). Fossil fuel divestment: a brief history. *The Guardian*, 8 October. Retrieved 9 March 2015 from www.theguardian.com/environment/2014/oct/08/fossil-fuel-divestment-a-brief-history

Vaughan, A. (2014b). Lego ends Shell partnership following Greenpeace campaign. *Guardian*, 9 October. Retrieved 2 August 2015 from www.theguardian.com/environment/2014/oct/09/lego-ends-shell-partnership-following-greenpeace-campaign

Young, I. (2014). Time to move to a post-carbon world. *Sydney Morning Herald*, October 13. Retrieved 9 March 2015 from www.smh.com.au/comment/time-to-move-to-a-postcarbon-world-20141012-114wmn.html

8   Protect yourself

Issues of privacy and regulation

In 2013, Seth Gordon's film, *Identity Thief*, found comedy in a phenomenon which, in that year alone, was reality for more than 11 million US citizens and which had been massively enabled by our collective willingness to share personal information. The data trail or "digital footprints" we leave behind as we move through the Internet has spawned new forms of crime and fueled public anxieties about privacy and security. Legislation and regulation lag far behind, while the ethical and legal dimensions of our participation in social media contexts are still being worked through by users, organizations and governments. In this chapter, we explore the unfolding debates and emerging issues and the way in which these debates and issues are impacting upon the practice of public relations.

The widespread sharing of the most intimate details of our personal lives that social media has enabled clearly poses substantial new challenges for societies and for regulators with responsibility for protecting information privacy (Ibrahim, 2008). However, even the more mundane aspects of our communication—the so-called "metadata" of who we connect with, who they connect with, and how often we interact—are of enormous potential value and are arguably in need of protection. Metadata mapping enables a detailed analysis to be undertaken of the communication lives of individuals that can be revealing or misleading (or both) as well as potentially incriminating. Social media sites, search engine queries, emails and telephone calls, are all rich sources of metadata. Given the degree of overt and covert surveillance that is occurring, one should take as a starting point that all such communications are likely to be monitored and may become public at some future time.

Privacy laws were originally enacted to deal with violations of physical rather than virtual space. Since then, lawmakers have struggled to keep up as each new wave of electronic and digital technology has brought new means of transmitting, eavesdropping, storing, tracking and hacking information. For example, Article 17 of the United Nations' International Covenant on Civil and Political Rights states:

> No one shall be subjected to arbitrary or unlawful interference with his [sic] privacy, family, home or correspondence, nor to unlawful attacks on

his [sic] honor or reputation. Everyone has the right to the protection of the law against such interference or attacks.

Just what the key words in Article 17—including "privacy," "protection," "interference" and "attack"—mean in virtual and social media contexts is unclear. Moreover, in the post 9/11 world, individual rights to privacy have been increasingly subordinated to national security goals. As a result, interference with privacy may be systematic rather than arbitrary and also lawful.

Internationally, the courts are struggling to make judgments due to the inadequacy of the legislation and the lack of precedents in areas in which social expectations and norms have yet to be determined. Meanwhile, the fast pace of technological change is itself a limiting factor as governments are reluctant to enact new legislation that is likely to be outdated before bills can work their way through the often sluggish and convoluted legislative processes. Even the concept of information privacy is a contested one (Smith, Dinev and Xu, 2011) that is variously presented as an individual right (Westin, 1967), the ability to control access to information (Altman, 1975), and as a commodity that may be traded (Davies, 1997). Depending upon the perspective adopted, different issues and solutions to issues will emerge. In this chapter, then, we tease out some of the complexities of information privacy and regulation, beginning with an analysis of the underlying power relations.

Power relations

Much has been written about the potential of social media to empower people, enabling us to freely share ideas and to organize resistance in the face of oppressive regimes. Less has been said about the way in which social participation "embeds users within relations of power" (Goldberg, 2010, p. 740). In referring to "relations of power," Goldberg is arguing that our participation in social media, albeit it through multiple acts that may appear trivial, may have far reaching consequences. In participating in social media, we are potentially opening our lives up to surveillance by governments, criminal networks, hackers and organizations of all kinds. In this section we consider the potential of social media to both shore up existing power relations and enable the exercise of what Castells (2007, p. 248) terms the exercise of counterpower through "mass self-communication," defined as communication that:

> reaches potentially a global audience through p2p [peer-to-peer] networks and Internet connection. It is multi-modal, as the digitization of content and advanced software, often based on open source that can be downloaded free, allows the reformatting of almost any content in almost any form, increasingly distributed via wireless networks. And it is self-generated in content, self-directed in emission, and self-selected in reception by many that communicate with many.

At one level, the characteristics of mass self-communication may be seen as profoundly democratic, enabling a peer-to-peer sharing of information and ideas that bypasses the gatekeepers of traditional mass media. The power to communicate globally now lies in the hands of everyone with access to an Internet-enabled device. For example, mass self-communication through social media appears to have played a significant role in the so-called Arab Spring which saw popular uprisings in Egypt, Tunisia, Syria and elsewhere. At the time, social media was labelled "liberation technology" because of its utility as means of organizing opposition to despotic regimes. Writing two years after the uprisings, however, Goldman (2013) is somewhat more measured in her analysis, noting that the role of social media may have been exaggerated by Western mass media who were reliant upon it as a source of information. Goldman also noted that social media was a tool for the regimes that activists were targeting. For example, Egyptian President Morsi issued major policy announcements via his Facebook page rather than through the filtering mechanism of the media conference.

The double-edged sword that is social media was highlighted by then US secretary of state, Hillary Rodham Clinton, in her now famous speech on Internet freedom, which was made in January 2010. In light of more recent events, including the Edward Snowden case discussed below, it is worth considering this extract from Clinton's speech:

> During his visit to China in November, for example, President Obama held a town hall meeting with an online component to highlight the importance of the internet. In response to a question that was sent in over the internet, he defended the right of people to freely access information, and said that the more freely information flows, the stronger societies become. He spoke about how access to information helps citizens hold their own governments accountable, generates new ideas, encourages creativity and entrepreneurship. The United States belief in that ground truth is what brings me here today.
>
> Because amid this unprecedented surge in connectivity, we must also recognize that these technologies are not an unmitigated blessing. These tools are also being exploited to undermine human progress and political rights. Just as steel can be used to build hospitals or machine guns, or nuclear power can either energize a city or destroy it, modern information networks and the technologies they support can be harnessed for good or for ill. The same networks that help organize movements for freedom also enable al-Qaida to spew hatred and incite violence against the innocent. And technologies with the potential to open up access to government and promote transparency can also be hijacked by governments to crush dissent and deny human rights.
>
> In the last year, we've seen a spike in threats to the free flow of information. China, Tunisia, and Uzbekistan have stepped up their censorship of

the internet. In Vietnam, access to popular social networking sites has suddenly disappeared. And last Friday in Egypt, 30 bloggers and activists were detained. One member of this group, Bassem Samir, who is thankfully no longer in prison, is with us today. So while it is clear that the spread of these technologies is transforming our world, it is still unclear how that transformation will affect the human rights and the human welfare of the world's population.

On their own, new technologies do not take sides in the struggle for freedom and progress, but the United States does. We stand for a single internet where all of humanity has equal access to knowledge and ideas. And we recognize that the world's information infrastructure will become what we and others make of it. Now, this challenge may be new, but our responsibility to help ensure the free exchange of ideas goes back to the birth of our republic.

(Clinton, 2010)

In her speech, Clinton emphasizes the open-ended nature of Internet technology, which can be used for multiple, sometimes conflicting, purposes. The same social media sites that may be deployed in the pursuit of social justice and freedom can be used by authoritarian regimes "to crush dissent and deny human rights." The sites can be used by such regimes to lure dissenters out into the open so that they can be identified and punished. The phenomenon is not new. For example, a similar tactic occurred in the pre-Internet era in China, during the reign of Mao Zedong, with the launch of the "Hundred flowers campaign" in 1956. Chinese citizens were encouraged to express their views on any matter—arts, science, even the Communist Party itself. This brief "flowering" of free speech was abruptly followed by a period of brutal repression. Hundreds of thousands of people were arrested and sent to "re-education camps," imprisoned or executed. Mao Zedong spoke of having "enticed the snakes out of their lairs" and of the need to distinguish "fragrant flowers" from "poisonous weeds" (King, 2012). There is no doubt that had a similar campaign been launched via social media, millions more would have been exposed as regime dissenters. As Deibert and Rohozinski (2012, p. 30) contend "linking technological properties to a single social outcome such as liberation or control is a highly dubious exercise." In short, social media like traditional media can serve many different purposes, including purposes that are illegal, unethical and antidemocratic.

In her speech, Clinton resolutely positions the US on the side of those who believe in Internet freedom and "equal access to knowledge and ideas." However, Clinton recognizes that such words are empty if not coupled with action and that "the world's information infrastructure will become what we and others make of it." In the next section we consider a case which renders these words somewhat prophetic and highlights the power relations at play in social media.

Edward Snowden and the NSA

On 6 June 2013, articles began to appear in the UK's *Guardian* newspaper that significantly changed the way in which we think about privacy on the Internet. Edward Snowden, formerly of the CIA and NSA, blew the whistle on the systematic monitoring of both domestic and international communications that was being conducted by the US with the cooperation of a number of other nations and corporations. Numerous overlapping programs were identified by Snowden but the program known as *PRSM* was given most prominence by the news media due to its potential implications for ordinary users of social media, email and search engines. The products of major Internet companies, including Facebook, Microsoft, Google, Yahoo, YouTube, Skype, and AOL were all implicated in the scandal. As the story unfolded, it became clear that the data and metadata being collected by the NSA on US citizens went far beyond that envisaged under the enabling legislation.

The US Government and its British ally reacted strongly to the security breach and the *Guardian* newspaper was ordered to either hand over or destroy the information it had received from Snowden. According to the *Washington Post:*

> On Saturday 20 July, in a deserted basement of the Guardian's King's Cross offices, a senior editor and a Guardian computer expert used angle grinders and other household tools to pulverise the hard drives and memory chips on which the encrypted files had been stored. As they worked, they were watched intently by technicians from the Government Communications Headquarters (GCHQ) who took notes and photographs, but who left empty-handed.
>
> (Peterson, 2013)

This episode was rendered more bizarre by the fact that the *Guardian* had declared it held copies of the encrypted files on servers located in other countries. Destruction of the London hard drives therefore did nothing to limit the *Guardian*'s access to the Snowden material. What it highlighted was the place-based nature of the relevant legislation, which meant that the physical location of hard drives was of primary importance—a fact that has particular implications for US-based companies such as Facebook, which is the largest global repository of social media data. Snowden himself had long since fled the US, first to Hong Kong and then on to seek political asylum in Russia.

The Snowden revelations created a political storm inside the US itself. A proposal to limit the collection of metadata and telephone records under the Patriot Act was put to the House of Representatives in July 2013 but failed narrowly to pass. One of the most surprising features of the proposal was that both support and opposition were bipartisan, with party leaders and the President opposed but a broad coalition of liberals and conservatives in support. Public opinion was also strongly opposed to the NSA programs according to a variety of polls, with opposition growing over time rather than diminishing

(Ehrenfreund, 2013). At the time of writing, the case was still unfolding with law suits under way by litigants ranging from large, activist organizations, such as the American Civil Liberties Union, to individuals, such as Anna Smith, a nurse from Idaho who was suing the President using her own resources (ibid). Whether Snowden has further revelations to make or will disappear into Russian exile as a historical footnote remains unclear. What is clear is that Snowden has fundamentally shifted our thinking about the possibility of privacy in digital communications.

There are a number of issues embedded in this case for public relations. The first is that social media sites and streams set up for public relations purposes are likely to be caught up in the general surveillance of Internet traffic. Inviting social media participants to share information about themselves or their opinions as part of, for example, games and competitions, is therefore also an indirect invitation to share this information publicly and permanently with unknown others. Your organization may fully comply with legal and ethical standards of information privacy and security but this is no guarantee that your data – and the data entrusted to you by your publics – is not being accessed by others, including your government. Moreover, the Snowden case reveals that this access is likely to be occurring during transmission. Your servers may be secure but the information shared with your organization by its publics was most likely monitored on the way in rather than hacked from your server.

The second issue is that the physical location of servers still matters—a lot. For example, if an organization located in Europe puts up a Facebook page that is hosted on a server based in the US, then the data associated with this page falls within US jurisdiction. The notion that such pages are located in "virtual" space is somewhat misleading. This issue is starkly illustrated by the UK *Guardian*'s experience of having its hard drives destroyed with angle grinders by agents of its own government on behalf of a political ally. On the flip side, when convicted murderers, Wolfgang Werlé and Manfred Lauber, successfully sued Wikipedia through the German courts to have their names removed from pages relating to their case, their goal was thwarted by the fact that Wikipedia has no operations inside German territory (Schwartz, 2010). Wikipedia is a nonprofit organization based in San Francisco. The German courts therefore had no jurisdiction over the company. Moreover, even expunging the names "Wolfgang Werlé" and "Manfred Lauber" from web site pages located on German servers could do nothing to block Internet searches by users from within Germany in relation to the murder case. The German court's ruling therefore seems as out of step with the Internet era as the UK Government's use of angle grinders to destroy a newspaper's server.

The third issue is that data traffic flows appear virtual but actually pass through servers with geographical locations. Even if you and the host servers of your social media site or stream are colocated, the data traffic that flows in and out may pass through multiple legal jurisdictions and therefore be subject to monitoring, control and/or collection. These flows are unpredictable, subject to frequent changes and largely invisible to users. One of the immediate repercussions of the Snowden revelations has been moves by more nations to regulate the flow of data. For example, in September 2013, Brazilian President, Dilma Rousseff, announced a plan to place an undersea cable between Brazil and Europe so that Brazilian data would not flow through US territory. This plan may never be enacted, partly because of the multibillion dollar cost of an undersea cable and partly because the US already reportedly has access to data flows through undersea cables. In June 2013, The UK *Guardian* reported that:

> Britain's spy agency GCHQ has secretly gained access to the network of cables which carry the world's phone calls and internet traffic and has started to process vast streams of sensitive personal information which it is sharing with its American partner, the National Security Agency (NSA).
>
> (MacAskill et al., 2013)

Even a dedicated undersea cable which you own is, therefore, no longer a secure vehicle for communication.

President Rousseff also foreshadowed moves to force Internet companies such as Google and Facebook to store all data related to Brazilian citizens on Brazilian-based servers. This proposal may not stop such data from being monitored but does give the nation legal jurisdiction over the activities of these companies. The case highlights the inherent and growing tension between Internet freedom and state sovereignty. Similar concerns have led the French data protection watchdog, CNIL, to begin formal sanctions against Google due to the company's refusal to inform users on how it processes and stores their data. Google's new practices enable the company to track user activity across the Google search engine, Gmail accounts and the Google+ social network. Google currently uses this tracking to better target users with advertising and users have little or no ability to opt out. Given the economic value of such tracking to Internet companies like Google, any moves by governments or international bodies to limit or control tracking will likely continue to be strongly resisted.

The fourth issue raised by the Snowden revelations, which is also highlighted by the CNIL vs. Google case, is that individual data may not matter as much as the aggregation of such data drawn from multiple sources. The potential power of data mining and the aggregation of information into what is now known as "big data," is discussed in the next section

Data mining and information privacy

The surveillance of Internet communications by governments, which has been highlighted by the Snowden case, is an important dimension of information privacy that is relevant for all public relations activities undertaken through social media. An associated, major issue is the use that public relations practitioners themselves make of the data provided by others. Public relations is no less immersed in "relations of power" when it engages with social media than any other participants (Goldberg, 2010). Indeed, public relations practices in social media contexts—including data mining and data sharing—may be in danger of falling on the wrong side of emerging legal and ethical standards in relation to information privacy and security.

Personal data is a valuable asset, often the major asset, owned by the Internet sites that collect it. For public relations practitioners, mining that data may assist the design of communication campaigns and the construction of messages most likely to resonate with the concerns of particular publics. It may also enable organizations to connect, not just with individuals but with entire networks of people with shared interests and connections. Public relations practitioners therefore often find themselves in the role of clients for the information available for sale from social networks and other Internet sites. The recent actions by Brazil, France and other nations in relation to the gathering of such information highlights the difficult ethical terrain that we cross in taking advantage of such data sets. In particular, the commercial uses that social media data may be put to—including its public relations uses—seldom coincide with the purposes for which the data was provided. Given that using personal data solely for the purposes for which it was collected is a fundamental principle of the information privacy regulations and policies of many nations, this mismatch is a serious issue for public relations.

Facebook provides a clear example of the tensions between the goals and expectations of individual users of social media and those of commercial entities. Users get free access to the Facebook site, which enables them to share their thoughts, ideas, photographs, current location, purchase choices, party invitations, marital status, religion, date of birth, home town and much, much more, with anyone they "friend." In return, Facebook gets access to all that personal information about user likes, dislikes, opinions and preferences, which they aggregate and on-sell to advertisers. Facebook has a simple business model based on deriving revenue from data mining. Every time one of Facebook's 1 billion plus users adds a post, they enhance the Facebook database asset and the ability of advertisers to customize their messages. The sheer scale of the Facebook enterprise and its data holdings was revealed when the company posted the following statistics on its own Facebook site:

Facebook Statistics May 2013
1.11 billion active monthly users
665 million active daily users
16 million business pages
4.75 billion content items shared daily
4.5 billion "likes" daily
4,900 employees worldwide
US$1.46 billion revenue first quarter 2013
US$1.25 billion advertising revenue first quarter 2013

(www.facebook.com/facebook)

Advertising is clearly the major source of revenue for the company. Targeted advertising on their personal pages is, then, the price that social media users pay for the utility of the otherwise free site. In this respect, social media may seem to differ little from free-to-air television, a domain in which viewers have long understood that it is the advertising that pays for the programs they enjoy. However, there are significant differences between old and new media, including the fact that your analog television was not collecting and transmitting personal information about you to the television station. Users have to trust that social media companies will strive to protect their personal data (from everyone but the company itself) because to allow it to be hacked into or stolen would reduce the value of the company's database for advertisers and, ultimately, reduce the value of the company itself for shareholders and investors. However, there have been numerous breaches of social media security, including a highly embarrassing admission by Facebook in June 2013—around the same time as the Snowden revelations—that a "glitch" in its software had led to data security breaches affecting around six million users. The level of Internet surveillance that is being undertaken by governments of all kinds, as revealed by Snowden, adds another layer of complexity onto the way in which users must think about privacy in social media contexts. A government agency may not have hacked your social media site but it has almost certainly monitored the data that has flowed in and out of the site and the links you have made and shared by "friending" or "liking" others.

There are no universal standards or laws relating to data privacy. As discussed above the nearest the world has come to a shared understanding of privacy resides in Article 17 of the United Nations' International Covenant on Civil and Political Rights. Article 17 was written prior to the Internet era and is of limited utility in the current context, especially in relation to social media. More than 80 nations do have their own information privacy laws, most of which now deal specifically with the Internet and digital technologies. In this regard, the US is something of an anomaly in having refused to introduce such legislation. Instead, there is an ever-changing patchwork of statutes targeting issues as they arise or focused on individual sectors of the economy or society. The reason for this rejection of far-reaching federal privacy legislation is likely to be the First Amendment to the US Constitution, which is interpreted to privilege the right to free speech above the right to privacy. As Hillary Rodham Clinton stated while US secretary of state, it is the US view that "our responsibility to help ensure the free exchange of ideas goes back to the birth of our republic" (Clinton, 2010).

In our discussion so far, we have primarily looked at privacy and regulation in digital and social media contexts from national and international perspectives. In the following sections we move our analysis to consider three different user perspectives; that of individuals, groups, and organizations.

Individuals

The value of social media sites for individuals stems in large part from their ability to connect us with others. The "others" may be friends, colleagues, or complete strangers with whom we share a common interest. The benefits of such sharing are manifest, ranging from entertainment, to the opportunity for socially isolated individuals to build relationships, to the chance to participate in broader social causes, even, as occurred during the Arab Spring, in social revolutions. Individuals experience their participation on the Internet as movement through virtual space. However, as discussed above, our virtual movements are captured and stored as metadata by the web sites we visit as well as by those who intercept and monitor data flows. Analysis of this metadata may provide an observer with a comprehensive picture of the relationships and communication patterns of individuals.

In the pre-Edward Snowden era, there was little evidence that the security of metadata was of concern to most Internet users (Belanger and Crossler, 2011). Instead, the privacy and security concerns of individuals were more often related to their ability to trust ecommerce sites, particularly in relation to financial information such as credit card details (Dinev and Hart, 2005). Public fears in relation to Internet security have been fueled by recent cases, such as the US Federal prosecution of a group of Eastern European hackers for US$300m in credit card fraud in 2013. Prior to this case, the largest known prosecution was in relation to the theft of more than 130 million credit card numbers in 2007 from a payment processing company, which was associated with around US$200 million in losses. J.C. Penney, 7-Eleven, Dow Jones and the French department store chain Carrefour, have all been targets of attempted or successful fraud involving stolen credit card numbers. Public concerns in relation to the privacy and security of their online interactions are certainly justified. Following the Snowden revelations, a broader range of concerns are likely to come to the fore as public awareness of Internet surveillance increases.

Despite our concerns and growing evidence for the validity of our concerns, we continue to share information online. Perhaps the Internet has become so ubiquitous that we feel that we must participate regardless of the dangers, just as we continue to drive our cars despite our knowledge of the frequency of car crashes. One explanation of our willingness to share personal information online, suggested by Vitak (2012, p. 451), is that social media use can lead to "context collapse: the flattening out of multiple, distinct audiences in one's social network, such that people from different contexts become part of a singular group of message recipients." Context collapse, Vitak argues, leads to "the blurring of public and private spheres," which simply means that we lose a sense of the line between our personal and public or professional lives (Vitak, 2012, p. 454). Moreover, while users may experience their participation in online forums as time-based conversations, their participation differs substantially from spoken conversations in leaving a permanent trace of data and metadata behind in terms of: what was said; who it was addressed to; and, potentially, who else may have accessed or commented on the discussion. A number of studies have found that awareness of context collapse leads users to either disclose less or disclose less information that is intimate (Stutzman et al., 2011).

Many social media users are very aware of context and do exercise caution in their choices of the people with whom they will share information. The potentially permanent nature of social media data may, however, create unintended issues for users in the future. In the US, for example, there is growing use of social media searches by employers seeking to hire future employees. Practices include requesting that job applicants provide access to their social media sites so that employers can make character checks (Sanchez et al., 2012). There have also been a number of law suits brought by employees who have lost their jobs following social media searches that have revealed negative comments about the employer. In some cases usernames and passwords have been obtained by coercion, in others access to social media has been obtained via third parties who have "friended" the complainant (ibid). In both cases, US courts have found in favor of the employees because the SCA prohibits employers from using such coercive or secretive means of obtaining information. However, where data is shared openly, users have far more limited legal protection or means of seeking redress. In establishing social media sites for the staff and clients of the organizations for which they work, public practitioners may therefore unwittingly expose the site's users to future career risks, especially if users choose to share criticisms of the organizations for which they work or may work in the future, or personal details that might negatively impact on their career options.

The privacy issues associated with social media sites are constantly changing as a result of increased awareness of such issues by users but also, partly, as a result of the expanded functions of the sites themselves. For example, when Facebook was launched, information was protected by the company and available only to site users (Tuten and Angermeier, 2013). Within five years, the onus to protect information had shifted from the company to the users themselves, requiring them to set up restrictive privacy settings in order to prevent most of their data becoming public information. A series of infographics developed by Matt McKeon, which trace the ongoing diminution of the default privacy settings on Facebook, show clearly that it has become significantly harder for users to ensure the security of their personal details, contacts and communications (http://mattmckeon.com/facebook-privacy/). It is worth noting here that, in 2010, Mark Zuckerberg, the founder of Facebook declared that privacy was no longer a "social norm" (Johnson, 2010).

Given the growing awareness of privacy issues on the Internet it is interesting to note that many users still do not use the privacy settings on social media sites. Studies have also found that fewer than half of those who user social media and other Internet sites ever read the site's privacy policies (Meinert et al., 2006). Belanger and Crossler (2011, p. 1031) argue that privacy policies are therefore more likely to provide protection for Internet companies against consumer law suits than they are to actually protect the privacy of site users. Certainly, one study of health-care web sites found that company objectives rather than consumer concerns were central criteria in the development of company privacy policies (Earp et al., 2005). In response to such criticisms, many social media sites, including Facebook and Google, have moved to provide explanations of their privacy policies in plain language. The policy includes clear instructions on how users may opt in or out of public data sharing as well as information on the organization's use of data and metadata, from which there is no "opt-out" provision. For example, the Facebook privacy policy states that the company will use the data its users provide "to measure or understand the effectiveness of ads you and others see, including to deliver relevant ads to you" (www.facebook.com/about/privacy/your-info). This key clause of the Facebook privacy policy spells out not just the way in which the site tailors its advertising to users, but also the unwitting participation of users in what could be seen as a mega-focus group for advertisers. There is no way of opting out of these commercial transactions other than by ceasing to be a Facebook participant. Of course, opting out of social media sites means also opting out of participation in social groups. The group perspective is considered in the next section.

Groups

The ability of individuals to form and join groups is a central, distinguishing characteristic of social media. Analysis of social media at the level of the group is, however, relatively sparse with most user-based research focused on either individuals or organizations (Belanger and Crossler, 2011). In the previous section, we discussed the phenomenon of context collapse that may occur, especially in omnibus social media settings (Vitak, 2012). However, groups may be seen to play an important role in establishing context within social media sites. Successful social media groups develop their own cultures and group dynamics, including norms in relation to what it is appropriate to share and the tone of communication (Hauptmann and Stegar, 2013).

Public relations has begun to make extensive use of social media groups for internal and external communication purposes. Some of the privacy issues inherent within social media that have been discussed above, including the unintended creation of a permanent data record, the potential for surveillance, and exposure of personal information to criminals, apply to both external and internal publics. From a privacy perspective, the issue of metadata is currently the most prominent one affecting groups. Metadata is not the content of communication but, as discussed above, is all of the information that can be collected in relation to communications sent and received. Mapping the metadata of Internet communication through, for example, email and social media, reveals the networks and patterns of communication of both groups and individuals. However, there are a range of other privacy-related issues that of particular relevance for internal social media groups.

Social media is used within organizational public relations primarily as a means of community building and knowledge sharing. The origins of social media as a vehicle for personal communication appears to spill over into organizational sites so that people will mix business-related and personal communication, just as they might, for instance, when chatting with coworkers. This slippage between work and personal life may serve to enhance connectedness with an organization. However, there are significant differences between the casual chat and a social media post, not the least being that the latter is both permanent and open for all site users to see. There is also evidence that younger and more junior members of organizations, who are likely to be more familiar with social media, may set the tone and agenda within such sites (Hauptmann and Stegar, 2013). This phenomenon reverses the behavioral norms of traditional organizational settings in which junior staff are likely to follow the lead of more senior organizational members, especially if they wish to progress their careers. Social media groups may therefore serve to subvert rather than reinforce organizational norms in ways that may be potentially damaging to both the organization and the careers of social media site participants. Internal regulation of social media sites through, for example, clearly stating the rules of engagement and setting the tone for participation, and continuously moderating the site, are significant roles for public relations.

Organizations:

The advent of social media has led to a lot of hyperbole about its potential to further the interests of organizations, particularly its ability to support public relations and marketing. There are numerous publications offering advice on the use of social media for the pursuit of organizational objectives (e.g. Bingham and Conner, 2010; Bradley and McDonald, 2011). Such books tend to focus on the how and why rather than the "why not" of social media. They also tend to say relatively little about the broader, privacy and regulation dimensions of social media. The hype has continued but the negative experiences of some organizations have provided cautionary tales with the related areas of privacy and security prime sources of such tales.

The most well-known of the cautionary tales is arguably the Twitter campaign launched by McDonald's under the hashtag "#McDStories." The company's objective appeared to be to motivate customers to tweet nostalgic stories about Happy Meals. Instead they got tweets such as:

"One time I walked into McDonalds and I could smell Type 2 Diabetes floating in the air and I threw up #McDStories"

"#McDStories I lost 50lbs in 6 months after I quit working and eating at McDonalds"

(Hill, 2012)

The #McDStories episode led Kashmir Hill of Forbes to coin a new social media term—bashtags, which has already made its way onto the Collins dictionary list of new words. Like all successful new technologies, social media is spawning a new vocabulary.

In addition to providing opportunities, participating in social media has opened organizations up to a plethora of new risks and liabilities. Some organizations have tended to avoid participation in social media on the basis that they have little power or ability to control communication (Verhoeven et. al., 2012). However as one public relations executive stated, organizations place themselves at greater risk if they "ignore social media and ... allow conversations to happen without awareness or participation" (DiStaso et al., 2011, p. 326). In the McDonalds case, the company's use of Twitter created a platform through which the company was attacked. While this phenomenon is concerning for organizations, from a legal perspective, a greater concern may be the use of organizational social media to attack and demean others. While the area is still evolving, organizations have been deemed responsible for the content posted on their social media sites. In Australia, for example, the social media pages of organizations are considered to be marketing communication tools and therefore subject to the same regulation as other forms of advertising. Organizations may not be expected to prevent postings from being made to their sites but they are expected to actively monitor such sites and to remove offensive postings that may, for example, be libelous or infringe copyright.

Facebook and Twitter constitute the dominant social media platforms with organizations as diverse as Harvard University, the World Economic Forum, the Canadian Tourism Foundation and NASA receiving hundreds of thousands of followers and page "likes." The use of popular social media sites offers many advantages to organizations, not least that millions of people are already active on these platforms and therefore constitute and easy-to-access source of participants. However, as discussed above sites such as Facebook have come under increasing scrutiny and critique for their privacy policies and practices. Organizations with sites or "pages" associated with these platforms therefore render themselves subject to the same critiques.

Despite the risks, externally focused social media sites through which an organizations can engage with their publics have become commonplace. They have also become a central component of public relations and marketing portfolios. In the early years of Facebook, when organizations established Facebook pages, the act of "friending" gave the organization access to personal data, including a connection to all of their friends' friends. The significant privacy issues that emerged led Facebook to create a new category of pages for organizations, with individuals able to connect to these pages by "liking" rather than "friending." The data and contacts of individual pages were thus no longer available, which protected the privacy of users as well as the commercial interests of Facebook. Given their business model, Facebook is not keen to share such valuable data with organizations for free.

Public relations, privacy and regulation

In this chapter, we have drawn attention to major information privacy and regulation issues that arise through the use of social media. We began by considering the power relations within which all social media users are embedded (Goldberg, 2010). Social media has enabled "mass self-communication," which means that individuals with access to an Internet-enabled device are able to share their ideas with the nearly 3 billion other people who have similar access (Castells, 2007). This phenomenon has been celebrated as "liberation technology" because of its enormous democratic potential (Diamond, 2008). However, social media participation occurs within the broader context of the Internet, which is itself enmeshed in a web of power relations that includes nation states, international bodies, commercial entities, activists, terrorists and criminal networks.

The Internet is global and, therefore, so is social media. However there is no global agreement on the regulation of the Internet or on data privacy issues that impact on the conduct of public relations through social media. Article 17 of the United Nations' International Covenant on Civil and Political Rights, which is the nearest the world has come to a shared understanding of privacy, is of limited utility because it was written prior to the Internet. Many nations do have information privacy laws that specifically reference the Internet and digital technologies. That these laws vary so much from nation to nation makes navigating the legal and regulatory issues associated with social media a highly complex undertaking. The situation is even more complex in the US which has eschewed federal regulation in favor of a patchwork of statutes, largely because the nation places a higher value on free speech than it does on privacy.

This chapter has also considered the Edward Snowden case at some length, due to its importance in shaping our thinking about privacy on the Internet. The Snowden case highlights four major issues for public relations practice. The first is that social media sites are almost certainly caught up in the general surveillance of Internet traffic that is being undertaken by governments. The second issue is that while social media may appear to exist "in the cloud," the physical location of servers remains an important consideration when it comes to regulation and control of the Internet. The third issue is that the data streams that feed into social media sites also pass through geographical locations where they may be subject to monitoring, control, collection and storage. The final issue highlighted by the Snowden case is that individual data may not matter as much as the aggregation of metadata, which may be used to track the relationships and communications of individuals and groups. All of these issues come into play whenever we set up a social media site and invite participation from our publics.

The Snowden case has served to amplify the privacy concerns of individuals, groups and organizations. These concerns were often financial in nature, an issue that has been fueled by revelations that hundreds of millions of dollars of credit card fraud has occurred by data theft. Identity theft, which is enabled by the willingness of millions to share personal information on social media sites, is another growing issue. However, despite the dangers, we continue to share such information through social media. One of the drivers may be what Vitak (2012) has termed "context collapse" whereby the boundaries between the public and personal spheres are blurred into one amorphous whole. Whether or not you agree with Facebook founder, Mark Zuckerberg, that privacy is no longer a social norm, there is no doubt that an unguarded approach to social media may have negative consequences for individuals.

Social media is, however, primarily about groups rather than individuals. For this reason, it has been harnessed by organizations for both public relations and marketing. Unfortunately, there is limited research available on the use of social media at the level of the group to guide organizational practices. In this chapter we have noted the pivotal role of group dynamics in setting context, including what it is appropriate to share and the tone of communication. Unregulated, unmonitored and unmoderated social media sites are a significant source of risk for both organizations and site participants. In this respect, public relations has a major role to play in setting the rules of engagement and in promoting communication practices that protect all parties.

The uncertainties, risks and cautionary tales associated with social media have not deterred billions of individuals and organizations from participation. For organizations, the lure of social media remains the highly valued opportunity to connect directly with both internal and external publics. Social media also constitutes a cost-effective vehicle for achieving a global communication presence. However, though social media is global, regulation is not. The plethora of conflicting national and international priorities and perspectives means that agreement on regulation is not likely any time soon, if ever. Meantime, the fast-moving social media landscape is constantly changing and, in the process, throwing light on new issues, particularly in relation to security and privacy.

References

Altman, I. (1975). *The Environment and Social Behavior: Privacy, Personal Space, Territory, and Crowding*. Brooks/Cole Publishing Company, Monterey, California.

Belanger, F. and Crossler, R. (2011).Privacy in the digital age: A review of information privacy research in information systems. *MIS Quarterly*, 35(4), 1017–1041.

Bingham, T. and Conner, M. (2010). *The New Social Learning: A Guide to Transforming Organizations through Social Media*. San Francisco, CA: ASTD & Berrett-Koehle.

Bradley, A. and McDonald, M. (2011). *The Social Organization: How to Use Social Media to Tap the Collective Genius of Your Customers and Employees*. Boston, MA: Harvard University Press.

Castells, M. (2007). Communication, power and counter-power in the network society. *International Journal of Communication*, 238–266.

Clinton, H. (2010) Transcript: Remarks on Internet freedom. The Newseum, Washington, DC, 21 January. Retrieved 3 August 2015 from www.state.gov/secretary/20092013clinton/rm/2010/01/135519.htm.

Davies, S.G. (1997). Re-engineering the right to privacy: how privacy has been transformed from a right to a commodity. In P.E. Agre and M. Rotenberg (ed.), *Technology and Privacy: The New Landscape* (pp. 143–165). MIT Press.

Deibert, R. and Rohozinski, R. (2012). Liberation vs. control: The future of cyberspace. In L. Diamond and M. Plattner (eds.). *Liberation Technology: Social Media and the Struggle for Democracy*. Baltimore: Johns Hopkins Press.

Diamond, L. (2008). *The Spirit of Democracy: The Struggle to Build Free Societies throughout the World*. New York: Times Books.

Dinev, T. and Hart, P. (2005). Internet privacy concerns and social awareness as determinants of intention to transact. *International Journal of Electronic Commerce*, 10(2), 7–29.

Earp, J., Anton, A., Aiman-Smith, L., and Stufflebeam, W. (2005). Examining internet privacy policies within the context of user privacy values. *IEEE Transactions on Engineering Management*, 52(2), 227–237.

Ehrenfreund, M. (2013). House proposal to curtail NSA in response to Edward Snowden's leaks fails narrowly. *Washington Post*, 25 January. Retrieved 3 August 2015 from www.washingtonpost.com/world/national-security/house-proposal-to-curtail-nsa-in-response-to-edward-snowdens-leaks-fails-narrowly/2013/07/25/b7117338-f54d-11e2-9434-60440856fadf_story.html

Goldberg, G. (2010). Rethinking the public/virtual sphere: The problem with participation. *New Media and Society*, 13(5), 739–754.

Goldman, L. (2013). Social Media Has Been a Mixed Blessing for the Arab Spring. *Personal Democracy Media*, 15 February. Retrieved 3 October 2013 from http://techpresident.com/news/wegov/23510/social-media-harming-arab-uprising

Hauptmann, S. and Stegar, T. (2013).A brave new (digital) world? Effects of in-house social media on HRM. Zeitschrift fuer Personalforschung. German Journal of Research in Human Resource Management, 27(1), 26–46.

Hill, K. (2012). McDstories—when a hashtag becomes a bashtag. *Forbes*, 24 January. Retrieved 12 November 2012 from www.forbes.com/sites/kashmirhill/2012/01/24/mcdstories-when-a-hashtag-becomes-a-bashtag/

Ibrahim, Y. (2008). The new risk communities: Social networking sites and risk. *International Journal of Media and Cultural Politics*, 4(2), 245–253.

Johnson, B. (2010). Privacy no longer a social norm, says Facebook founder. *Guardian*, 11 January. Retrieved 3 October 2013 from www.theguardian.com/technology/2010/jan/11/facebook-privacy

King, G. (2012). The silence that preceded China's great leap into famine. *Past imperfect: Smithsonian Blogs*, 26 September. Retrieved 3 October 2013 from http://blogs.smithsonianmag.com/history/2012/09/the-silence-that-preceded-chinas-great-leap-into-famine/

MacAskill, E., Borger, J., Hopkins, N., Davies, N. and Ball, J. (2013). GCHQ taps fibre-optic cables for secret access to world's communications. *Guardian*, 22 June. Retrieved 1 October 2013 from www.theguardian.com/uk/2013/jun/21/gchq-cables-secret-world-communications-nsa?guni=Article:in%20body%20link

Meinert, D., Peterson, D., Criswell, J., and Crossland, M. (2006). Privacy policy statements and consumer willingness to provide personal information. *Journal of Electronic Commerce in Organizations*, 4(1), 1–17.

Peterson, A. (2013). Here's how the British Government made the Guardian destroy its computers. *Washington Post*, 20 August. Retrieved 1 October 2013 from www.washingtonpost.com/blogs/the-switch/wp/2013/08/20/heres-how-the-british-government-made-the-guardian-destroy-its-computers/

Sánchez Abril, P., Levin, A., and Del Riego, A. (2012). Blurred boundaries: Social media privacy and the twenty-first-century employee. *American Business Law Journal*, 49(12), 63–124.

Schwartz, J. (2010). Free speech vs. privacy. *New York Times Upfront*, vol. 142, February 8. Retrieved 30 september 2013 from http://teacher.scholastic.com/scholasticnews/indepth/upfront/features/index.asp?article=f020810_wiki

Smith, H.J., Dinev, T., and Xu, H. (2011). Information privacy research: An interdisciplinary review. *MIS Quarterly*, 35(4), 989–1016.

Stutzman, F., Capra, R., and Thompson, J. (2011). Factors mediating disclosure in social network sites. *Computers in Human Behavior*, 27, 590–598.

Tuten, T. and Angermeier, W. (2013).Before and beyond the social movement of engagement: Perspectives on the negative utilities of social media marketing. *Gestion*, Mai-Juin, 69–76.

Verhoeven, P., Tench, R., Zerfass, A., and Vercic, D. (2012). How European PR practitioners handle digital and social media. *Public Relations Review*, 38, 162–164.

Vitak, J. (2012). The impact of context collapse and privacy on social network site disclosures. *Journal of Broadcasting and Electronic Media*, 56(4): 451–470.

Westin, A, (1967). *Privacy and Freedom*. Atheneum, New York.

9 Know your risks

A collective orientation

Risks abound. They are a defining, perhaps the defining, aspect, of the human experience (Beck, 1992, 1999; Douglas, 1992). In fact, a case can be made that how well the members of each or any society collectively cooperate to manage the multitude of risks they encounter determines the quality, the efficacy, of that society. Is the community smart, efficacious, proactive, and resilient? Does it have the knowledge foundation and communication infrastructure to protect its citizens? And, in the context of this study, the question is, how and how well do social media frustrate or support such collective risk management?

Community (as culture, infrastructure, and discourse arena) is a crucial theme for the discussion throughout this book, and especially on matters of risk. Community is a physical, conceptual/perceptual, and virtual experience. Social media are particularly important for the functionality of this risk assessment, management, and communication experience. This point is summarized and defined this way: Social media are "collaborative online applications and technologies that enable participation, connectivity, user-generated content, sharing of information, and collaboration amongst a community of users" (Henderson and Bowley, 2010, p. 239).

Introduction to social media and risk

By that logic of community as the basis for risk management, such discussion needs to recognize how societies are organized as well as create, derive, and allot authority for judging and responding to risks based on a huge array of sociopolitical roles relevant to risk management. By that logic, a community becomes variously structured and empowered by the following kinds of risk managers and communicators: scientists, teachers, religious thinkers, philosophers of all kinds, police and fire personnel, food inspectors, garbage collectors and disposal experts, doctors and nurses, researchers of all kinds, accountants, engineers, communication specialists, lawyers, legislators, regulators, and adjudicators. On and on the list grows.

Teachers, for instance, provide education about science, ethics, politics, social science, health, and cognitive skills that help students develop problem-solving skills. They even provide instruction about such basic health-related matters as proper techniques for hand washing as a way of battling the transmission of germs.

Engaging in the analysis of risk, anthropology is, among other disciplines, interested in how peoples historically protected themselves, built alliances and developed other means of within and across group relationships, as well as fed and sheltered themselves. The artifacts of anthropology typically are those of survival—risk management, and include those which deal with the uncertainties, mysteries most fundamental to life: Birth, death, creation, the past, the future, the now, and "sustainability" in all of its dimensions including the challenges to survive as a species. Risk, by such analysis, is the study of survival at minimum and sustainability in the large. Such artifacts focus on food, enemies, predators, naturally occurring events, and reproduction as survival.

All of this consideration is shaped by the discursive influences at work in each unit of collective experience, with the family as the most basic, and with community, nation, and globality as the "big picture." As such, a basic discursive challenge confronting each unit of analysis is the formulation of the ideas, the meaning, needed to identify, foretell, and recover from risks as they manifest themselves. These could, for instance, include killer storms that create mass damage, geological events such as earthquakes and volcanoes, illness, and war. They would focus attention on sources and safety. So, one starting point in understanding risk is to gain insights into how communities engage collectively to define, understand, and respond to such risks.

That topic necessarily arouses an interest in the infrastructures that exist, are created, or need to be created so that members of the society can communicate about such risks. Even a brief glimpse into anthropology, for instance, leads us to recall how the matriarch's or patriarch's hut or similar structure, often highly symbolic places, becomes the "infrastructure" of group discourse. Since the dawn of human existence, such places have become variously defined and reshaped through discourse processes and media. Today, social media is such a place. It is a "hut," a place where risk is analyzed.

However much one might assume that the importance of social media is its role as channel; the truth is that risk infrastructures are all of the means by which humans interact, communicate, with one another. Again, we find a long list: legislative and regulatory arenas, courts, scientific research and the processes of peer review, emergency planning, and role-specific training (think in terms of the roles noted above). We have networks for violence counseling and prevention. We find arenas such as hearings, lobbying, protest, and "public meetings or hearings." We have community advisory panels. Infrastructures are created so that risks can be discussed and concurrence achieved. This is the case because individuals want as much control as possible over the risks they perceive, those which involve them as decision makers.

Some channels, media, infrastructures are "created" by leaders and even endowed with authority. Social media may be "part of" or a "kind of" such infrastructures, but they are empowered, once designed, by the users, not some authority.

The media, print and electronic, contain infinite arrays of risk messages, even marketing content on automobile safety, insurance plans, diet tips, and ways to improve personal hygiene. Think about the news on crime and health, for instance—even entertainment programming. Consider programming relevant to investing. Citizens employ standard media and the Internet, various social media, to learn about and manage risks. This might include weather prediction and storm alerts, and real time monitoring of shelter-in-place as well as evacuation. It can include "mommy sites" where women gain information relevant to their pregnancies and children's health and well-being. Such infrastructures help people manage their banking and learn about good places to eat, including the menus, addresses, and reservations. Throughout such infrastructures, interpersonal communication is vital, whether as information sharing and friendly advisory discussions, or interactions with experts such as doctors, social workers, or police. Even the family table or the park bench is a place where risks are analyzed.

Relevant to this book's central topic, we are interested in how the new media, Internet driven social media, become part of the discursive and infrastructural analysis of risk. These means not only connect people to large organizations such as corporate businesses and governmental agencies, but also to one another in fairly small networks. But, we cannot understand risk communication as discourse and infrastructure if we do not acknowledge how fundamental the topic is to the collective human experience. And, although public relations practitioners have a responsibility and an impact on sociocultural practices and discourse transformation (Motion and Leitch, 1996), it is apparent that such practices and transformations occur in social media, with or without the participation of public relations.

In such discussions, Self (2010) recommended relying on the ideas of Hegel and Habermas to formulate a dialogic sense of communication as means for understanding "the public" in the new media era. His sense of Habermas featured the notion

> that the public, to be viable, had to exhibit several essential characteristics: Members of the public had to be of roughly equal status, they had to be educated and informed, they had to debate and decide issues without interference or influence from either the state (government) or from the estates (powerful moneyed interests that negotiated directly with the state and exhibited their agreements to the public for its acquiescence).
>
> (p. 79)

It's interesting to ponder how much of these communicative conditions are driven by the empowering of social media design and enacted engagement.

To explore such quandaries, Self (2010) reflected on an Hegelian position that is comfortable to rhetorical and discourse approaches to appreciating and empowering the challenges of publics engaged in deliberative democracy. Self reasoned that instead of employing a static or segmented view of "public" that matter is best conceptualized this way: "The public flows across networks of dialog in an unending battle for universality" (p. 89). Drawing inspiration from philosophy as well as from the emerging characteristics of the new media environment, Self conjected

> that notions of a stable public operating as an essence within a public sphere might always have been better understood as a constantly evolving flow of communication activity—assertion, rereading and reassertion of the universal aspiration of particulars—in a never-ending struggle for recognition.
>
> (p. 90)

And, one could add that the challenge of engaging with such flows is that which faces government and business because the technologies allow publics to define issues, engage on them, and do so without dependence on the authority of external influence (see also, Agostino, 2013, on the challenges of engagement given the autonomy of networks which are self-empowered).

These themes, often tangled and interconnected, offer the foundation for the remainder of this chapter. A brief glimpse into one of the many advocacy battleground of risk management and communication can help frame and ground the discussion that follows.

A case to frame the social media discussion of risk: Product contents labeling as "right to know"

The Web is alive with risk-related messages. One moment in that battle circulated on the Web in early October 2013 at *Organic Bytes* which reports "Health, Justice and Sustainability News from the Organic Consumers Association" (Paul and Cummins, 2013). The Organic Consumers Association is an NGO engaged in various themes relevant to the GMO battle. This group provides information and commentary in an online publication. It also solicits donations and encourages public policy actions.

This specific moment, as well as many others, caught the attention of those concerned in citizen participation in battles regarding the influence of corporate bias in how societies collectively manage risks. This case points to several important themes, including the gender and even age biases that occur as we think about how stakeholders play out their interests against those of others, especially targets of their "risk rage." Such moments, reported in NGO blogs, for instance, are information for "standard media" reportage. As such, the personnel supporting the blog engage in the investigations that are less and less a capability of standard media as budgets for reporters are slashed.

This moment in the GMO battle occurred when Moms for Labeling, a concerned consumer grassroots NGO, concluded that the Grocery Manufacturers Association (GMA, a trade association) was breaking campaign finance disclosure laws. They brought a formal complaint that GMA was concealing the identities of corporations that were providing funds that could be used to finance political campaigns to oppose labeling.

The GMO labeling battle is not new, and takes different trajectories in different communities, and even around the globe. For instance, GMO companies have strongly opposed labeling in the US on the assumption that it would harm their marketing efforts. Engaging in consumer protection, European Community countries see labeling as important information consumers have a right to receive. Some countries, such as France, aggressively defend labeling because they deeply oppose GMO agriculture. Such battles, therefore, are not only local to a community or nation but have trade relationship consequences between nations.

Such battles are an ongoing effort in the US and abroad to force companies engaged in agriculture to disclose, in this case, GMO contents in processed food. The logic of the Moms for Labeling is to inform the public (or compel product labeling to do so) and thereby let consumers decide, which seems to be wise consumer policy. This incentive parallels the risk decision-making logic of the precautionary principle.

Precautionary principle as sound science and common sense

What is called the precautionary principle is a battleground of "sound science" and common sense. This principle was developed as a result of the advocacy and counteradvocacy efforts to balance the roles of scientific probabilities and values considerations in risk analysis.

The fundamental precautious approach sets the hurdle for approving GMO ingredients, for instance, as the ability of science to prove that such food ingredients do no harm. The assumption is that, unless and until the case can be made through peer-reviewed scientific investigation that a technological change does no harm, policy change, in this instance food safety, should not be approved as the standard operating principle. Thus, to the extent that critics of GMO are not convinced that such ingredients will not lead to negative effects—classic harms that only reveal themselves as unintended consequences over time—then the change in food ingredients should remain in the test stage. Consequently, companies should be forced to identify by label if processed food contains GMO so consumers can decide.

This cautious use of the principle fits the metaphor, "look before you leap." The "look" is especially relevant, advocates of caution reason, when or if the consequences of risk manifestation are irreversible. What if some change, they ask, would result in health harms that simply could not be foretold and never be undone? Such harms would become, in each specific case, the new norm.

The contrary view of this cautious use of the precautionary principle is based on another metaphor, "the early bird catches the worm." Too much precaution can, advocates claim, prevent the realization of the benefits of a technology. Thus, they would point to changes such as inoculation, for polio, for instance. If a medication seems promising, but has not been "absolutely" proved to produce such benefits and to do so without unintended consequences, when should a decision be made, advocates of change ask. The question is how much scientific data need to be produced and of what kind for a community to enjoy the benefits of some scientific-driven change? As far as GMO goes, its supporters (and they are not only corporations) reason that apparent food supply benefits can be demonstrated while at the same time no harms have so far appeared that would warrant more precaution than what has occurred.

Providing an excellent theoretical and applied analysis of the precautionary principle, Maguire and Ellis (2009) emphasized how it is necessarily a concept that is examined, used, and contested discursively. It underscores the importance of ongoing scientific research and careful attention to the cultural implications of risk decisions. It focuses attention only on implications for risk for those who create them but also on the bearers who can, do, or will suffer the risk manifestation. By this reasoning, it is important "to conceive of risk communication as a highly multilateral process" (p. 133). It adds the cultural and political dimensions to the scientific discourse. In doing so, it enlarges that discussion and presumes that critics should not be marginalized, nor should they stop change when precaution has become evidently sufficient for topic-specific risk management.

That approach to risk communication underscores its connection to the current investigations of deliberative democracy. Such investigation presumes transparency and joint analysis of risks.

Stakeholders of risk

For decades, agribusinesses of all kinds have opposed labeling of all kinds because such labels (that "share" information) are likely to harm their ability to market products. They worry, for instance, that even something so simple as putting labels on packaging of meat that indicate which packages contain growth hormones and which do not will cause consumers to turn away from the former even though "no evidence exists" that the hormones are harmful. GMO has a similar labeling problem.

When the Moms for Labeling brought their case, even claiming they had a whistle-blower who would testify as to the campaign funding impropriety, the judge dismissed the case on a technicality. The suit had been filed under a Washington DC campaign finance law. The suit alleged that funds were being illegally funneled through a Washington DC lobbying group. That technicality was based on the judges' opinion that only the state district attorney-general could bring a campaign-finance suit within Washington DC.

Once that verdict was handed down, the industry which had raised millions to battle labeling through lobbying as well as advertising campaigns against states seeking to require labeling brought a countersuit. The outcome of that countersuit was a judge's decision to fine the Moms $10,000. The basis of that fine was a law that was supposed to protect citizens from frivolous suits by large corporations.

And Moms were up against 300 large companies, as members of GMA, such as Kraft, Kellogg's, Monsanto, DuPont, Starbucks, PepsiCo, Coca-Cola, ConAgra, and General Mills. The irony, of course, is that such battles reported and discussed in social media allow those who oppose GMO ingredients to monitor such companies as well as engage in political discourse.

Such cases, and they abound in various iterations, are relevant to the discussion of risk communication and new media. In many ways, such battles are not new, but one of the new dimensions to such battles is how they get fought, often outside of the "public" eye in blogs and various other e-publications. Organizations and blogs link to such discussion sites creating discursive networks in which risk topics are ground into meal. They become the fodder of social media.

Even though this moment, GMO labeling, is not unique or extraordinary, it helps illustrate several key points relevant to the challenges of stakeholders of risk. For 30 years, stakeholder analysis has been part of the business ethics and public relations literature. In 1984, Freeman pointed to the necessity of organizational planners and policymakers to acknowledge that their efforts occur in a multiple-stakeholder environment. Policies and actions by organizations of all sizes and natures are judged by myriad stakeholders. Stakeholders are important to organizations' *right to reward* and *right to operate* because those stakeholders possess resources that can be used to reward or punish organizations.

These stakes can be tangible, such as monetary, or symbolic, such as organizational reputation. Organizations, by this logic, are stakeseekers. There can be no stakeholders without stakeseekers, and vice versa. So, stakeseekers are also stakeholders who calculate whether they should grant or withhold the resources they hold in exchange for various stakes that they seek. As strategic approaches are applied to management policy and operation, Freeman reasoned, attention must be paid to the constraint and reward role stakeholders play as they scrutinize the ethical choices of management.

Such stakeholder networks are of various density, the tightness of the networks. Friendship and familiarity, for instance, increases such density as does the organizational memberships that investigate various risks. Density, as it increases, does so because the network couplings allow stakeholders the opportunity to carefully interact to scrutinize some issue of risk. One of the ways to conceptualize such density is by examining the network of nodes through which risk analysis passes from an originating point to where it can affect some end-user far from the original point of risk discussion.

What's also very important to understand in terms of risk analysis is how the risk manifestation impact and the organizational risk bearer may be several conceptual steps downstream from the organization that created the risk. Thus, for instance, if the health impact of bisphenol-A, an ingredient that plastic packaging often contains, is debated, such debates often go on in the scientific community considerably removed from the discourse arena of customers. Scientists engaged in the peer review process debate, often in very complex ways that elude the understanding of lay audiences, the safety of such a product ingredient. Analyzing such a case, Heath et al. (2012) modeled such discourse arenas as having several staged, multilayered nodes. Each deliberative node moves closer to the end user of a product or technology and further away from scientific expertise.

- Scientific node A is within the organization or industry (GMO or bisphenol-A; ironically bisphenol-A was originally developed to be a birth control product because it is an endocrine inhibitor or interrupter. Critics of that ingredient worry that children's developing endocrine systems can be harmed by high dose response to bisphenol-A.)
- Scientific node B is enacted when others outside of the original organization examine the science and even conduct independent research to verify the levels of risk concluded by the players in node A. Node B, thus, might be other companies in an industry, independent scientists such as those working at a university, or regulatory bodies.
- Regulatory node A, for instance, can bring trade association scientists as well as those engaged by NGOs into the discourse. The question is whether science is sufficiently sound to approve something (an ingredient in plastic bottles or a GMO) for consumption.
- Regulatory node B consists of litigators, regulatory and other review bodies that continue the examination of the risk as its analysis moves from the point of origin, for instance, to the time when it enters (or does not) the food/consumption stream.
- The marketing communication and news reporting node contains statements, as marketing, which "sell" the product, even with warnings, as in the case of pharmaceuticals. The reporters, depending on editorial policy, variously examine the evidence that they find or is made available to them. This content can, at this point, become reported in news and editorial statements.
- The consumer node is that where customers examine the information they have, and apply whatever risk heuristics they employ, to make product purchase decisions. Thus, mothers and grandmothers can be daunting monitors of products as they do their best to assure that children are nurtured as safely as circumstances allow. Such decisions are typically culturally driven, even if science is part of such culture, because the science, regulation, and litigation are reported in ways that provide the end user decision heuristics.

Following the analysis of this book, these nodes are important because they model the decision-making process as it moves from maximum scientific judgment to minimal comprehension of the science as science. That does not, however, preclude the important risk assessment roles of those at the later stages of the model. Manufacturers and retailers of soft drink or water beverages can have their sales affected by consumer perceptions of product safety. These organizations are risk bearers whose stakeseeker well-being can be constrained or rewarded by risk decisions at the final risk decision stage. Thus, in this fairly complex process risk creators and arbitrators are variously engaged in precautionary battles at various points in a product development, processing, and consumption chain.

Such analysis, returning to the case in point, is relevant to food products that contain amounts of GMO (or do not). For the purposes of the analysis of the role of social media and other communication technologies the question is whether and how risks are discussed and whether the known science is variously sufficient for decisions at various points in a consumption chain.

The question, one of the most fundamental to risk, is how safe is safe and how fair is safe? And, we ask how safety and fairness, as grist, survive the grinding of social media and discussions in other technologies.

Risk Communication Frameworks and Conceptualizations

Although infrastructures are "networks," they are more than networks. The concept of network is as old as the early days of information theory. The early conceptualizations and recurring discussion of the topic suggests that networks are at heart a means by which information flows within, between, and among systems (supra, system, and sub) (Reddy, 1993). Many evaluative variables have developed to analyze network quality, but the essential theme is the efficiency and effectiveness of a network to allow/foster flow, create linkages to that end, and result in end-user satisfaction.

Infrastructures, similar in some ways to networks, refer to the quality of networks, as information processing units, and most importantly as they aided or frustrated discursive elaborations and frames of the information. Rather than conduits, networks become infrastructures when they become places, such as meeting rooms and legislative halls, as well as media in which deliberation occurs and decisions are made. Such infrastructures are affected by membership and access as foundations of power. Who is engaged in each infrastructure, how does membership influence the discourse about the information? Such questions, as well as technical issues of linkage/interconnectivity, density, and even bandwidth help define the strength and usefulness of social media infrastructures of risk communication and management.

"Information communication technologies (ICTs) such as the Internet have enabled citizens to create and share information and content without having to rely on traditional intermediaries such as government and the press," observed Seo and Thorson (2012, p. 345). So analyzed, networks are neutral. Infrastructures, as enacted decision-making networks, are not. They discursively support decision-making in a hierarchy from the individual, to group, to community, to nation, to globe. They not only facilitate interconnection and information flow but generate, share, and debate ideas and norms.

Given the nature of infrastructures and the roles they serve, public relations can work to include as many people as possible in each infrastructure. They can determine who should participate or they can encourage participation to avoid the claim, and actuality, that they are playing the power game of inclusion and exclusion.

Infrastructures, viewed through the developing lens of deliberative democracy, are challenged to be useful for government, business, NGO, and even marginalized publics' decision-making. They function in various ways to more or less effectively provide stakeholder oversight regarding business activities. Such deliberation presumes that the quality of public policy, corporate policy and practice, and individual policy must occur in an arena where competing voices of the powerful and the much less powerful are heard, understood, and appreciated. But the question is: On whose terms, what power rationale?

Such infrastructures require, at minimum, that participants are able to know, consider, and respond to matters from what is called the perspective of the "other." In one sense, othering can be a way of marginalizing a voice. "This battle is us versus them, the other." Or, why should we care about "them," the other? The legitimating role of social capital, however, Freeman and Gilbert (1988) concluded, presumes that "effective strategy will be formulated and implemented if and only if each player successfully puts himself or herself in the place of other players and endeavors to see the situation from the others' perceptions" (p. 91). So, infrastructure, unlike networks, are not merely means or places where adjustive behavior (and a theme underpinning some views of public relations) occurs, but arenas wherein stakeholders seek and analyze the relevant ethics of some matter.

Such infrastructures are defined by at least two key dimensions. The first is what do social media and other communication technologies lend to the challenges of discursive/deliberative democracy? And, how does that discussion comply to the prevailing principle, at least in the United States, of consumers' right to know.

Discursive/deliberative democracy in social media

Over the past several years, a concerted effort has been devoted to understanding the conditions of sociopolitical deliberation. One recent approach is called deliberative democracy (or even discursive democracy). This concept refers to a deliberative process that ideally empowers and incorporates all relevant voices. Relevancy is not determined by one player, but by the extent to which voices achieve and maintain relevancy regarding the discursive examination of some matter, an issue of public safety for instance. The ideal, as Palazzo and Scherer (2006) reasoned, rests upon how others in the discourse field judge corporate legitimacy as a deliberative matter. In addition, how well organizations engage deliberatively with one another becomes a factor in how legitimate they are in the minds of those engaged in this discourse field. Scherer and Palazzo (2007) adapted a Habermasian perspective to this problem which couples corporate social responsibility, commitment to deliberation, and legitimacy. Legitimacy, and that of positions taken, becomes subjected to a discourse arena of varying degrees of openness and comprehensiveness. Such discursive processes become the authority by which individual and organizations make decisions.

Democracy is often conceptualized as a governance style. Deliberative democracy enlarges the legislative process, for instance, and even marginalizes legislators as the essence of democracy. Instead of their "owning" the process, this concept empowers the discourse field of a society, those individuals who engage in the discourse and the conclusions to which it leads. Law or regulation, by such analysis, becomes the defined opinion of the governing, but not necessarily the "governed."

Such analysis features the distinction between the public policy created by government, but that does not deny a parallel public policy of societal enactment. As such, how, when, and why organizations participate become part of the deliberation of corporate social responsibility and legitimacy. These concepts come together in ways that generate the evaluative criteria of an organization's right to reward and its right to operate.

The existence of useful and valid information, so this line of analysis argues, is the precondition for sound judgments of corporate social responsibility and legitimacy. But, whereas social media are useful tools for making such information available they also are prone to "bad" information, such as hoaxes, that produce dysfunctional decision-making. Since there are no gatekeepers other than the members of the group, false information can get into the discourse. However, as well, the gatekeeping aspect of social media can prevent outsiders from putting "bad" information into the system as though it were "good."

As much as factual claims are relevant to legitimacy, so too are actions, the rationale for actional legitimacy (Boyd, 2000), the challenge and rhetorical ability of the organization to reason about and enact itself in ways that justify or restore its legitimacy. Thus, by taking actions of socially mediated redemption and renewal, an organization, confronted by a hoax can prove its legitimacy by demonstrations of responsible and responsive enactment. Thus, for instance, social media can give that participative community access to the organization's operations so they can judge for themselves whether the alleged hoax has merit (Veil et al., 2012).

Given such logics, and adding dimensions to the matter of hoax-driven crisis, this analysis offers a daunting challenge for organizations, such as those that support GMO but do not believe that labeling is a communicative right of product end-users. By such actions, the legitimacy of their claims of "safety" may fail to bear up to the standard expected by stakeholders. The organization's transparency and enactment claims can lack legitimacy, trustworthiness and corporate social responsibility. Such enactments can have the sort of veracity that arises when a child says "Nothing" in response to a suspicious parent's question, "What are you doing?"

Social media adds important dimensions to this deliberative process because, in one way, they remove it from the control of any entity. It becomes a self-realizing tool of the community, a commons, where voices are heard without institutional filtering such as the gatekeeping involvement of reporters or legislators. However, and whether, such discourse leads to larger, substantial decisions, such as those regarding corporate planning and policy or legislation or regulation, is another matter. Such discourse can serve the advocates of the deliberative advantages of social media. Communication technologies diffuse and instantiate power as deliberative processes free from such discourse from institutionalized decision-making. However, that does not mean that the players in institutionalized decision-making necessarily heed the voices in social media, especially when there is little to no tendency to produce consensus or even concurrence.

But, the rationale is that the voices unincorporated in formal public policy decisions do affect the more informal public policy. Such analysis differentiates the public policy process as that "owned" by community decision makers, from that typically the purview of government. This dynamic includes the corporate planning which affects public policy by what and how businesses operate even if the public policy process makes no particular decision regarding their actions.

However, the voices in social media, even if they don't immediately or directly affect institutionalized public policy, have a public policy effect. This occurs as those voices affect consumption practices and processes, for instance by raising concerns and questions about what risks are safe and fair. Thus, the discursiveness of the voices in social media, for instance, enjoy a life and power that is constrained only by their influence (large or small) and not by the specific impact on or by the governmental or corporate process. However, as opinions form, government and corporations are likely to use such ideas as fodder for institutionalized decision-making. Thus, if social media helps people organize protest to products, that becomes a kind of public policy, a powerful one. Corporate and governmental powers cannot extend to prevent or end boycotts.

The implications of such deliberative democracy are too vast and complicated to analyze in totality in this current discussion. However, suffice it to say that since the discourse exists, and can be shared at the speed of transmission and bandwidth, with pictures and comments, it is never irrelevant even if it is inconclusive as to its institutionalized policy implications. The key to such stakeholder empowerment, thus, is not whether this discourse plays directly into corporate or governmental planning or policy but its impact on daily lives, consumption patterns.

As risk is a counterpart of uncertainty, control, and involvement, it is relevant to discussions of how individuals avoid, accommodate to, or collaborate in regard to risks in their community. The logic is that if risk is sufficiently capable of creating an aura of fear, people may avoid discussions of it, or engage the topics by indirection. However, as is evident in the notion of risk management as collective activity, communities long for efficacy, a means for being able to discursively and by taking actions and implementing policies been empowered to deal with risks. As Heath et al. (2009) observe, individuals' levels of risk tolerance depend on their sense of how efficacious they are. The same standard is applied to determine how efficacious experts are as well as the community is in dealing with risks. Quite relevant to social media impact, it is important to note that risk and efficacy assessments are influenced by the extent to which individuals participating in such discourse are similar to one another and the extent to which messages are sensitive to the decision heuristics being employed by those engaged in the discourse.

Social media add message sensitivity and source similarity as well as density to the potency of risk discussions and decision-making. That observation has substantial implications for those engaged in emergency management and communication. It is also relevant for the discourse field in which voices are engaged over matters of risk, in the consumption chain, for instance, such as GMO or bisphenol-A.

These media, as well, seem to be influenced by how "external" voices seek to engage with the various interlocked/interlinked social media networks. The grist for the discussion seems most valued when external sources communicate quickly with the network, are credible/trustworthy, accurate, simple, complete, and engage in ways that help the discourse to be broad in its appeal and inclusive in its reach (Freberg et al., 2013). The value of any external voice's engagement in a net's discourse presumes that the participants make decisions among themselves. Thus, for instance, emergency management serves communities best when it helps social media communities obtain the information, opinion, and advice they want to be efficacious in their decision-making and emergency enactment.

In such engagement, authenticity becomes not only useful, but arguably the price of engagement. As Gilpin et al. (2010) observe, "Authenticity is particularly important in the public sphere, and public institutions are increasingly engaging with social media as a means of connecting with constituencies" (p. 258). One of the key aspects of authenticity is the identity that emerges through the discourse of the network participants. "Identity is thus a processual quality that emerges through interaction, as a narrative strand that may change over time but maintains a reliably identifiable subject" (p. 265).

A second communicative feature is transparency. One dimension of transparency entails making an organization available for public scrutiny. The second aspect is an extension of the first. Making information available for public scrutiny fails to achieve authenticity if that information's accuracy and decision-making value cannot be verified, as by a third party. Thus, does the information hold up under scrutiny.

Such discourse conditions presume engagement. "In a social media context, engagement means that there is interaction among the actors who make up the virtual community, which may or may not include the organization providing the virtual discussion space" (Gilpin, et al., 2010, p. 266). This view presumes communication is not linear but a group activity. Information is not definitive, but grist for the social media mill. Such engagement constitutes evidence that a group legitimizes the discourse by how interaction occurs. Such interaction presumes that the group "owns" the discourse.

Getting risk related information to people at risk is a crucial part of this challenge. Knowing a risk potential is part of the equation. Thus, sirens, for instance, have often been employed to call people's attention to a risk as it is manifesting itself. Likewise, social media can be a means for getting such information to potentially affected parties. Thus, there are social media alerts to risks.

That technology takes many turns. One recent innovation in Australia has been to monitor GPS-tagged sharks and use those tags as part of a system for warning swimmers and others in the surf of the presence of such a threat. Called Surf Life Saving Western Australia (@SLSWA) a group uses Twitter, for instance, in this way to tweet eminent threat. Scientists have tagged more than 300 individuals of three kinds of sharks (white, tiger, and bull) in the waters near Perth, Australia. (See www.examiner.com/article/shark-warnings-via-twitter-real-time-shark-tweet-warns-australia-beach-goers, retrieved 27 December 2013.)

That idea is the basis of right to know and failure to warn information, two principles central to the legacy of risk communication.

Information sharing, right to know

Based on one of the basic principles of risk communication, analysis of information sharing, in the US context, flows from two interconnected principles of legislation, regulation, and litigation: right to know and failure to warn. The argument against the public health damage of the asbestos industry gave rise to the principle that an industry is ethically and legally liable when it *fails to warn victims of the health consequence of its products*. That logic led to warning labeling battles over cigarettes and other tobacco products as well as alcohol beverages. It has been part of the battle over ingredient labeling which includes presumptions regarding the usefulness of recommendations by serving sizes. For instance, the food and beverage industry negotiated the policy that it can report ingredients based on a standard of daily consumption. The question is what part of a daily diet should include the products' ingredients? Such packaging often states "per serving" even though a product, such as bottled beverage, may typically be consumed by one person and all at one time. Even when a consumer is "warned" that contents may be packaged for two or more "servings," marketers know that it is often not shared. Also, the question is how the ingredients should be presented, what is the informational value of each product ingredient presentation? Thus, even when a package contains ingredients, has the company "failed to inform"?

In the US, right to know is a stated principle of law at least as old as the 1960s, but older still in common law. Taking a seminal stance on modern risk communication strategies and policies, the National Research Council (1989) espoused the principle that "a major element in risk management in a democratic society is communication about risk" (p. ix). How well or badly that study and subsequent ones have improved risk communication, it did establish that minimally risk communication is obligated to raise "the level of understanding of relevant issues or actions for those involved and satisfies them that they are adequately informed within the limits of available knowledge" (p. 2).

Right to know and failure to inform become heuristic topics of risk communication in social media. Social integration in discourse is consequently not an outcome but a mandate of such networks and infrastructures. The underlying principle of such integration is to help citizens realize the communicative implications of social capital. Although focusing on news, the claim that Rojas et al. (2011) made is sufficiently solid to embrace all risk communication, which includes "news." They argued that "integration occurring at the system level via news consumption and at the individual level via interpersonal communication is amplified by ties at the community level" (p. 689). Such community perspective squares perfectly with the conceptualization of the collective management of risk as a community obligation and challenge. These ties become the magnetic attraction for information, opinion, and means for community efficacy, even if the community is limited to each or any network of social media. The goal is to collectively achieve social capital.

On matters of integrating sound science with cultural perspectives and communication effectiveness, social capital becomes one of the hallmarks of risk communication, amplified through social media. Consequently, "commercial practices are not merely matters of economic legitimacy but also of political legitimacy" (Heath et al., 2012, p. 136). As such practices occur in ICT contexts, such as social media, they become more owned and applied to the service of the media users than to some commercial interest that seeks to use public relations to shape and control messages and decision makers' access to them. Interestingly enough, discursive democracy can be conceptualized as a community-based, risk bearer and risk arbiter centered approach to how the wheat of risk gets ground into the flour of personal and collective decision-making.

Such processes are what they are by the ability of social and other new media to expand the cognitive complexity and capacity of communities.

Holding many ideas collectively in mind

Each individual can only think about and hold in memory and consider a limited amount of information, opinion, and ideas at a time. This capacity can be modified, for instance, by increased anxiety during risk experiences. As humans get to the limits of what they can think about, each either loses capacity (can't get our thoughts together) or focuses like radar on one matter, shutting out all that is distracting (such as the focus a mother might have while searching for a lost child and not attending to comments unrelated to that task). By this logic, public relations theory must, then, recognize and attempt to reconcile the tensions inherent in operating across organizational boundaries, and within public spheres and private spaces where individual capacities are combined, multiplied, and enriched.

Stress and anxiety are two factors that affect capacity and load. So does individual efficacy, expert efficacy, and community efficacy which are key influences in how individuals approach risk decision-making collectively.

Social media are discussion rooms. They allow some network of individuals to hold many ideas at one time. They increase the information, opinion, and advice that are collectively available for the members to use to make optimal decisions.

Because nets are variously permeable to "outsider" opinions and information, such outsiders can seek to intrude in various ways to inject information and opinions. Such injections might be spurious or self-serving without appearing to be such. Similarly, insiders look outward for information which they believe might be useful to their network partners.

Such social media discussion rooms, however dialogic they are, do not necessarily or inherently produce consensus or even concurrence, but perhaps that is an advantage insofar as they may help individual decision makers to continue to seek, evaluate, and share thoughts on the matter. Capacity, therefore, is not limited to that of one person, but is augmented by the mediated group.

Cognitive capacity and cognitive loads are two dimensions of the human experience. Capacity refers to the ability to hold information and ideas, recall it and use that information for decision-making. Load refers to the number of matters that a mind can attend to at the same time, or nearly simultaneously. Similarly, agenda-setting theory is a well-established explanation of what is at the top of mind and why. Do media or other influences prompt what people think about, even if such sources cannot predict what people will think about those matters?

Adopting ideas such as these and implementing them to explain and operationalize issue monitoring, Naisbitt (1982) developed the concept of megatrends which he operationalized by using content analysis to determine how important an idea is to a society by examining the proportion of all ideas discussed against one another. The assumption is that what topics are being discussed by the media become those most top of the mind for those who see, read, and listen to such coverage. The research protocol derived from efforts to monitor the thinking of other governments, such as the Soviet Union, to determine what it was thinking about, and to some extent what thoughts it had on such matters.

Cognitive capacity was in this way defined as the media news hole (Naisbitt, 1982). That concept referred to the total amount of coverage of all topics, defined by the pages in print as well as the minutes of news and editorial coverage on radio and television. Given the limits of the news hole, a society can only "think" about some topics, not all of them, and in weighted proportion to one another.

Using that reasoning as a foundation, it can be argued social media expand the news hole and thereby expand individuals' and communities' cognitive capacity and load capability. And, instead of having to go to a library, find and retrieve an article or newspaper, wait for such coverage to come sailing by, or "call a friend," the logic is that with ICT a search engine can deliver a plethora of information and opinion by the click of a button. And, within each social media community, the importance of a topic is the amount of attention given to it. Such capacity expands as more people engage in that topic providing more information and opinion, but doing so in ways that the messages come from sources similar to the user and expressed in ways that are sensitive to the user.

Such conditions have profound implications for the discussion of topics, such as GMO and labeling. Within a dense network, people grind the topic into manageable units of thought and thereby generate solutions to problems. They share and vet ideas, and cocreate meaning. Social media socially construct an enactable world.

That analysis, however, applies to many or all circumstance of risk communication and management. A case in point, a person moving to hurricane prone Houston, Texas in the early 1970s would sooner or later have to acquire information and learn emergency planning and responses to an approaching hurricane. Media provided some of the information, in various formats, but it also came from friends and acquaintances who were a storehouse of knowledge and advice. Thus, networks operate infrastructurally to serve individual and collective needs for information, opinion, and actions in the face of risks. As much as these once were limited to personal or telephonic interaction, today they are the playground of social media.

Forty years later, social media have come to serve as emergency management tools for the preparation for and notification of emergency response. This is as true of the community emergency management experts and politicians as it is for the friends and family on whom individuals rely in such circumstances. And, with the mobility of devices such as smartphones, people have mobile sources of expert and familiar advice as well as means for coordinating responses (as long as transmission towers remain intact). Families, for instance, can monitor one another's location and emergency management response.

Such media use is beginning to show up in public relations practice and research. When a series of emergency response and planning studies were started in the early 1990s, none of the respondents indicated the likelihood they would be notified of an emergency event by email/text, simply because such tools did not exist. These studies were conducted to examine residents' knowledge and responses in the face of emergency events in communities where some of the world's greatest concentrations of petrochemical facilities are surrounded by residential neighborhoods. A study in such a communication in 2012, found that 20.4 percent of the respondents said they were highly likely to be notified of emergency events by email or text. A smaller segment, 15.2 percent, said they were somewhat likely to be notified by that means. Given the trajectory of new media adoption and use, it is likely that this number will increase, assuming the willingness of local industry and government to use the technology.

Age often plays an important role in such studies. Younger members of a community tend to believe they will get information and advice through new media, social media, and from people who are similar to them providing messages that are sensitive to their emergency response needs. As well, they believe that such information and advice will come from family members and friends. Thus, the social media generation is more confident in its functionality and serviceability.

In the US, as many as 31 percent of the population was using online platforms including blogs, social networking, text messaging, and portable digital devices to get risk and crisis information and opinion. They were using social media of various kinds for this communication. (For a literature review on the rate and extensiveness of the adoption and application of social media for risk and crisis communication, see Veil et al., 2011).

Trends are confirming the popularity and usability of new media for risk and crisis. Freberg et al. (2013) examined that topic by studying communication patterns regarding H1N1 flu virus. One of the patterns, which situationally can have a positive or negative impact on community control of information and advice, is the fragmentation that can occur because of the nature of social media. It also is variously permeable to sources that are not closely connected to each media community, some of which should, or even must, play a constructive role in the dialogue. Thus, because of the nature of social media as used, primary organizations that should be most useful to some risk may not be. One way of tracking such discourse is to examine patterns of bookmarking. Bookmarking allows users to store, highlight, and share information via social media.

Of related importance is the challenge by an organization seeking to use social media to achieve what can be conceptualized as mutually beneficial outcomes—a win–win scenario. The challenge is to achieve and maintain the authenticity of the communicators as a condition that predicts access to a community through social media. Use of social media can be harmed if a corporate communicator seeks to control the discourse and cannot maintain authenticity of voice (Henderson and Bowley, 2010). Powers of inclusion/exclusion are traditional factors affecting group dynamics. Even though a corporate source gains access to a network, that does not mean that it is authentically included in the dialogue.

Dialogue, as has been widely discussed, is a multidimensional, multilevel and socially constructed process. It also, in a somewhat tautological manner, is itself socially constructed through the ways in which the participants enact such media discursively. It has an underpinning of technology, but the discursive forms and issue themes frame, reframe, and define as well as result from the enactment of discourse processes.

Participation, therefore, is not only essential as a way of contributing to discourse, it is perhaps even more vital as a means for monitoring such discourse. Attempting to position such challenges and public relations practice in harmony, Kent et al. (2011) reasoned that "Web analysis data should be a staple research tool in capstone, management, campaigns, and similar courses, as well as used in student-run agencies to gather data on behalf of clients" (p. 536). Such observations, working to bring the complexity of new media into the classroom, suggest that teaching techniques need to be sensitive to how well they prepare students to qualify for professional roles in the new media environment. This sort of pedagogical paper presses faculty members (and senior practitioners) to understand the dynamics of new media. It also presumes a challenge to the very paradigms that drive the understanding of how to teach and practice public relations.

Conclusions

Risk and crisis are fundamentally socially constructed narratives. They concern characters, plots, themes, tensions, conflict, harmony, coordination, chaos, and all of the other narrative elements. Thus, it can be reasoned that "a crisis event constitutes a rhetorical exigency that requires one or more responsible parties to enact control in the face of uncertainty in an effort to win key publics' confidence and meet their ethical standards" (Heath, 2004, p. 167). This sort of thinking builds on the notion that a crisis is a risk manifested.

The challenges of discursive democracy, made possible through new media, not only point to the need for alternative best practices but challenge theorists to refine their understandings of the nature and role of public relations. Social media demonstrate how discursive processes take on a life of their own. They suggest that ideas and expectations are very much a part of the experience of stakeholders. However otherwise powerful organizations are, they only gain access to discourse by invited engagement.

References

Agostino, D. (2013). Using social media to engage citizens: A study of Italian municipalities. *Public Relations Review*, 39, 232–234.

Beck, U. (1992). *Risk Society: Towards a New Modernity*, Sage, London.

Beck, U. (1999). *World Risk Society*, Polity Press, Cambridge, MA.

Boyd, J. (2000). Actional legitimation: No crisis necessary. *Journal of Public Relations Research*, 12, 341–353.

Douglas, M. (1992). *Risk and Blame*, Routledge, London.

Freberg, K., Saling, K., Vidoloff, K.G., and Eosco, G. (2013). Using value modeling to evaluate social media messages: The case of Hurricane Irene. *Public Relations Review*, 39, 185–192.

Freburg, K., Palenchar, M.J., and Veil, S.R. (2013). Managing and sharing H1N1 crisis information using social media bookmarking services. *Public Relations Review*, 39, 178–184.

Freeman, R.E. (1984). *Strategic Management: A Stakeholder Approach*. Boston, MA: Pitman.

Freeman, R.E. and Gilbert, D.R. Jr. (1988). *Corporate Strategy and the Search for Ethics*. Englewood Cliffs, NJ: Prentice-Hall.

Gilpin, D.R., Palazzolo, E.T., and Brody, N. (2010). Socially mediated authenticity. *Journal of Communication Management*, 14(3), 258–278.

Heath, R.L. (2004). Telling a story: A narrative approach to communication during crisis. In D.P. Millar, and R.L. Heath (eds.), *Responding to Crisis: A Rhetorical Approach to Crisis Communication*, pp. 167–187. Mahwah, NJ: Erlbaum.

Heath, R.L., Lee, J., and Ni, L. (2009). Crisis and risk approaches to emergency management planning and communication: The role of similarity and sensitivity. *Journal of Public Relations Research*, 22, 123–141.

Heath, R.L., Palenchar, M.J., McComas, K.A., and Prouthreau, S. (2012). Risk management and communication: Pressures and conflicts of a stakeholder approach to corporate social responsibility. In A. Lindgreen, P. Kotler, J. Vanhamme, and F. Maon (eds.), *A Stakeholder Approach to Corporate Social Responsibility*, pp. 121–140. Surrey, England: Gower.

Henderson, A. and Bowley, R. (2010). Authentic dialogue? The role of "friendship" in a social media recruitment campaign. *Journal of Communication Management*, 14, 237–257.

Kent, M.L., Carr, B.J., Husted, R.A., and Pop, R.A. (2011). Learning web analytics: A tool for strategic communication. *Public Relations Review*, 37, 536–543.

Maguire, S. and Ellis, J. (2009). The precautionary principle and risk communication. In R. L. Heath and H. D. O'Hair (eds.), *Handbook of Risk and Crisis Communication*, pp. 119–137. New York: Routledge.

Motion, J. and Leitch, S. (1996). A discursive perspective from New Zealand: Another world view. *Public Relations Review*, 22(3), 297–309.

Naisbitt, J. (1982). *Megatrends: Ten New Directions Transforming Our Lives*. New York: Warner Books.

National Research Council (1989). *Improving Risk Communication*. Washington, DC: National Academy Press.

Palazzo, G. and Scherer, A.G. (2006). Corporate legitimacy as deliberation: A communicative framework. *Journal of Business Ethics*, 66, 71–88.

Paul, K. and Cummins, R. (2013). Moms fight back against GMA money laundering. *Organic Bytes*, 398, 10 October,. www.organicconsumers.org/organicbytes.cfm

Reddy, M.J. (1993). The conduit metaphor: A case of frame conflict in our language about language. In A. Ortony (ed.), *Metaphor and Thought*, 2nd ed., pp. 164–201. Cambridge: Cambridge University Press.

Rojas, H., Shah, D.V., and Friedland, L.A. (2011). A communicative approach to social capital. *Journal of Communication*, 61, 689–712.

Scherer, A.G. and Palazzo, G. (2007). Toward a political conceptualization of corporate responsibility: business and society seen from a Habermasian perspective. *Academic of Management Review*, 31, 1096–1120.

Self, C.C. (2010). Hegel, Habermas, and community: The public in the new media era. *International Journal of Strategic Communication*, 4, 78–92.

Seo, H. and Thorson, S.J. (2012). Networks of networks: Changing patterns in country bandwidth and centrality in global information infrastructure, 2002–2010. *Journal of Communication*, 62, 345–358.

Veil, S.R., Buehner, T., and Palenchar, M.J. (2011). A work-in-process literature review: Incorporating social media in risk and crisis communication. *Journal of Contingencies and Crisis Management*, 19, 110–122.

Veil, S.R., Sellnow, T.L., and Petrun, E.L. (2012). Hoaxes and the paradoxical challenges of restoring legitimacy: Dominos' response to its YouTube crisis. *Management Communication Quarterly*, 26, 322–345.

10 Navigate the issues
Situating power/knowledge within public relations

Following World War II, especially in the United States, public relations had reason to feel good about itself and the organizations that it represented. Governments, businesses, and NGOs had supported one another in amazingly collaborative ways to bring a successful end to the war and start the process of healing and rebuilding. The Marshall Plan even contained provisions for promulgating public relations practices to help countries rebuild, restore their reputations, and deal with issues that posed impediments to a solid future of democracy and civil society. GIs returned home and commenced the lives they had dreamed during long hours of combat—and the logistical tedium before and after action. Suburbia beckoned with the promise of a new car in the garage of a tract house bracketed front and back with a manicured lawn.

But, in the US as elsewhere, this glowing success would soon give way to knotty issues that would disrupt the general tranquility and cause changes in public and private policies. The war left civil rights in a tangle. It ended with the dawning of the nuclear era which launched a penetrating debate about the peaceful and military use of nuclear power. Soon, women's rights, environmental rights, consumer rights, employee rights, and definitions of civic responsibility would become daily headlines. Cold war tensions increased. Governmental and civic leaders felt compelled to smoke out the Reds and end subversion at home. Eisenhower warned of the military industrial complex. At least in the US, these narratives marked the end of an era of deference toward the power of industry and democracy.

Such tensions and increasingly less domestic tranquility got further upset with the war in Vietnam that dragged young men from their homes and transported them to a grinding and inglorious military tour in jungles denuded of foliage by agent orange. Helicopter power as well as a modern version of chemical warfare played out on the nightly news. Napalm became a weapon of evil, as did carpet bombing delivered by enormous bombers.

Every aspect of the society was being examined. That genie, once out of the bottle, continued to play the devil with political careers, corporations' reputations, and the democratic process. Protests became extraordinary— then ordinary. Genres of music increasingly mixed entertainment and protest.

Identities and issues that once were trivial now were undergoing redefinitions that tore families and political parties apart. Such turbulence became an incentive for a collaborative search for order out of chaos.

Especially relevant to the themes of this book, this was the era of issues and their management, and impact on management, as power/knowledge constructions. As smug as they had been, large and small organizations, public and private, looked to public relations as a kind of final resort for solutions. The broad assumption was that if public opinion was turning against business and government, public relations could put matters right by engineering a new era of consent. That kind of solution had spurred President Eisenhower's 1950's call for businesses to engage more effectively in public affairs. Thus, the Public Affairs Council was born as Eisenhower brought together business executives and leading Democrats and Republicans committed to bipartisanship.

By the 1970s, the call that Eisenhower had issued was becoming more salient to senior practitioners and academics. Trends and tensions motivated public relations leaders to create the *Public Relations Review* as a scholarly publication bringing practitioners and academics together. One of their first undertakings was the crafting of a new definition of public relations. Public and private policy issues had always been part of the portfolio of senior practitioners, but now they realized they needed to sit down, scratch their heads, and redefine the mission and vision of the industry.

In that spirit, Rex Harlow (1976) sought to refocus the practice of public relations; his proposed definition championed an issues approach to reflective management, societally focused public relations and CSR:

> Public relations is a distinctive management function which helps establish and maintain mutual lines of communication, understanding, acceptance and cooperation between an organization and its publics; involves the management of problems or issues; helps management to keep informed on and responsive to public opinion; defines and emphasizes the responsibility of management to serve the public interest; helps management keep abreast of and effectively utilize change, serving as an early warning system to help anticipate trends; and uses research and sound and ethical communication techniques as its principal tools. (p. 36)

This definition fits nicely with academic training in rhetorical theory, journalism and mass media studies, social theory, and critical study that examined the democratic clash of voices and collision of ideas, a power/knowledge struggle.

This definition illuminated the notion that public relations could be a constructive force in society, not merely a pawn playing to the self-interest of the highest bidder. Within less than two decades, voices from a diverse array of disciplines had designed a discipline that worked to enact strategic business planning, advancements and adherence to corporate social responsibility, issues monitoring, and issues communication (Heath and Cousino, 1990).

Issues as power/knowledge debates

The reconceptualization of public relations fostered creation of a "new and improved" discipline named issue(s) management. One question was whether issue should have an "s" in its name. Another was whether it rehabilitated public relations or replaced it as the totality of management planning and operations needing a public relations specialty. Whichever, it innovated a new sense of what public relations as a practice and discipline can do to make organizations effective and society more fully functioning. This discipline championed a dialogic and reflective management approach to intersections of power and knowledge. These ingredients for democratizing the private sector and public policy arena offered a foundation for reconceptualizing the directionality (one-way and two-way) and symmetry of communicative and planning engagement in more discursive and less inherently instrumental (structural and functional) ways. Publics became collaborative partners rather than targets of change and compliance.

Just as the discipline was getting a sense of how issues played out in the standard print and electronic mass media, it found itself challenged by the Internet, the Web, and eventually by a panoply of social media. Upon these foundations, this chapter explores strains in the societal fabric to examine how new media help and hinder the socially responsible discussion and collaboration regarding topics of narrow and broad interest. All of these tensions require the collaborative "management" of issues relevant to the quality of society as power/knowledge enactment.

Over the years, cases, studies, and publications have advanced the enthusiasm for this sense of society, and for public relations' role in achieving it. This new narrative opened a discussion regarding what practitioners do, how and why. As Auger (2013) considered the dynamics of advocacy in social media, she concluded, "Nonprofit organizations contribute to a democratic society by allowing those with diverse opinions to assemble and voice these ideas" (p. 369). Advocacy organizations gain voice through social media. Change management continues to be daunting, but becomes more promising as the Internet causes channel factors to become more fluid and dynamic.

Other changes over the years have occurred as the discourse arena has changed. Any arena where discourse occurs is shaped by the infrastructures in which discourse occurs, such as the mass media and legislative debates and hearings—and includes public relations activities such as media relations. The other dimension of the arena is the discursive fabric, meaning construction, composed of social constructions, narratives, themes, discourse resources, languages, cultures and such.

As the discourse arena changed, large and powerful entities began to have less power to dominate discussions, a trend that enables democratic decision-making. Exploring this theme 15 years ago, Heath (1998) examined the Web-based debate over the disposition of the Brent Spar, an oil-gathering vessel in the North Sea. As the vessel aged, it needed to be taken out of service.

An industry-led, collaborative, multidisciplinary, and multinational dialogue examined the problem and recommended that the vessel be scuttled. This solution led to a protest by Greenpeace which changed the dialogue in the traditional media and moved it to the Web. This online dialogue between Shell Oil Company and Greenpeace served as a town hall meeting on the topic. The traditional power/knowledge disparity between large corporations, governments, and NGOs was leveled by this communicative platform.

In similar fashion, Coombs (1998) explored the ways the Internet as channel/medium helped any ostensibly powerless group and/or NGO to be less easily ignored. Reflecting on the communication and public policy decision-making dynamics of the 1990s, he concluded , "Now activists have a new weapon which can change the organization-stakeholder dynamic—the Internet" (p. 289).

Continuing this topic, Kent and Taylor (1998) investigated the Web as a format for building dialogic relationships. They proposed several principles regarding how the Web could and would change the power/knowledge dynamics of society. One way is its ability to facilitate the dialogic loop as interactive relationships. A second way is users' ability to determine the usefulness of information that is endlessly available on the Web. The Web increased interested and cognitively involved publics' ability to get information that had not been framed by and filtered through standard media. A third way is the generation of return visits whereby information acquisition can be facilitated and stored on users' computers by earmarks and email storage. Such power dynamics are influenced by the ease of the interface and the conservation of visitors who are not misdirected into unproductive searches.

The invention, development and evolution of the Internet, in these and other ways, were natural and inherent means by which each society could reconfigure its power/knowledge relationships. Whereas large organizations had the power, often through skilled media relations, to frame and even control information flows needed for societal discourse, the communication commons aspect of the Web opened, enlarged, and reformed those power/knowledge dynamics.

Over the years, it has been interesting to note how governments, especially authoritarian ones, have sought to frustrate, block, and maliciously distort the Net to their power/knowledge ends. Such efforts have come about because the Internet allowed more voices to be heard, questions to be raised, information to become part of the "public record," and interpretations to be expressed. If power results from the ability of any entity or faction of society to determine what is said, on which matters, when, and by whom, the Net changed those power/knowledge dynamics. In doing so, it even allowed for offensive expressions and misinformation (and disinformation) to become part of the discourse arena. The Web needed a sign that read "user beware" alongside one that said, "enjoy the communication commons."

The practice of public relations during the last half of the twentieth century was called on to keep managements informed about conditions, opinions, pressures, and issues that were occurring and developing outside the organizations. The organization needed formal and systematic issue monitoring. It required insights into how the Internet was changing the deployment of power/knowledge resources in the collective management of issues. By participating in social media, organizations could monitor and participate in the development of power blocs and discourse resources.

Unpacking Harlow's definition

To understand new-era public relations changes that are resulting because of social media, it is important to unpack Harlow's definition. Even if the definition should be found to be at odds with current thinking, it is an important stepping stone on the path leading to where we are today. It formed a transition to an era of interest in issues management, crisis management and communication, and risk management and communication. Issues, risks, and crises were not separate topics. They were linked. Crises could produce issues. Issues regarding risks could become crisis. And risk management was the heart and soul of issues management, and public affairs.

The definition symbolizes the sociopolitical turbulence of the last half of the twentieth century. From battles over nuclear power (military and industrial) and harmful chemicals in the environment, risks manifested themselves as crises and became issues tug-of-wars. Crises occurred as medical researchers produced statistics that connected smoking to health problems. That issue matured into public policy in the US in the mid-1960s when the Surgeon General's report outlined the tobacco-health hazard and suggested public policy changes.

The issue of smoking and health risk became a crisis for the industry. Nuclear power, introduced to the world at the end of the battle for Japan, took two courses. One was the prospect of global destruction by nuclear weaponry. The other was brought to light by the crisis at Three Mile Island generating facility in Pennsylvania, March 28, 1979. Another iconic moment of risk manifestation occurred when lethal amounts of MIC were released at the Union Carbide plant in Bhopal, India, December 1984 (the same year that books on issues management began to be published). The risk-manifested crisis of Bhopal was not only relevant to that region of the world. That chemical, manufactured by the same "open-loop" process, posed a risk in other locations, including the petrochemical manufacturing complex near Houston, Texas. Once the Bhopal incident became discussed as an industrial tragedy, "closed-loop" manufacturing processes were implemented in Texas and West Virginia. Managements realized that issues management required policy and procedure changes as well as, and even instead of, public policy debates.

Drawing on senior practitioner expertise, Harlow correctly framed the discipline of public relations as a management function. That does not mean that public relations could manage issues, but it could help executives understand the public affairs and public policy implications of their missions, visions, and business plans. The goal, for communication, was to establish and maintain mutual lines of communication and to generate and support means for open public policy deliberations. That was not easy for traditional command and control oriented managements or for public policy arenas that preferred elitist decision-making process to something more along the lines of what is called deliberative democracy.

Deliberative communication was championed because of its ability to foster mutual understanding, acceptance and cooperation between an organization and its publics, so that managements could act responsibly (corporate social responsibly) and serve the public interest. Issue monitoring, early warning systems, were needed to spot and anticipate trends so that appropriate action could be taken as soon as possible. Issue communication needed to be dialogic; participatory engagement replaced elitist decision-making. Well, at least that was the aspiration of those who saw the need for a new discourse arena. It was inspired by the ancient Greek tradition of the good person speaking well in the public arena. This was the essence of a democratic culture.

In this way, public relations became invested with the responsibility of helping organizations to effectively and ethically utilize change management. Change depended on research as well as sound and ethical communication techniques. It required the creation and meaningful use of decision-making infrastructures. Candor and transparency became new CSR standards, even if they often were easily avoided by large institutions that defined and implemented decision processes favorable to their interests and did so with paradox and double-edged ambiguity.

These tensions provided the outline that led to the discipline Howard Chase (1984) called issue management. Although advocates of this discipline could not agree whether it should have an "s" issue, they concluded that it was a substantial improvement for the disciplines of public relations and/ or public affairs. It linked public relations and public affairs with thoughtful, savvy planning, and wise navigation of the issue driven public sector world of "the public interest."

Issues management was not crafted overnight or in a singular meeting. It was driven by concerns over the "public interest." What is the public interest and how can it be understood and used to shape corporate and political policies? Can large and powerful organizations observe, define, and respond to the public interest, or must it bubble up through unfettered and unfiltered discourse? Such consideration acknowledged that the tensions of issues, crises, and risks were not just a matter of the interest of one organization or segment of society, but part of the power/knowledge discourse of entire societies.

Along with other senior practitioners, John W. Hill (cofounder of Hill and Knowlton) had for years been interested in the concept of public interest. On this topic, Hill (1958) warned,

> It is not the work of public relations—let it always be emphasized—to outsmart the American public in helping management build profits. It is the job of public relations to help management find ways of identifying its

own interests with the public interest—ways so clear that the profit earned by the company may be viewed as contributing to the progress of everybody in the American economy.

(p. 21)

This sage advice emphasized that "the public interest" was created, owned, and applied by the "public." Such acknowledgement emphasized how power/ knowledge is a collective matter.

Social media, to make a thematically current point, has become a commons in which the public in various ways defines its interests. Or, perhaps it should be stated that it is a means by which publics express, define, and negotiate their interests. Obviously, a multiple public view would suggest that there are multiple publics' interests. That theme is exactly the tension addressed under the rubric of power/knowledge.

Given this history of the discipline, and with the window open to connecting it with social media, it is fair to observe that today two broad challenges face organizations: The right to operate and the right to reward. Both rights are derived from the "people," and either large organizations shape and tailor their interests to others or that is the task and purview of the "people."

These dynamics of the public interest underscore the rationale for organizational legitimacy. Featuring that concept from the public perspective emphasizes how multiple interests become the rationale for legitimacy, rather than organizations enjoying the privilege to define and enact their standards of legitimacy.

The legitimacy gap, given the multiple tensions within any planning, management and communication arena, anchors the assessment of whether and how each organization is aligned with the community(ies) where it operates. Such analysis asks whether organizations bend the community to serve their interests or bend themselves to serve the public interest.

That matter is contestable—an issue—the topic that is explored in the next section which examines how dialogue, issues, power/knowledge and public policy decision-making can play out in the new media society over the issue of the environmental impact and regulation of fracking.

Fracking: An issue playing out in social media

"The hills are alive with the sound of music." So are the media full of advocacy for and against the use of hydraulic fracking to produce natural gas in the US (and elsewhere around the globe), especially from specific shale formations. Fracking is an issue because it is required to crack formations to allow natural gas to flow. Such engineering processes have been criticized and debated because industry believes them to be more environmentally sound than critics of this process do. Social media are alive with this controversies' sights, sounds and texts.

Employing the infrastructural nature and textuality of legitimacy, Smith and Ferguson (2013) addressed the issue of fracking safety as it plays out in the public policy issue debate in Pennsylvania. This commonwealth has been the center of the controversy over this natural gas production technique in its Marcellus Shale region. The voice of critics of this industrial process is called the Marcellus Protest (MP); an amalgam of 90 environmental and community organizations that adds the adjective "toxic" to frame fracking. The Marcellus Shale Coalition (MSC) serves as the voice of the industry; its supporters include landowners and neighbors whose properties are or can produce natural gas. Both organizations have a web site that contains public relations texts, "including news releases, statements, testimony, presentations, reports, organization-produced magazines and newsletters, and links to news articles and other groups that supported each organization's position" (p. 379). MP's web site reveals its Facebook, Twitter, YouTube, and Flickr sites. MSC offers similar communication venues as well as job portals, executive board members, public policy venues, conferences, and technical impact statements.

These sites are fed by and feed social media and other media outlet discussions. At issue are questions of what policy is best and what government agencies are the legitimate protectors of the public interest. Advocates for both sides seek what they believe to be the most enlightened choices. They present issues positions, calendars of events and meetings, deliberation venues, and videos. In the traditional narrative of issue debates, these sites provide facts which are framed and analyzed. They express a range of values and discuss which policies best serve the public interest. Their messages foster supportive and oppositional identifications, that are differentiating.

Key themes presented in Smith and Ferguson's (2013) analysis include self-legitimatizing themes advanced by the opponents and proponents of fracking. They adopted Heath and Palenchar's (2009) claim that "Legitimacy is a (perhaps *the*) central theme in issues management" (p. 9). And, important to their analysis, they focus on the legitimacy of public policy formation as deliberative and collaborative process. To support their discussion, Smith and Ferguson emphasized the point that voices on important issues are predictably and strategically attentive to how members of various publics examine the legitimacy of issues and issues advocacy as well as the legitimacy of those advocates and the decision-making processes they support and oppose.

To develop their discussion, they adopted Coombs's (1992) taxonomy of legitimacy tools and tactics that are foundational to "the public acceptance of the political order's claim to authority" (p. 105). To examine the legitimacy of the advocates and public policy processes regarding the regulation of fracking, they employed these legitimacy frames:

1 tradition: legitimacy derived from the history of how things have always been done;
2 charisma: dynamism, values, and personality characteristics of individual and organizational voices as issue advocates;
3 bureaucracy: authority of traditional public policy decision-making processes, discursive themes, and infrastructures;

4   values: universal judgements as to what is right and just including princi-
    ples each society or culture finds important;

5   symbols: textual signs that represent concepts and ideas that frame deci-
    sions and guide judgments;

6   delegitimacy claims: positions advocated by one discourse partner that are
    used to attack the legitimacy of opposing voices, processes, and motives;

7   credibility: examination of own and opponents' expertise and
    trustworthiness;

8   rationality: contests and claims regarding the quality of evidence each side
    uses as it seeks to bolster its claims about the legitimacy of an issue and
    proposed policy resolutions;

9   emotionality: texts used to elicit an emotional response; in the context of
    social media, videos present damages and atrocities that can evoke mes-
    sages that legitimize one side and attack the other;

10 entitlement: rhetorical appeals that feature the issue managers' direct expe-
    rience with a particular issue.

(Smith and Ferguson, 2013, p. 378)

In this contest of legitimacy over the practice and discussion of and decision-making regarding fracking, Smith and Ferguson discovered that both sides preferred to keep the focal point of public policy decision-making at the state and local levels. Those policymaking and implementation venues were closer to the direct experience of competing interests than would be the case of the federal government. Not only did local policymakers appear more legitimate because they were closer to the cultural text of the battle, but they were also thought to be "influenceable" by both parties.

By that textuality of legitimacy, this process seemed to carry and enact the authority of democratic local self-governance. But as the process seemed to be collaborative win-win decision-making, the industry pressed for and obtained a state legislative ruling that local governments could not use their zoning authority to constraint the use of fracking. That decision outcome was viewed by MP to favor MSC interests, and not those of the "public." Thus, the issue stays alive.

Is there a public, and if so, who speaks for its interests? This case study reveals how issue discourse is necessarily multilayered, multitextual, multivocal—and multimedia. Available media enlarge the discourse field to allow more voices to influence power/knowledge relationships and outcomes. Those are the legitimate dynamics of a community's struggle to manage its sense of the public interest. In this case, the issue was whether fracking democracy had prevailed. That currently is the grist for public discussions, including social media.

From this case, and the literature that informs it, the theme of legitimacy can be seen to have several discursive dimensions:

1   Legitimacy as the willingness and ability of an organization to meet others'
    corporate social responsibility expectations.

2 Legitimacy as change management that presupposes that argument and agreement will affect how public policy decisions will be reached and implemented in the "public interest."

3 Legitimacy as change management among competing organizations to earn the right to operate and the right to reward.

4 Legitimacy as a critical standard by which to discuss and determine the authority of organizations, of all types, roles, structures, functions, and values as constructive members of a community of shared interest.

Such conceptualizations about the nature and role of legitimacy in society and organizational agency can be even better understood by examining the societal tensions of power/knowledge. Standards and assessments of legitimacy are inseparable from considerations of each organization's and society's power/knowledge culture. That topic is explored in the next section.

Legitimacy and its relationship to power/knowledge dynamics

Throughout the discussion of this chapter, the concept of power/knowledge has been used in anticipation that it would be discussed in detail to solidify and clarify that discussion. By this analysis, legitimacy becomes a turning point of power, knowledge, performance, collaboration, and such. It is inherent to the discursive processes of socially constructed policy both public and private.

Critical discourse analysis, Motion and Leitch (1996) reason, offers potentially corrective critical insights at all levels of society. "At the societal level, discourse transformations emerge out of the discursive struggles engaged in by competing institutions and groups over sociopolitical practices" (297). Such discussion becomes even more valuable as it can address the ways in which social media enlarges the discourse arena allowing more voices to contest with one another to affect the rationale of organizational, institutional, community and communicative legitimacy.

Sociopolitical practices are fundamentally discursive but not totally random. They are strategic to discourse and policymaking practices that address themes of power and knowledge. Herein lies the rationale for understanding power/knowledge as social construction.

Power is multilayered, reasoned Foucault, as he pointed to ways that expertise crafts knowledge in support of power; power commissions knowledge that empowers it in return. Noting this tautology of power and knowledge, Motion and Leitch (2007) pointed to Foucault's reasoning that knowledge is "both a creator of power and a creation of power" (p. 265). Ironically, the expertise that can free and empower people can also be used to shape their judgements and those of important others on key matters in ways that marginalize and disempower them.

By this logic, experts contest positions advocated by other experts, sometimes aided by communication professionals who have an incentive to either lead to some privileging outcome or continue a discussion which in process fails to resolve matters at hand. Reviewing the twists and turns of such power/ knowledge, Bourne (2013) expressed confidence that the "changing nature of global media has certainly transformed the interaction between laypeople and expert systems" (p. 677). She reasons that new media, because of their global reach, transcend national and cultural boarders to serve as discursive kaleidoscopes.

Turns of textual prisms open discourse participants to alternative expertise which confirms and challenges other expertise. Given the discursive variety of social media, each or any institution or organization has less opportunity to inject and tailor knowledge into the discourse arena in ways that narrowly privilege its interests. That process has the potential of enlarging the interests that empower the generation and contest of knowledge as well as be empowered by that knowledge as it grows, declines and changes.

Fundamental to such conclusions is the manner in which discourse enacted through expertise shapes perceptions, interpretations, and enactments of ideation, identity, and relational matters (Motion and Leitch, 2007). Those three aspects of the human condition correspond to ones George Herbert Mead postulated to be fundamental to the human condition: mind, self, and society (Heath et al., 2010). Combined, such analysis produces these social construction combinations: mind/ideation, self/identity, and relationship/society.

Accordingly, the resources of power/knowledge become those discursive practices that socially construct ideas about mindful interpretations of reality/ experience, self-identity, and the relationships that enact society. Viewed in this way, the fundamental tension is whether organizations bend society to their interests or their interests to those of society.

In terms of the fracking controversy, the MP and MSC contest each other's power resources of knowledge and the expertise that generates and is further empowered (or disempowered) by such knowledge. Also, and ironically so, the discourse arena is shaped by a profound empowering or disempowering construction. The underpinning question guiding such discourse is who bears the burden of proof relevant to the risks of fracking. Does the power/knowledge construct of the specific discourse community empower companies, for instance, to operate as they prefer until their processes have been indicted as and proven to be unsafe? Or do such companies have to prove sufficiently (recall the precautionary principle discussed in Chapter 9) that their processes and operations will produce no harm before they are allowed to be put into operation? Cultures are variously defined by such foundational texts. These texts necessarily shape the conditions, and even the legitimacy of voices, in each community.

Such tensions correspond to the conditions and discursive substance of issues and their collective management, the topic of the next section.

Issues: Discursive grist of public discourse

By all standards, such as those emphasized in the case on fracking, legitimacy is fraught with challenge, uncertainty and risk. Legitimacy is not a fixed, universal standard, nor is it static. It evolves, and even devolves, but always is fluid given the changing circumstances and discourse resources at each moment in the life of a community. Whether an organization, issue, voice, or deliberative process is legitimate becomes a problematic matter. It is variously contestable as are the standards for judging legitimacy.

This notion of contestability and matters needing resolution provides the essential and compelling character of issues. Heath and Palenchar (2009) championed the tradition that views an issue as a contestable matter. What is contestable is the quality of the discourse, whether it enlightens choices and provides legitimate turning points in the collective efforts to arrive at some decision and resolve some matter. The view favored by Heath and Palenchar features, by that logic, the discursive, disputational contestability of fact, value, policy, and identification. That is a big ballpark with multiple dimensions and layers of textuality. By this logic, issues are inherently discursive matters relevant to resource dependencies and risk management. They acknowledge a discourse arena where supporters and opponents of some matter are both cognitively involved to learn about, discuss, and collaborate for some conclusion in the public interest.

The innovator of issue management, Howard Chase (1984) defined issue as "an unsettled matter which is ready for decision" (p. 38). Crable and Vibbert (1986) mused that "An issue occurs when a problem becomes focused in a particular question that calls for dispute and some sort of resolution" (p. 62). Turning this kaleidoscope another turn brings up two more definitions worth viewing: (1) It is evidence of "a public dispute in which the public interest is unclear" (Stanley, 1985, p. 18). (2) It results from or "leads to confrontations and political battles" (Lerbinger, 1997, p. 318).

Assessing these *disputational* approaches to issue, Jaques (2010) offered two other views for consideration. He reasoned that disputation alone might be inadequate in the understanding of issues because an issue can exist prior to or without its being a matter of disputation. Thus, one might imagine that human's need for energy is a matter needing resolution which is not inherently debatable as such. (Narratively, Prometheus was the fire-bringer in Greek mythology. He thought he was serving a public interest as he speculated, if they only had fire.)

One of the alternative views of issue, Jaques treats as an expectation gap, a variation of the legitimacy gap. It focuses on the "gap between the actions of the organization concerned and the expectations of its stakeholders" (p. 437). The second, which he calls the impact theme, was promulgated by the Conference Board, which early on embraced and engaged the topic of issues management: "An issue is a condition or pressure, either internal or external to an organization that, if it continues, will have a significant effect on the functioning of the organization or its future interests" (Brown, 1979, p. 1).

Thus, issues, as issues, can be viewed in slightly different ways, but all versions focus on their discursive nature. One view features their dispositional/disputational character that flows from and supports the paradigm of deliberative democracy. The second view emphasizes their management and planning nature as challenges to the mission and vision of organizations' enactments of their business plans. The latter version of issues is receiving rich analysis as foundations for the reflective management and neoinstitutional views of organizational agency. In both cases, it is important to realize that issue positions as well as being problematic conditions for any organization can both be a challenge to one or more organizations as well.

It is important, and paradoxical, that what is an issue/issue position preferred by one organization and a problem needing solution can variously justify the purpose of other organizations. NGOs, for instance, can and do view the problems that they identify as legitimacy challenges to which other organizations need to attend in varying degrees of reflectiveness.

As reasoned by neoinstitutional theory, the discourse surrounding an organization's need for resources and agency become a discursive reaction by that organization to itself in the discourse arena. As much as they interpret and work to define their operational arena, they are a product, discursively created, of the forces, tensions, problems, opportunities, and issues in that arena. Therefore, by extension, they need to reflexively control and shape discourse as they know they must respond to it in self-fulfilling ways.

Social media reduce their ability to control discourse. These media increase the incentive for the organizations to adapt to and participate with the discourse. For that reason, issues management presumes an issue monitoring function that can be viewed in a cybernetic manner. By that logic the monitoring can lead the organization to adapt its behavior to the discourse, but such nondialogic adaptation can presume that the organization cannot or need not participate in the discourse.

That failure undercuts deliberative democracy since the adaptation may be less genuine, even disingenuous. It is not transparent and engaging. As such it even suggests that by not engaging it actually marginalizes other voices. And, it can presume that if the organization lies low the tempest will pass and it will eventually not need to change. For these reasons, social media are a powerful authentic discursive means for organizations to adapt society to them through the honest and candid effort to bend themselves to society.

As organizations are resource dependent, they seek stakes from stakeholders. Issues become the legitimating rationale for each organization's business plan. They are defined and enacted to attract stakes and define the protocols for exchanging stakes with stakeholders, because they themselves are stakeseekers. This dialectic of stake exchange is inherently discursive. In the fracking case, the community's need for energy (and kinds of energy have environmental relevance discursively managed) predicts that energy companies will develop and enact business plans intended to solve the issue of safe, cost effective, and reliable energy supply.

The organization's legitimacy, consequently, becomes a tension generated by discussed and disputed stakeholder expectations as conditions for granting or withholding its stakes. Thus, in the fracking case the MP seeks to hold the stakes energy organizations seek regarding where, how, and whether fracking is used. But MP members, and the community at large needs energy, a resource the energy companies can provide. Such issue tensions, legitimacy resources, and stake exchanges are essential power/knowledge resources.

Thus, energy organizations commission studies to determine environmental and financial cost effectiveness of fracking as an empowerment of their business planning. They seek sound science but predictably tend to prefer studies and researchers who confirm a model favorable their business plan. If fracking can be proven to be financially and environmentally cost effective, that line of reasoning is reinforcing. Its enactment of power/knowledge dynamics support industry operations.

One key aspect of issue deliberation and legitimacy is the extent to which the discourse preferences of the industry (or the opposing NGOs) become tautological, a closed circuit, cybernetic loop, that can disrupt collaborative decision-making. Thus, how issues are debated, within the power/knowledge context, determines the extent to which they become self-serving or evidence of an honest and candid effort to bend to the community. Similarly, if the discourse is either inconsistent or leads to conclusions the energy organizations do not favor, it can seek to exploit and exacerbate such discourse resources.

If such discourse seems to lead in ways that are collaborative and seem productive to mutual benefits for all voices engaged, the energy organizations can destroy their legitimacy and the legitimacy of the deliberative processes by turning the narrative only to its interests. By that means, the energy organizations leave the fundamental issue unresolved and process proclaimed to be nonlegitimate if they settle, through the power/knowledge resources of government, to get a local decision that only favors their interest. If they work through the discourse, arrive at the conclusion that local decisions are more constructive, they harm that entire process if they short circuit the process by embracing/ enacting a decision that seems to (and does) marginalize other voices.

To expand that analysis, it is important to understand the compelling nature of stakes. Mitchell et al. (1997) defined stake as

> something that can be lost. The use of risk to denote stake appears to be a way to narrow the stakeholder field to those with legitimate claims, regardless of their power to influence the firm or the legitimacy of their relationship to the firm.
>
> (p. 857)

A sense of what can be gained, and lost, offers a substantial reality to how organizations engage to seek stakes and embrace the interests of stakeholders. If stakes are expressions of values and interests, a multiple-objective decision analysis is required to achieve effective stakeholder participation (Merrick et al.,

2005). By this logic, issues management emphasizes the inherent stake dependency of organizations engaged in instances of issues discourse. It offers a means and discourse arena for contesting the nature, value, and exchange of stakes.

MP argues that the risk (loss of stakes) is sufficiently great to refine, reduce, constrain or prevent the use of fracking that it considers toxic. Thus, problematic challenges to the legitimacy (legitimacy gap) of the energy industry arise through power/knowledge contests regarding the contest of issues of fact, value, policy, and identification. Such discussions (enacted textually—thematically and narratively) focus on the science, expertise, discussion and decision venues, decision processes, discussants, and relative power resources which can be brought to bear on some matter that needs resolution and conditions of stake exchange. Stakeholder theory suggests that the ethics of legitimacy define the discourse arena. Social media change at least the discourse dynamics if not those leading to concurrence regarding policy.

Activists and other NGO voices raise and advocate issues positions. Those positions can either focus on a condition challenging other organizations or they can themselves serve as such challenges. That which is proposed by one voice can oppose and be opposed by another voice. That paradigm is the essence of the rhetorical theory of public relations that presumes the discursive dynamics of statement and counterstatement—the element of dialogue. However supported by issue substance and played out dialogically, this view presumes differences of fact, value, policy, and identification (Heath and Palenchar, 2009).

Reflecting this normative theme, Gregory et al. (2005) observed, "Multiparty deliberative processes have become a popular way to increase public participation in public policy choices" (p. 4). The legitimacy of such processes "depends on participant's ability, first, to understand the issues facing them and, then, to form and express their own positions on them. These tasks pose significant cognitive and emotional challenges" (p. 4). The principle of deliberative democracy recognizes public engagement that addresses conflicts of interest and marginalized stakeholders, which is central to legislative and regulatory decision-making. Such deliberation presumes that the quality of policy and business practice must occur in an arena where competing voices of the powerful and far less powerful are heard, understood and appreciated (Heath et al., 2009; McComas, et al., 2009; McComas, 2010; Renn, 2009).

Power/knowledge conditions not only examine the discourse that becomes the grist for collaborative decision-making, but they also emphasize the legitimacy requirements of the discourse arena. That topic is developed further in the specific discussion of the role issue analysis plays in deliberative democracy. Social media, it is important to note, offer a discourse arena in which and where interdependent voices seek mutual benefits.

Issues and deliberative democracy

The incentive to enact deliberative democracy grows from the need for understanding and agreement as a foundation for practicing sound management at all levels, individual, organizational, and societal. It also offers challenges for issues communication to move beyond efficiency to a societal instrument for amalgamating diversity into coherent unity. Such analysis tends to fall victim to such incentives as power resources are discursively contested.

However relevant that theme is to the normative nature of discourse infrastructures it seems, and probably is, amplified by social media. In Chapter 9, we emphasized a fundamental principle of risk democracy as the right to know, for instance. Framed in terms of issues management, the principle of right to know is or becomes the right to participate. And, from a dialogic perspective, dialogue can at one end of the continuum be an expression among other expressions of issues perspectives. It can be like conversation, an interaction over matters of concern and problems, but that does mean that it arrives at any conclusion, concurrence, or consensus.

These rights challenge organizations of all sorts, but especially businesses, to adopt a political conception of corporate social responsibility that aspires toward the Habermasian principle of deliberative democracy. That view of participatory democracy can move beyond the ethical vacuity of institutionalism's positivity and avoid the problems of postpositivism: relativism, foundationalism, and utopianism (Scherer and Palazzo, 2007). Discursiveness guided by desire to build social capital is an incentive and reward for seeking advantage for society rather than for any organization/industry and its peculiar interests.

Discussing interconnected themes such as these, Sommerfeldt (2013) examined the challenges of public relations in a new media era as offering challenges and opportunities for public relations. He reasoned that "the normative role of public relations in democracy is best perceived as creating the social capital that facilitates access to spheres of public discussion and in maintaining relationships among those organizations that check state power" (p. 281). Civility in discourse, perhaps given incentive by social media, opens society to the opportunity for a generalized trust, the building of weak ties through discourse themes, the engagement of discourse by subaltern counterpublics, and the recreation of society as an iterative process.

Discursively approached, corporate social responsibility provides standards and critical points in the judgement of an organization's legitimacy. For that reason, Palazzo and Scherer (2006; see also, Gamper and Turcanu, 2007, who championed a multicriteria analysis of socially responsible planning sensitive to future impacts) called for a shift to moral legitimacy from a commitment to a model based on efficiency standards of input/output and power ratios. Such a shift moves from an approach that privileges powerful organizations to one that presumes a deliberative approach to problem solving rather than one driven by elites. However much organizations have an incentive toward diversity in all forms and fashions, social media provides additional motive because so many voices create a dialogic arena that presumes that no force can predetermine the policy outcomes. Given that dynamic diversity, it becomes problematic when organizations of any kind can and do use their influence infrastructurally to deny the discourse arena.

Such participation calls for an infrastructural approach to issues management and risk communication by which robust, collaborative decision-making enables deliberative democracy. The principle of deliberative democracy recognizes public engagement that addresses conflicts of interest and the need to listen to and appreciate the voices of traditionally marginalized stakeholders. Such communicative empathy is central to legislative and regulatory decision-making. The chaotic, random nature of social media suggest how important it is for each interest to presume first that they must listen and acknowledge points of view and resist the tendency to turn the discourse to their interests. Such deliberation presumes that the quality of policy and business practice must occur in an arena where competing voices of the powerful and far less powerful are heard, understood and appreciated. Kent suggested that there may not be quick fixes that practitioners can apply to staunch the flow of information, evaluation, policy positions, and calls for identifications.

Deliberative democracy raises the ante to the level of collaborative outcomes through stakeholder participation. Work by Renn (1992) has helped frame advances in public participation in risk management. It stresses the importance of social networks for societal risk assessment and mitigation. Along this line of thinking, Rowley (1997) observed, "Since stakeholder relationships do not occur in a vacuum of dyadic ties, but rather in a network of influences, a firm's stakeholders are likely to have direct relationships with one another" (p. 890).

Media of all kinds and communication challenges of power resource management and public policy decision-making institutions serve as important points of interaction and ties among influencers and decision makers. As much as these are defined by traditional media and public policy institutions, they are reshaped by social media. Kent (2013) reflected upon this current era as a post-mass media society, made so because of social media. As noted throughout this chapter, new media have not only changed the standard role of media as gatekeepers, but suggest now that social media are the "new gatekeepers." Information is abundant. Traditional gatekeepers do not have the ability to vet it all, so it enters the public discourse as grist rather than refined meal. Such conclusions have powerful implications for power/knowledge dynamics. The mass mediated view presumed, especially for public relations practitioners, the opportunity to prevent information from entering the public arena, and once it had to frame it and gain third-party opinions that could (and did) privilege a particular power/knowledge body of expertise.

Analysis of the issue theory of social movement activism suggests that discourse occurs for various reasons and is expressed by varied and competing voices. The issues stages can be conceptualized as having the potential to be motivated by strain. As noted above in the discussion of power/knowledge, how such strain is voiced, felt, and defined can variously motivate movement. It might be defined by elites, risk creators and arbiters, but it is improved by a grassroots component. The motivation of shared strain (differences between what is and what ought to be) can lead to the other four stages: mobilization, confrontation, negotiation, and resolution (Heath and Palenchar, 2009).

Institutionalized power resources are managed to constrain and guide choices. (Recall the various roles of risk bearers and issues managers investigated in

Chapter 9.) As society collectively organizes to manage risk, it does so to manage crises and issues. The question, however, is the extent to which such infrastructures and voices (discourses) lead in competing, confounding, or collaborative directions. This topic of public engagement is explored in the next section.

Participation and collaboration

Collaboration and participation have a tautological relationship. Decades ago, Arnstein (1969) worried that community engagement failed when public participation was attempted without a redistribution of power. Infrastructures of decision-making tend to be constructed by and dominated by power elites to control discourse and public policymaking, Hearings, town-hall meetings, advisory councils, blue ribbon panels: All of these forms of infrastructure are power resources elites deploy in their efforts to seek and accomplish control of community engagement and ostensibly grassroots decision-making.

In the face of such issues oriented infrastructures, generations of practitioners and academics have delved into the structured discursiveness of various opportunities for engagement, participation, and collaboration to determine when and why they succeed or fail. Citizen participation or not: more than a parallel to Shakespeare's line for Hamlet, the underpinning theme of the nature and quality of citizen participation tend to be the cost-effective and qualitative ratio of input to output. What do the citizens get from the engagement? McComas et al. (2006) suggested that civility and input/outcome discourse trust are essential.

Social media enrich the opportunity for many voices to weigh in on public policy matters. They are a means for creating and sharing the kinds of strains that are motivating for social movements, and even become important to the identifications that arise from such movements. They can create opportunity for mobilizing actions and calling for engagement. They can help to create confrontation and even lead contesting parties toward compromise. Such is the dialogic richness of issues oriented discourse in social media. But they do not necessarily lead to decision-making.

Such decision-making is influenced by the prevailing power/knowledge dynamics. Social media can reshape such dynamics, but skilled public relations practitioners can engineer and re-engineer the points of engagement, the deliberative criteria, and bring power resources to bear on one outcome in preference for others. Thus, social media enrich issues communication and can help reflective management monitor community opinions. But the incentive to make society more fully functioning is the singular incentive that drives collaborative decision-making. If organizations use the process to bend society to serve their interests, such engagement becomes frustrated and itself can suffer legitimacy gaps.

Conclusion

Throughout this chapter, with issues connected to the challenges of power/knowledge, a concerted effort has been made to understand how social media figure into that mix. M. T. Brown (2006) offered insights into that problem as he discussed corporate integrity. He approached "the question of corporate integrity and leadership from a civic perspective, which means that corporations are seen as members of civil society, corporate members are seen as citizens, and corporate decisions are guided by civic norms" (pp. 11). Corporate planning, operations, and communication are necessarily challenged to understand and facilitate the sorts of discussions now possible with social media. In this framework, the challenge is to be engaged without presuming the ability to control process and outcomes.

References

Arnstein, S.R. (1969). A ladder of citizen participation. *Journal of the American Institute of Planners*, 35(4), 216–224.

Auger, G.A. (2013). Fostering democracy through social media: Evaluating diametrically opposed nonprofit advocacy organizations' use of Facebook, Twitter, and YouTube. *Public Relations Review*, 39, 369–376.

Bourne, C. (2013). Power/knowledge and public relations. In R.L. Heath (ed.), *Encyclopedia of Public Relations*, 2nd ed., pp. 676–677. Thousand Oaks, CA: Sage.

Brown, J.K. (1979). *The Business of Issues: Coping with the Company's Environments*. New York: Conference Board.

Brown, M.T. (2006). Corporate integrity and public interest: A relational approach to business ethics and leadership. *Journal of Business Ethics*, 66, 11–18.

Chase, W.H. (1984). *Issue Management: Origins of the Future*. Stamford, CT: Issue Action Publications.

Coombs, W.T. (1992). The failure of the Task Force on Food Assistance: A case study of the role of legitimacy in issue management. *Journal of Public Relations Research*, 4(2), 101–122.

Coombs, W.T. (1998). The Internet as potential equalizer: New leverage for confronting social irresponsibility. *Public Relations Review*, 24, 289–303.

Crable, R.E., and Vibbert, S.L. (1986). *Public Relations as Communication Management*. Edina, MN: Bellwhether Press.

Gamper, C.D., and Turcanu, C. (2007). On the governmental use of multi-criteria analysis. *Ecological Economics*, 62, 298–307.

Gregory, R., Fischhoff, B., and Daniels, T. (2005). Acceptable input: Using Decision analysis to guide public policy deliberations. *Decision Analysis*, 2(1), 4–16.

Harlow, R.F. (1976). Building a public relations definition. *Public Relations Review*, 2(4), 34–42.

Heath, R.L. (1998). New communication technologies: An issues management point of view. *Public Relations Review*, 24, 273–288.

Heath, R.L., and Cousino, K.R. (1990). Issues management: End of first decade progress report. *Public Relations Review*, 16(1), 6–18.

Heath, R.L., Motion, J., and Leitch, S. (2010). Power and public relations: Paradoxes and programmatic thoughts. In R.L. Heath (ed.), *Sage Handbook of Public Relations*, pp. 191–204. Thousand Oaks, CA: Sage.

Heath, R. L., and Palenchar, M.J. (2009). *Strategic Issues Management: Organizations and Public Policy Challenges*. Thousand Oaks, CA: Sage.

Heath, R.L., Palenchar, M.J., and O'Hair, H.D. (2009). Community building through risk communication infrastructure. In R.L. Heath and D.H. O'Hair (eds.), *Handbook of Risk and Crisis Communication*, pp. 474–490. New York: Routledge.

Hill, J.W. (1958). *Corporate Public Relations: Arm of Modern Management*. New York: Harper & Brothers.

Jaques, T. (2010). Embedding issue management: From process to policy. In R.L. Heath (ed.), *Sage Handbook of Public Relations*, pp. 435–446. Thousand Oaks, CA: Sage.

Kent, M.L. (2013). Using social media dialogically: Public relations role in reviving democracy. *Public Relations Review*, 39, 337–345.

Kent, M.L., and Taylor, M. (1998). Building dialogic relationships through the World Wide Web. *Public Relations Review*, 24, 321–334.

Lerbinger, O. (1997). *The Crisis Manager: Facing Risk and Responsibility*. Mahwah, NJ: Lawrence Erlbaum.

McComas, K.A. (2010). Community engagement and risk management. In R.L. Heath (ed.), *Sage Handbook of Public Relations*, pp. 461–476. Thousand Oaks, CA: Sage.

McComas, K.A., Arvai, J., and Besley, J.C. (2009). Linking public participation and decision making through risk communication. In R.L. Heath and H.D. O'Hair (eds.), *Handbook of Risk and Crisis Communication*, pp. 364–385. New York: Routledge.

McComas, K., Besley, J., and Trumbo, C. (2006). Why citizens do and don't attend public meetings about local cancer clusters. *Policy Studies Journal*, 34(4), 671–698.

Merrick, J.R.W., Parnell, G.S., Barnett, J., and Garcia, M. (2005). A multiple-objective decision analysis of stakeholder values to identify watershed improvement needs. *Decision Analysis*, 2, 44–57.

Mitchell, R.K., Agle, B.R., and Wood, D.J. (1997). Toward a theory of stakeholder identification and salience: Defining the principle of who and what really counts. *Academy of Management Review*, 22(4), 853–886.

Motion, J. and Leitch, S. (1996). A discursive perspective from New Zealand: Another world view. *Public Relations Review*, 22, 297–309.

Motion, J. and Leitch, S. (2007). A toolbox for public relations: The oeuvre of Michel Foucault. *Public Relations Review*, 33, 263–268.

Palazzo, G. and Scherer, A.G. (2006). Corporate legitimacy as deliberation: A communicative framework. *Journal of Business Ethics*, 66, 71–88.

Renn, O. (1992). Concepts of Risk: A classification. In Krimsky, S.,and Golding, D. (eds) *Social Theories of Risk*, pp. 53–79. Westport, CT: Praeger.

Renn, O. (2009). Risk communication: insights and requirements for designing successful communication programs on health and environmental hazards. In R.L. Heath and H.D. O'Hair (eds.), *Handbook of Risk and Crisis Communication*, pp. 80–98. New York, Routledge.

Rowley, T.J. (1997). Moving beyond dyadic ties: A network theory of stakeholder influences. *Academic of Management Review*, 22, 887–910.

Scherer, A.G., and Palazzo, G. (2007). Toward a political conceptualization of corporate responsibility: business and society seen from a Habermasian perspective. *Academy of Management Review*, 31, 1096–1120.

Smith, M.F., and Ferguson, D.P. (2013). "Fracking democracy": Issue management and locus of policy decision-making in the Marcellus Shale gas drilling debate. *Public Relations Review*, 39, 377–386.

Sommerfeldt, E.J. (2013). The civility of social capital: Public relations in the public sphere, civil society, and democracy. *Public Relations Review*, 39, 280–289.

Stanley, G.D.D. (1985). *Managing External Issues: Theory and Practice*. Greenwich, CT: JAI Press.

11 Reshape policy
Public–private clashes and collaborative dialogue

Social media have changed the dynamics of what is "public" and "private." Likewise, the clash between public and private shape social media. Such observations draw attention to the notion of "commons." The Internet is a communication "commons," a space shared by individuals who are willing to pay to play in cyberspace. Once an individual or organization enters the "commons," they have moved from private to public space. Likewise, the public space can not only allow for them to engage in important ways with person and private policies but also be asked to participate in specific ways. Through social media, they enter the public discourse arena where public policy is formed and enacted.

Social media is central to the formation and enactment of sociopolitical change, public policy formation and implementation. Consider how they relate to political change as Howard and Parks (2012) concluded; they consist of

> (a) the information infrastructures and tools used to produce and distribute content that has individual value but reflects shared values; (b) the content that takes the digital form of personal messages, news, ideas, that becomes cultural content; and (c) the people, organizations, and industries that produce and consume both the tools and content.
>
> (p. 359)

The boundaries between public and private are often so blurred that it is difficult to know whether they actually exist, should exist, and can exist especially through the new communication commons.

The 2013 National Security Agency surveillance controversy in the United States is but one of many examples of this tension. Given such tensions between private realms of discourse and the public arena, this chapter begins with a discussion of the boundaries of public and private, progresses to discuss policy "clash" and ends by examining the ideal of "collaborative dialogue." If the discussion arrives successfully at a sound resolution of this topic, it will do so by showing separations and overlaps of "public" and "private" as collaboration.

The paradox of public and private

Philosophies of what is public and what is private address a necessarily complex set of opinions that center on discursive senses of culture, subculture, and an infinite regression of subs to the level of two individuals engaged in "conversation." These philosophies focus on issues, risk, risk management, and problems of creating a fully functioning society.

The crux of the matter is the norms that allow and constrain how individuals occupy the same space while espousing compatible and opposing ideas, cocreating meanings, and enacting processes that lead to similar and divergent purposes. These conditions are very human. Therefore, the future of social media to foster or inhibit collaboration is no better or worse than that of any other mode for interaction that humans have invented to that end. But, for public relations practitioners, sorting out those tensions and dynamics is becoming vital to their implementation of plans, strategies, and discourse resources.

Where does private end and public begin? Private traditionally means that which an individual or organization can think or own which is not public— someone else's, can be protected from becoming public or being someone else's, and serves society best when it remains private. Here are some tantalizing examples.

- In the USA, people can think what they want about the president, but it is a crime to voice a threat (going public) against the president, members of his/her family, and other government officials. A person can think "in a threatening way," but once thoughts are made known, even on social media, they can lead to criminal charges.
- Similarly, a teenager can think how much she/he "hates his/her parents"; silence keeps that opinion private.
- Businesses are allowed to have private, proprietary information and plans. That is a limited privacy. They can keep product ingredients secret, but must make them "public" to regulatory bodies, such as the Federal Drug Administration. In fact, they may have to develop and publicly proclaim plans, such as how they will protect food safety, deploy emergency response because of their "public actions," and give regulatory bodies information about product ingredients.
- Organizations as members of the private sector necessarily are subject to all manner of public policies relevant to how a community manages collective risks.
- Governments can have "top secret" plans and act accordingly. Disclosing top secrets can be treason, but also a courageous act by whistle-blowers who are "protected." Whistle-blowers can and should reveal plans, information, and actions by private corporations which have "public" impact. Thus, whistle-blowers have revealed product development and marketing activities by tobacco companies, pharmaceutical companies, and financial agencies, for instance.

- When is sexual behavior no longer merely a "private matter" (for instance adults engaging with children on social media)?
- When must a reporter reveal the sources for a story? What if the reporter discovered the story through social media?
- If we believe that a spouse cannot be forced to testify against a partner, does that same protection apply to same-sex couples if they are not "married"?
- When does not disclosing private information, such as a plan to harm another person and/or government official, move from "private conversation" to conspiracy and cover up?
- If a person writes a tweet but does not send it, can that message be "forced" into public view? If a person sends a tweet, does the privacy of that act end the person's right to privacy on other matters relevant to that tweet?
- If a person complains on social media about a boss or attacks a business activity, does that comment become public and potentially suffer reprisal that is "legitimate"?
- Do we assume that information gathered as we use social media, even the online routes we take as we move about and/or our GPS coordinates, is sold for marketing purposes? Do we assume that such information is (should be) available to governmental surveillance agencies? Do we assume that our messages and searches are monitored for terms that can serve marketing purposes (such as travel-related discussions) or surveillance related to terrorism (including online searches about terrorism and for academic research purposes)?
- As managements of organizations discuss topics about products and/or processes when and why do those discussions become and need to be public?

Lawyers, communication scholars, and philosophers have eternally discussed such matters and likely will forever. When do private choices and practices necessarily become public?

Such illustrations point to rubrics useful for differentiating what is "private" policy from "public" policy. That tension, recall Chapter 10, became vital to the public discussion regarding corporate behavior during the last decades of the twentieth century. Such discussions focus on the public interest. It is of public interest when actions by the private sector offend stakeholders to the point that they seek public policy relief. For instance, monopoly is allowed, and often regulated, insofar as such private sector activities make an economy more efficient in ways that serve the public interest. Monopoly violates the public interest when it distorts the capitalist system so that normal competitive advantages of supply and demand no longer are "rational."

As private standards and actions change or the criteria by which they are judged matures so does public policy. Once such collisions occur, public policy remedies are likely to be developed and implemented. To better understand those tensions, the next section explores the intersection of what is public and private.

Intersection of public and private

As we discussed in Chapters 9 and 10, risks, crises, and issues intersect. How and when they intersect reveals tensions between private and public realms. For instance, businesses are allowed to engage in private planning sessions during which they develop policies regarding product (safety, for instance), services (such as decisions about whether clients/customers/employees will be profiled by race, age, or gender), and policies (such as manufacturing safety including allowable "violations" of employee safety codes). At some moment, plans and policies necessarily become grist for the public policy grinder and social media enter the narrative.

Asbestos

Brodeur (1985) explained how litigation revealed asbestos company executives' knowledge of the health effects of asbestos. Courts gained access to planning documents that revealed what the executives knew and what actions they took (and did not take). For years, lack of such information in the public arena allowed worker safety standards to be ridiculously inadequate. Companies violated employees' right to know. A trust fund was established to fund employee health programs. Such litigation led corporations to declare bankruptcy to avoid liability to workers and their families that had been exposed to asbestos.

Enter social media

On 5 December 2013, the Asbestos Disease Awareness Organization launched an asbestos mobile app. This organization created the app for persons who suffered from asbestos related health problems and the fear of life-threatening disorders:

> The Asbestos Disease Awareness Organization (ADAO) is committed to replacing those feelings of fear, loneliness and confusion with the knowledge that there are others who share your experience and want to support you. We want you to have easy access to information about medical resources for asbestos-caused diseases. **Now this connection can be made immediately with a touch of your iPhone.**
>
> (Retrieved 9 December 2013 from
> www.asbestosdiseaseawareness.org/archives/23794)

Tobacco

Jeffrey S. Wigand rose to the position of vice president of research and development at Brown & Williamson tobacco company, Louisville, Kentucky. He worked on the development of reduced-harm cigarettes. On 4 February 1996, he appeared on CBS news, *60 Minutes*. He claimed that his company had knowingly and intentionally manipulated the blend of its tobacco in ways that would increase the levels of nicotine, a highly addictive substance, in cigarette smoke.

Enter social media

The National Cancer Institute's web site discusses issues of tobacco and health and advises smokers on ways to become smoke free. Its QuitPal app provides tools to help smokers to stop smoking, including support group assistance. The advice is segmented, for instance, by themes and practices relevant to women and to teens.

Health insurance

Wendell Potter (2010) argued that public relations practitioners, the target of his book, created messaging strategies intended to confuse and reassure persons who bought health insurance that the plans were good and the companies were committed to customer well-being. He alleged that corporate public relations works tirelessly to kill health-care insurance changes and deceive customers about its merits.

Enter social media

Today, healthcare fraud investigators use social media. At what point does some matter that was private become public? And, vice versa? Modern Business Associates (MBA) is a human resources company headquartered in St. Petersburg, Florida; its web site offers the following warning:

> Privacy experts say the information gathered online helps companies understand the risks involved of the person they would potentially insure. Companies use posts and tweets to see what people's hobbies are and to investigate worker's comp or disability claims. Experts say people should think twice before posting information that could ever be held against them in a fraudulent claim. Even something innocent could be misconstrued.
> (Retrieved 9 December 2013 from mabfro.com)

So when people think they are "being private" they may be standing naked in a socially mediated public.

Texting, Bullying and Sexting

Each month some innovation in communication technology offers promise for enhancing the education experience of children. This can be especially true for those who study in remote areas of nation or region. In that same context, however, social media pose many, but most importantly, three real dangers that lurk in the lives of school-age children. One is texting while driving, another is bullying, and the third is sexting. These ostensibly private actions occur in public space and have real public policy implications.

Enter social media

Enough-Is-Enough is an NGO program partly funded by the Office of Juvenile Justice and Delinquency Prevention, Office of Justice Programs, US Department of Justice. Along with other sites, it warns young adults of the costs and hazards of driving and texting.

Its homepage reports statistics such as "95% of social media–using teens who have witnessed cruel behavior on social networking sites say they have seen others ignoring the mean behavior; 55% witness this frequently" (citing PEW Internet Research Center, FOSI, Cable in the Classroom, 2011) (retrieved 10 December 2013 from www.internetsafety101.org/cyberbullyingstatistics.htm). Young people not only ignore such behavior, some even join the bullying. That piling on is a kind of diffusion of responsibility—not my responsibility. Such sites offer tons of careful, thoughtful public policy oriented research. They provide advice for parents/guardians, responsible adults such as teachers, and teens to resist, avoid, and report such behavior.

Along with bullying, sexting is prevalent. It often begins with "private" exchanges between dating teens or those interested in dating someone by providing alluring pictures. One teen can lure another into sexting on the "promise" of dating. Topic-oriented sites advise parents to ask their sons or daughters what they think will happen with those pictures or videos once the "romance" breaks up. Again, private exchanges have public policy implications.

These are a few examples where public and private matters collide and intersect. These strains offer opportunities for public policy engagement via social media.

Policy at the intersection of private and public: The heart of public policy

Conventional wisdom argues that communication technologies grow and change (and are used) in ways that serve community. Telephone service, shortly after its invention, lacked specific incentives needed for commercialization. Why should someone want a telephone when it was rude to interrupt a friend or neighbor at home, unannounced and without forewarning? Why should someone want to pay for a phone to call a neighbor when one could (and should) walk to their home, sit and visit, and even enjoy a beverage?

The answer was convenience. What if you need to speak to a friend or neighbor during a rain or snowstorm? Isn't it convenient to converse by phone? What if you need to reach a doctor? Isn't it better to call and have the doctor come to your home than to send someone to the doctor's office or home and then have the doctor have to come to your home? Thus, public policy is formed to frame, ground, and guide personal actions.

Conventional wisdom argues that lack of timely communication allowed the 13 American colonies to be able to foment appeals for revolution and independence since communication between the colonies (colonial governors) and Parliament or the King took weeks by water transportation. Once police gained the use of portable radios, their ability to fight crime increased. And, of course, we now know that battlefield tactics are ordered and coordinated in real time by helmet cameras, built in headphones, and GPS coordinates. Military personnel can use Skype and other technologies to communicate with friends and family—in real time across long distances.

Communication technology changes the nature of community—time, space, information availability, relationships, coordination, and cocreated meanings. Today a couple shopping can find one another in a store or mall by phone. They can let one another know what a product looks like by using programs such as FaceTime. Teens can bully one another. Friends can defend one another against rumor and bullying. They can provide pictures (video and sound) that strengthen personal bonds. They can plot and initiate terrorist attacks while moving about.

All of these possibilities for interaction, in one way or another, make their way into narratives created by popular culture. How many movies in the last decade have used an electronic communication device as a key part of the plot and character development? Sites such as those operated by Enough-Is-Enough provide statistics, cautions, advice, and support. The mission and strategy of many organizations is to create social media applications that educate, equip, and empower customers.

So, given what social media can do, for better or worse, can it help people collaborate in the creation of public policy? One of the themes that emerges in the case vignettes above is that public policy is essentially connected to the collective management of risk, issue debate, and crisis response. That topic was featured in Chapter 10. At what point does some private act, or some matter of privacy, no longer deserve to be "private" for the good of the community? Answering that question requires consideration of the nature of public policy, the theme of the next section.

Public policy: The nature of the beast

What is public policy? In a world that prizes privacy, the fact is that there is more to the human condition that is "public" than "private." Thoughts are private. Statements are public. Actions are public because they at least have communicative potential.

Public policy comes in all sizes, kinds and shapes. Some constrain behavior. Others allow and even demand behavior. Some is formal, instituted by governments, businesses, or churches. Others are societal norms, lived culture. All kinds can carry penalties for violation, and even earn rewards for violations. Protest, for instance, may be contrary to current public policy but rewardable insofar as it seeks to change that policy.

Action may enact compliance to policy. Attribution theory argues that individuals "decode" others thoughts by what and how they communicate, including how they act, what they do. Thus, it is easy to create a short narrative for each of the persons on a bus or subway. Our mothers told us that we can't tell a book by the cover, but that advice does not keep us from trying. We actually believe we are quite good at it because we assume that what people do is purposeful, including the clothes they wear, the items they carry, and today how they use social media. And, think just a moment what crosses your mind if someone on that bus takes your picture with a cell phone. Can you imagine, for instance, that seconds later your image will be posted somewhere for others to interpret as they may.

We assume that the public sector is different that the private sector and then look for the differentiating seams. Companies believe they are private enterprises, but lose that status because they operate, enact themselves, in public. Is a drilling rig/ship (Deepwater Horizon) operating (by BP with the technological assistance of Halliburton) in the Gulf of Mexico a "private" or a "public" operation? To what extent does a government entity, another company, an NGO, or individual have a right and responsibility to assure that the "private" actions meet the standards of operations in the public arena?

Eggs get broken, a rationale for public policy. On 24 March 1989, the oil tanker Exxon Valdez struck Bligh Reef in Prince William Sound, Alaska. Over the next days and weeks, media accounts and images became increasingly available to the world. On 20 April 2010, a gas kick from the drilling operations being conducted by BP on the Deepwater Horizon ignited and exploded. The explosion killed 11 workers. Over the next months, the company struggled to cap the well, stop the flow, contain or disperse the oil that flowed from the well, and protect the Gulf wildlife, beaches, and businesses.

There are many similarities and a lot of differences between the Valdez incident and the Maconda Well event. One is the presence of social media. Alaska is remote compared to the Gulf, but both had seafood harvesting vessels that could record the event. Cell phone camera technology, however, made nearly everyone a "reporter" in days after the BP spill. So, what was "private" became public very quickly. Images spread and went viral and global. Risk bearers had substantial incentive to document the event, serving their self-interests.

One of the daunting challenges, perhaps the most important, of public relations is the ability through management and communication to help organizations (however private) to operate in the public arena. Such tensions revolve around matters of legitimacy and trust (social capital) framed as the right to operate and the right to reward. And, although people have rights as a natural citizen (whatever those are by culture), an organization only (or similarly) has rights granted by the authority of the community where it exists and operates. It is beholden to the public policy of the community as it attempts to shape how the community is beholden to the organization.

As NGOs, such as environmental groups, work to publicize that which is or was private, public relations professionals (and other disciplines such as general counsel) work to "privatize" that which is public. Here is the tension of crisis, risk, and issues management and communication. By what rights and authority are operations deemed "OK"? Are such matters normative, and therefore battles over norms? Are they matters where clarity (or obscurity) becomes relevant to the need for and development of public policy?

Public policy has at least two distinguishable dimensions, both of which are normative: norm based actions and judgements or evaluations regarding the appropriateness of such actions. These norms are framed as socially constructed narratives. These norms are essential to the societal and organizational standards of legitimacy and corporate social responsibility.

One type of public policy is that developed and enacted as legislative, regulatory, or judicial norms. This type would include the dictates of a monarch, despot, or ruling oligarchy—or representative democracy. It refers to the regulatory law of the land. This sort of prescribed norm is intended to demonstrate power, exert control, and regulate specific types of interactions. These norms can apply to individuals, organizations, or both. For instance, even though in the US the Supreme Court has defined certain rights of free speech to businesses as citizens, those "citizens" cannot hold office. They can elect, but not be elected. Some see that as a public policy paradox or irony, but it is "the law."

Some of the strongest pro-industrial operational public policies are driven by the need for warfare materiel—the narrative of national defense. Near Climax, Colorado in the United States are the remains of a mountain, Bartlett Mountain, that was basically dismantled first to obtain molybdenum for WWI armament and later for many other metallurgical applications.

Before and after pictures offer startling contrasts to those who love Colorado's mountains. Molybdenum became a valued material once it was learned that the German military industry was using this material to strengthen steel during WWI. The norm of national security sanctioned the mining of this material, even though it required destroying a mountain and creating massive tailing ponds that will never be remediated. That action was done in the sanctioning narrative of wartime public policy, the norms of risk management. And, this dismantling took place at 11,500 feet in the central Rocky Mountains, far from the public view (Voynick, 1996). Cameras did not record and disseminate the environmental damage associated with this project as they have for other such mining operations.

One more example of sanctioned environmental damage, but in the view of social media: various norms sanction such behavior. Sanction is one of the many ironical words in the English vocabulary. It can mean to impose (or threaten to do so) a penalty for nonnormative behavior. It can also be a grant of official permission. Thus, by sanction coal mining companies can engage in controversial hilltop mining whereby soil and rock are removed from above the seam of coal, a process that became increasingly popular in the Appalachian Mountains of the US starting in the 1970s. After the overburden is stripped away and the coal is removed, the companies need to only minimally restore the mountain by some reclamation. They do not need to rebuild or restore the mountain but engage in minimal remediation. This sort of sanction is often justified as a source of community income, jobs, and solutions for the need for energy. But, of course, the sanction is a means for generating profits.

One difference in the battle over mountaintop mining is the constant scrutiny and documentation of the process on social media. One web site discusses the process and offers information about it. It includes pictures that show the environmental impact, and calls on users to contact Congress to protest this process (iLoveMountains.org, retrieved 27 January 2014; see also ApplachianVoices.org). The National Resources Defense Council opposes the sanctions that allow, even encourage this process. It advocates with the tag-line: "In the Sierras, they climb them. In the Rockies, they ski them. In Appalachia, they level them" (www.nrdc.org/energy/coal/mtr/, retrieved 27 January 2014).

As these two examples testify, public policy can authorize industrial activities. One difference, however, between Climax and various hilltop mining operations is that the pictures and text about the latter is very much alive and part of the current public policy debate. That debate has slowly led to public policy changes by which hilltop mining is today more carefully regulated. Motive for such change occurred in part because the soil loosened by the mining process has harmed area towns' water supplies. Citizens have used social media to document this damage for the world to see. The process was making communities near the operations less fully functioning.

These examples illustrate the sorts of public policy that allow behavior rather than prohibit or restrict it. Restrictions obviously are an important type of public policy. Corporations are told what they cannot do, how their operations are restricted and guided by public policy. Similarly, automobile drivers are told to not drive faster than stated speeds at various locations in each community. They are told not to text and drive. That sanction (the limiting rather than permitting kind) is even more extreme and better enforced near school zones. So, societies create formal public policies which are promulgated. Punishments are set for those who do not obey. Enforcement measures are stated and applied to "force" compliance.

Nevertheless, public policy norms are routinely ignored, even flaunted—thus essentially nullifying the policy by enactment. That kind of public policy refers to norms that are created and sanctioned by convention. Traffic in large cities often flows at speeds that are faster than posted speeds. Going with the flow is normative. So is texting while driving. Just don't get caught. But if so, one can think, even if not say, but most people speed or text, as the case might be.

Even more germane to social media use are the norms (unofficial but powerful public policy) regarding communication behaviors. How quickly after receiving a text must the receiver respond to avoid being "rude." Social exchange theory of interpersonal communication points to the norms of exchange as predictors of interpersonal relationship quality. If someone says, "Hello," the norm is to respond, "Hello." Other responses are available but according to social exchange theory are negotiated as rewardable and there-fore continued or discontinued behavior. If a person does not reply properly, they may be seen as less cordial, costing more than they are rewarding. Thus, teenagers work out very careful norms ("public policy") that regulate private behaviors done in public. Such regulations are important because they allow for knowable and rewardable norms of behavior.

Students, therefore, are likely to text and drive because they are normatively expected to respond, even though they are driving. They want to be seen and treated as a friend. Similarly, they post information in a normative fash-ion. They exchange information, in a normative fashion. And, they use social media to impose norms on one another. Such norms, even though they violate other norms, predict behaviors that parents would not approve.

These norms can have other implications. If a person posts a complaint about an employer or boss, can the person be fired? If the person complains about a landlord, can the person's lease be terminated? If the person complains about a product, can the vendor or manufacturer sue for defamation?

An online search using the terms "norms and social media," will generate dozens of hits. Such hits even suggest that authors are addressing topics such as "do mass media create social norms or merely reflect them." Substitute the term social for mass and the same question gets addressed. The former is a topic of media effects. The latter is a matter of social media effects.

All have public policy implications of both kinds: the formal kind prescribed as law and the "informal" kind which reflect customs, cultures, and protocols that are created by users even though they may violate the first type. Relevant to such norms, it has become the custom that if something happens someone armed with a "camera" must immediately take the picture/capture the video and post it. Such was the case during the 2012 presidential campaign in the US when a cell phone or camera captured presidential candidate Mitt Romney's dismissive comment that since 47 percent were takers and not makers they would not vote for him and he would not court their votes. Thus, that which is "private" can quickly become public, and affect public policy such as a presi-dential election.

As these examples suggest, public policy can approve or restrict behaviors, corporate or individual. Similarly, powerful public policies prescribe individual behaviors as variously socially approved or disapproved. Human society can only function by such rule based, normative, and predictable behavior. And as the next section explains, social media are not only the targets of such policy but key players in policy changes.

Social media and governmental public policy

Societies face recurring attacks on authority, focused protest for some public policy change by social movement activists. During the days leading up to the downfall of Hosni Mubarak in Egypt, activists posted comments and images on various social media such as Twitpic, Facebook and YouTube. Issues were discussed. Claims were made about his character and political leadership. In these formats, a case was made for public policy change.

During the uprising in Egypt, social media were used to record and share images of violent clashes with the authorities. As such, social media become judge and jury. As had been the case during the civil rights movements in the US during the 1960s, such images had a veracity of authority and authenticity because they were actual, often unfiltered. As pictures become shared, images of persons in authority could be shared quickly and widely condemned.

In situations such as these, communicators for the authorities create counterimages. This is a modern, viral, virtual, and dramatic form of rhetoric, the clash of statement and counterstatement. Such media outlets allow for street-level discourse, the voice of the people. This is a discourse in which voices occur at the street level. Those voices can also be blocked as was allegedly the case with Twitter in Egypt.

Hamdy and Gomaa (2012) used the analytical tool of framing narratives to differentiate between how various media interpreted and reported the 2011 January uprising in Egypt. Government-sanctioned newspapers interpreted the activism as an attack on the authority of state and state leaders. Social media frames emphasized social justice and revolution acts calling for freedom. Independent newspapers used both frames at various times and ways. The key finding of the study was that social media give voice to alternative and competing perspectives in times of unrest. Such perspectives are generated by the images themselves even though they may subsequently be debated and judged by other frames, including those of journalists.

Under such conditions, governments not only can supply counterfootage but also have at least two countermeasures. One is to block activists' ability to use servers to disseminate their images and messages. The other is to feed disinformation and misinformation into the social media venues being used. Thus, confusion can occur among activists as competing images are presented and as venues and times of protest are changed. These may be changed strategically by activist organizers who adapt to the measures taken by government officials and police/army (and street bullies). But such changes can also occur as officials put out what seem to be activist bulletins either leading to clashes with well-prepared police, or call organizers and activists to meet at the wrong place and/or time. Social media, in this public policy venue, becomes a cat and mouse tug of war. Its political and agitational impact can not only voice protest but also encounter various kinds of governmental and corporate interest constraint (Youmans and York, 2012).

Such mediated communication not only occurred in real time but also supplies content for other media users. Some outlets were standard print. Others were international electronic media (radio, television, and Internet news). Both or all sides used supplied discourse content details that could end up on web sites and blogs. The fact, however, that "both" sides give out details and interpretations as well as expressions of outrage is important. Lim (2012) reasoned that oppositional movements in Egypt between 2004 and 2011 used social media "to expand networks of disaffected Egyptians, broker relations between activists, and globalize the resources and reach of opposition leaders" (p. 231).

Valenzuela et al. (2012) considered the advantage and role of social media to younger activists. First, it fits their lifestyle better than it does older members of a community. It plays an important role beyond being a means for self-expression and outrage. It serves to spread news and facilitate social bonding.

Governments of all types, but primarily those with high control incentives, work to shape public policy and public discourse. On matters of public interest and policy, therefore, they work to control news and policy narratives. During the SARS outbreak in China from November 2002 to July 2003, government political and health officials worked to maintain a narrative that shifted blame to public hygiene and away from government public health narratives. Media coverage internal to China presented the theme that the virus originated with animals, thousands of which were killed. Such responses are often used as a means for thwarting what could become a pandemic, but they are also potentially not only ineffective but counterproductive.

Details on the mysterious disease were posted outside of China; they painted a different picture. That alternative narrative even pointed out how clumsy public health measures were causative to the spread of the disease rather than useful for its containment. China's tight reporting hampered the public health response efforts by national health organizations (Heath et al., 2008). In these ways, blogs that are unfettered can serve both as safety valves and pressure cookers (Hassid, 2012).

Fast forward one decade. In part due to the humiliation of the failed proactive response to SARS, a genetic research firm called BGI (formerly Beijing Genomics Institute) has raised China's and the world's ability to respond quickly and effectively to public health problems resulting from mysterious virus and bacteria. BGI has become a global leader in understanding the genetic fingerprints and characteristics of such health threats. Its prowess was brought to bear in 2011 when a deadly strain of E. coli bacteria emerged in Germany and then spread to Denmark and Sweden. Once BGI received a sample of the bacteria, it was able to determine its nature and effective response in three days. And, quite relevant to the theme of this book, it released its conclusions through Twitter (rather than an academic peer-reviewed journal, for instance) so they could be subjected immediately to peer review. Speed, as well as accuracy, is vital in meeting the threat of a pandemic. Social media can facilitate global communication within a community of public health scientists (Specter, 2014).

Because of their ubiquity and ostensible freedom from establishment control, social media are lauded as the "voice of the people." Citizens can express themselves in ways that provide details that authorities seek to hide. They offer interpretations and opinions that attack governments' credibility. They give users a view of the world that at least seems authentic, credible, and therefore powerful. And, they help create means by which some or all parts of a society collaborate, if not immediately then later.

To understand collaboration and public policy the next section investigates how they interconnect in the joined effort to make enlightened choices.

Collaboration

Collaboration and collaborative decision-making presume various kinds of coming together. Collaboration might lead to consensus, but concurrence is also likely. So is a failure to come together. So, social media are no magic elixir, but they are also not inherently dysfunctional as people engage in (or at least attempt) collaboration.

Coming-togethers inherently, and with varying kinds of structuration, produce the discourse and decision processes by which people can collectively identify and solve problems and implement solutions. By this logic, two individuals can enact the process of shopping "together" via social media. They could, for instance, use FaceTime to chat about a product. One could show the other in real time the various choices available at a store counter. A collaborative decision could be made although the two persons are only linked by social media and not standing in a store at the same counter.

Understanding collaboration entails appreciating the standard approaches for managing issues discussed in Chapter 10. There several types of issues were identified: the discursive, disputational contestability of fact, value, policy, and identification; solution of a problem and its solution; public dispute; battles over legitimacy gaps; and consideration and response to conditions that have impact on the functioning of an organization. These views of issues point to the collective (and therefore collaborative) need for enlightened choice.

One of the key factors of collaboration is sharing. Sharing gives people a means and an incentive to come together (or divide from one another, and even stay apart). Sharing opinions and motives occurs when a similar or same narrative interpretation brings individuals into a situation where collaboration is needed and possible.

Even though people have an incentive to collaborate that does not mean they will. The writing of history has been granted to the victors, but that does not mean that those disempowered or marginalized no longer carry and add to or modify the various narratives of conflict. Conversation, crafted senses of the past, failed memories, and distorted stories are part of this discourse fabric. Postconflict discourse can consist of a collection of narratives that never become one metanarrative.

How a society heals, if it does, can have a lot to do with how it remembers its past. Museums, for instance, can be a repository of the past facts and feelings. Similarly, social media can offer a mix of permanent artifacts, images and interpretations as well as be a lively forum for current/contemporary postings. However difficult, it is improbable that a society/community can heal without a narrative that contains all rather than some of the elements of its divided past. James (2013) analyzed social mediated reflections of civil unrest and postconflict civil life in what was once Yugoslavia. She found that images of the Sarajevo Roses, street memorials to victims and violent acts, have become part of tourists' socially mediated photographic records. All of the statements about the past, plus what individuals post about their interpretations of the past appear alongside contemporary reflections. This pointing to the past mixes with commentary to become the postconflict narrative. She observed how

> images posted online are available for sharing, thus keeping memories alive and providing opportunities for the community of memory to change over time as people with different perspectives find and comment on the images of the Roses, "Don't Forget," and other monuments a decade and more postconflict.
>
> (pp. 988–989)

So, in postconflict situations, social media reflects on the past while commenting on the present and while setting coordinates for future policy.

Social media serves important purposes for collaborative crime solving. In an era fascinated by the popular culture of superheroes, each individual can become one, probably without intention. Individuals can seek collaborative interpretations of past crimes as well as work together to solve current ones. Pictures, text, and film recalling the assignation of President Kennedy, for instance, help citizens interpret important events as though they were eyewitnesses. Such digital museums store iconic images that reinforce and dispute expert interpretations of such events. Lay crime stoppers ponder solutions to crimes without leaving their armchairs.

So too, social media allows individuals to be superheroes of current crimes. During the Boston Marathon on 15 April 2013, bombs were detonated in the midst of crowds gathered to witness this competition. Within minutes, images from the street became posted that, once added to surveillance video, helped police to identify the alleged bombers. Once those images were posted online, they became a "wanted" poster for police and citizens. Eyewitness accounts were not trivial, but served as a probable cause for arrest and as evidence to be used in court. Images caught by digital media were invaluable. Cases of this kind happen every day somewhere around the world. Networks of law enforcement officers become enlarged by citizen cell phone technology. The eyes of the community are everywhere and never sleep as all members of a community become collaborative crime investigators.

To facilitate collaboration, the Amber Alert system was established several years ago in the United States. Each day across the country, such alerts provide real-time details people need to become crime solvers; these alerts can occur on radio, television, roadside electronic signs, posters, flyers, computers, and cell phones/tablets. A cell phone, for instance, beeps to announce an Amber Alert that a child is missing and might be abducted. Social media facilitate collaborative enactment of the search. If a traveler receives an alert and subsequently sees the vehicle it specified, with its license plate fitting the description, that person has just become vital to law enforcement. Purely random events justify the omnipresent vigilance of social media devices.

Such media help emergency response personnel to alert community members in ways that allow them to take defensive measures. Experts alert citizens to some problem and coordinate activities such as shelter in place or evacuation in the face of a violent storm. The latter is especially important, for instance, when the time has come to enact community level emergency response. Similarly, if a chemical plant experiences a fire, explosion, or serious release of hazardous material, members of a community can be almost instantaneously alerted to the event and advised as to the best emergency response. Later, people can conveniently be notified when the danger has passed.

Centuries ago, the town crier would announce that all is well. Or, a fire alarm would announce a fire. A hurricane alert could be posted on radio or television and the Internet. Today, social media routinely facilitate these traditional forms of collaborative risk management and communication. They add reach to formal networks and put information (or capture it) within seconds and at a user's fingertips. There is a randomness to this model, a real example of chaos theory, but the media offer structure through networked relationships; individuals can become more tightly coupled into collaborative response for the common good.

The sorts of collaborations discussed in this section suggest how connections are inherently available through the nature and use of social mediated networks. The next section directs attention to the controversial, but utopian solution, potential for dialogue to achieve collaborative problem-solving.

Social media and public policy collaborative decision-making

For decades, theories regarding collaborative decision-making have been pounded into text, articles, chapters, and books—as well as the minds of practitioners. Consequently, it is reasonable that public relations theory and practice today are moving away from a linear media relations paradigm of collaboration to determine whether social media are the Holy Grail of collaborative decision-making. In such discussions, dialogue is a capstone concept and scholars as well as practitioners want to know how social media help or harm the processes and discursiveness needed to collaboratively solve sociopolitical problems.

Before continuing to discuss how well social media lead to collaborative decision-making, it is worth pausing to consider the requirements for and steps of the process. The process is discursive, driven by ideas and evaluations, not merely processes. It is not only a process guided by narratives but one that results in one or more narratives. One of the outcome narratives can be that the decision did not resolve the controversy. Another outcome is the decision that the solution crafted to the problem is only marginally better than the problem (Heath and Coombs, 2006). Social media may help, but the human dynamics of community are both the rudder and broken compass of collective decision-making.

For nearly 40 years, five management styles have been offered to explain conflict resolution: avoidance, accommodation, competition, compromise, and collaboration. Parents send children to time out until their conflict has quieted or become resolved by avoidance. Accommodation results when one conflict partner gives ground to the other ("OK, we'll do it your way," a viable solution to a binary decision that offers no option of compromise, but one that does not actually "solve" the problem). Competition is a win-loss game that may be zero sum: both sides can lose. Compromise presumes giving ground to gain support for a preferred part of a decision. Collaboration presumes that those engaged in decision-making have the will and can find a way to achieve mutually satisfying solutions or issue resolution (Kilman and Thomas, 1975).

Collaboration presumes several conditions: openness, trust, commitment to demonstrate cooperation, alignment of interests (shared self-interest), and compatibility of views and opinions. These conditions are typical of dialogue which can be expressive and nonpropositional or highly propositional and contentious (see Heath et al., 2006). Dialogue not only presupposes the possibility of commitment to collectively develop an idea, but also entails a network of relationships that dispose communicators to prefer points of view recommended by their preferred relational partners.

Kent and Taylor (2002) concluded that "since dialogue involves 'trust.' 'risk,' and 'vulnerability' dialogic partners (and publics) can be manipulated by unscrupulous organizations and publics" (p. 24). Dialogue can fail when participants cling to prior commitment (preference for one idea) for a specific point of view. If they merely interact with the limited goal of gaining adherence (concurrence) to one point of view such narrowness of purpose will produce communication dysfunctions. Dysfunctional dialogue can result in win-loss outcomes. Another dysfunctional kind of dialogue occurs when participants are more engaged in deceit than the honest brokering of collaborative engagement.

But propositional dialogue can also mean that participants truly listen to and learn from one another as well as share information and vet ideas with a mutual benefit spirit leading to a win-win outcome fostering truly aligned interests. Such a review of dialogue types and incentives suggest that "dialogue" alone is not a solution unless the concept is defined as being inherently normative toward mutual benefit.

Bringing together themes such as these provides an explanatory logic and incentive to follow stages of collaborative decision-making.

- Identifying, understanding, and agreeing with the goals of those in dialogue and collaborative decision-making.
- Discovering and agreeing to common ground; determining which ideas lead to disagreement as well as concurrence.
- Uncovering points of disagreement.

- Determining degrees of commitment to agreement and disagreement.
- Identifying impediments to collaboration.
- Seeking to eliminate impediments.
- Focusing on positive incentives for agreement.
- Proposing solutions to problems and differences in ways that are based on agreement and do not collide with points of disagreement.
- Agreeing on options to be analyzed and tested.
- Analyzing and testing options.
- Determining which options best address and solve the issue and build concurrence.

These steps can help issue discussants achieve outcomes that are agreeable to all while wrestling with a manageable amount of disagreement. That is of course the theory.

Within that line of analysis, substantial amounts of discussion have addressed the connection between public relations and dialogue, and the accompanying role of social media in dialogue, or vice versa. It is important to appreciate how well this model fits the incentives that connect persons through social media to achieve collaboration.

Of related interest to those themes is the nature of community and the community building role of public relations. Can and does public relations have a role in building a fully functioning community? Hallahan's (2004; see also, Kruckeberg and Starck, 1988) leadership on this topic is important; he offered this overview:

> Community offers the potential for organizations to become more socially responsible by heightening awareness of the greater whole of which the organization is a part. Community shifts the organizational emphasis from the cold treatment of impersonal, often adversarial publics, to a warmer, more enlightened emphasis on collaboration and cooperation with others.
>
> (p. 264)

The goal is to understand and appreciate communicative and ideological empowerment and engagement as a process and discursive goal. Such discussion wonders how communities can be strategically cooperative and how such discussions are enriched by appreciating and understanding the role of emerging technologies.

Kent and Taylor (2002) have explored how dialogue is an ideology as well as model for "understanding how organizations can build relationships that serve both organizational and public interests" (p. 21). As an orientation and guide to practice, dialogue features five concepts: mutuality, propinquity, empathy, risk, and commitment. Furthermore, organizations can implement and demonstrate their commitment to dialogue by how they engage mass-mediated and social media channels. Such conditions, Kent and Taylor reminded us, do not assure ethics and collaboration, but "increase the likelihood that publics and organizations will better understand each other and have ground rules for communication" (p. 33).

Cases such as the one regarding fracking (discussed in Chapter 10) suggest that no matter how much discourse occurs through social media, the ultimate resolution of issues is likely to rest with decisions promulgated by some authorized deliberative body (regulation, legislation, or judicial). Discussion prior to, and even following, such decisions is important but not predictive of a universally superior outcome. The nature of the decision reflects each set of public policy dynamics as norms become promulgated within a society.

Many cases can be used to examine the role of collaborative decision-making and social media. One current case where public policy is being collaboratively forged centers on cell phone use during a flight on an airplane. On 12 December 2013, the US Federal Communications Commission (FCC) voted (3–2) to lift its ban on cell phone use during flights. On that day, the federal Department of Transportation and members of Congress began measures that would prohibit those calls. Even given the FCC decision, airlines would be able to allow or prohibit such calls as they wish. Airlines polled customers and invited social media commentary.

Airlines have reported that the commentary is leading them to be cautious or hesitant about implement this change. They have announced that they do not plan to allow cell phone use except under extraordinary circumstances. Such dialogue can even lead to alternatives beyond the binary choice of allowing or not allowing. Texting, for instance, might be allowed, but if so, can that occur responsibly. That means that customers would have to self-police their use of cell phones. Perhaps an annoyed seat mate might video an offender and post it to a site: Do social media make people socially responsible? Examples such as this suggest the potency of social media for collaborative decision-making regarding public policies.

So, the study of social media and dialogue continues. Kent (2010) applied his principles of dialogue as norms for investigating social media use and societal impact. He noted the problem of moderation, the condition whereby those who administratively control social media sites can determine who participates and even how they do so. He critiques this practice, "social media is *antisocial*. Social media create the illusion of knowing what someone is doing by seeing the posts by others on their social networking pages and reading the comments to their own posts" (p. 646).

Having posts available does not mean, however, that they are read and given much regard. Readers may be disinterested in most posts. That can allow their outrage to overwhelm reason or be cautious in expressing thoughts because they are overheard by folks who could be friends or foes. "Their public nature precludes intimateness, self-disclose, and genuine sociality. Intimacy requires privacy" (p. 646). These and many other challenges, Kent cautioned, are important as practitioners and academics define, research, and employ social media's dialogic potential as "a place of genuine dialogue and peace" (p. 656).

One dialogic impact of social media is the opportunity people (laypersons, corporate spokespersons, and managers) have to get unfiltered information, even though a plethora of comments on some matter the discussion of which tends toward chaos and uncertainty rather than to a collective sense of some matter. That problem is a challenge. Its resolution is vital to the future role of social media in dialogic collaborative decision-making. As Kent (2013) recently observed:

> With the shift away from mainstream media and professional gatekeepers who made editorial decisions, citizens have increasingly come to rely on a greater diversity of news sources (some more credible than others), and more idiosyncratic voices that appeal to individual citizens' unique interests. Without the aid of credible gatekeepers and media professionals, democracy is hobbled, just as it is by having its media controlled by only five mega-corporations.
>
> (p. 338)

As the media landscape, and that of public relations practice changes, can technologies add or detract to the societal need for collaborative decision-making?

That observation can lead practitioners as well as academics to believe in "dialogue" and social media without much of a critique. Kent (2013) warned against a naive approach, as he concluded that:

> the professional use of dialogue is a sophisticated, technical skill, not simply a matter of talking to other people. In professional practice, many mistakenly believe that dialogue is just communicating with others: tweeting status updates, posting content to one's Facebook account. Ultimately, dialogue is a one-on-one relational tool. Dialogue is not about mass communication. Dialogue represents a relational give and take that occurs between two people, or in small groups, that observe strict rules of decorum to maintain fairness, trust, and the opportunity for all involved to express their opinion. Dialogue is an orientation toward communication with others, not a simple procedure or process. Dialogic encounters can build long-lasting relationships, but dialogue as a professional tool is much more.
>
> (p. 341)

Reflections such as this emphasize how important it is to move thoughtfully into the social media era to obtain purposeful, engaging, and productive uses of such discourse. Beyond the value of social media for expressions of feelings and opinions, which can facilitate issue monitoring, the real challenge is know how to integrate social media into public policy decision-making infrastructures.

From the organization's public relations team's perspective then, Kent (2013) hit on an essential theme. If an organization wants to be good and communicate well, its use of "social media needs to be genuinely social, or not at all" (p. 341). That means that the organization needs to communicate about what users want to communicate about. It should be enacted so that the organization communicates with individuals as thoughtful and concerned persons, not as stereotypes. The discourse as enacted needs to serve the social media community's interests not those of the organization, at all or only.

Can social media be used to make discussions and discussants more authentic (Gilpin et al., 2010; Henderson and Bowley, 2010)? The challenge seems to be how and how well discussants share social media space, discourse space, and societal space so that all voices that need to be heard are heard and listened to (Sommerfeldt, 2013).

Old media allowed, and perhaps required, that organizations speak self-interestedly. The new era of social media and dialogic decision-making is less about the organization per se and more about the individuals engaged in the dialogue. It is more about community and others than narrowly about self.

Conclusion

The future of public relations and collaborative public policy decision-making is like a train coming downhill with a tentative person at the brakes. The future is approaching, and may have just passed. The old notion of mass-mediated communicators affecting the agenda and content of issue discussions and gate-keepers has become reshaped. Those facts, however, do not signal a future without peril or difficulty. The key to collaborative decision-making is the ways that the players engaged in public policy deliberations and enactments play together, authentically and collaboratively. Does social media mitigate the role of self-interested deliberation making such efforts more "democratic" or does it merely rearrange the deck chairs. To know the answer to that puzzler, one must stay tuned and be vigilant.

References

Brodeur, P. (1985). *Outrageous Misconduct: The Asbestos Industry on Trial*. New York: Pantheon.

Gilpin, D.R., Palazzolo, E.T., and Brody, N. (2010). Socially mediated authenticity. *Journal of Communication Management*, 14, 258–278.

Hallahan, K. (2004). "Community: as a foundation for public relations theory and practice. In P.J. Kalbfleisch (ed.). *Communication Yearbook 28*, pp. 233–279. Mahwah, NJ: Erlbaum.

Hamdy, N. and Gomaa, E.H. (2012). Framing the Egyptian uprising in Arabic language newspapers and social media. *Journal of Communication*, 62, 195–211.

Hassid, J. (2012). Safety valve or pressure cooker? Blogs in Chinese political life. *Journal of Communication*, 62, 212–230).

Heath, R.L. and Coombs, W.T. (2006). *Today's Public Relations*. Thousand Oaks, CA: Sage.

Heath, R.L., Li, F., Bowen, S.A., and Lee, J. (2008). Narratives of crisis planning and infectious disease: A case study of SARS. In M.W. Seeger and T. Sellnow (eds.), *Crisis Communication and the Public Health*, pp. 131–155. New York: Hampton Press.

Heath, R.L., Pearce, W.B., Shotter, J., Taylor, J.T., Kerstein, A., and Zorn, T. (2006). The processes of dialogue: Participation and legitimation. *Management Communication Quarterly*, 19, 341–375.

Henderson, A. and Bowley, R. (2010). Authentic dialogue? The role of "friendship" in a social media recruitment campaign. *Journal of Communication Management*, 14, 237–257.

Howard, P.N. and Parks, M.R. (2012). Social media and political change: Capacity, constraint, and consequence. *Journal of Communication*, 62, 359–362.

James, D. (2013). Social networking Sarajevo Roses: Digital representations of postconflict civil life in (the former) Yugoslavia. *Journal of Communication*, 63, 975–992.

Kent, M.L. (2010). Directions in social media for professionals and scholars. In R.L. Heath (ed.), *Sage Handbook of Public Relations*, pp. 643–656. Thousand Oaks, CA: Sage.

Kent, M.L. (2013). Using social media dialogically: Public relations role in reviving democracy. *Public Relations Review*, 39, 337–345.

Kent, M.L. and Taylor, M. (2002). Toward a dialogic theory of public relations. *Public Relations Review*, 28, 21–37.

Kilman, R. and Thomas, K. (1975). Interpersonal conflict behavior as a reflection Jungian personality dimensions. *Psychological Reports*, 37, 971–980.

Kruckeberg, D. and Starck, K. (1988). Public relations and community: A reconstructed theory. New York: Praeger.

Lim, M. (2012). Clicks, cabs, and coffee houses: Social media and oppositional movements in Egypt, 2004–2011. *Journal of Communication*, 62, 231–248).

Potter, W. (2010). *Deadly Spin*. New York: Bloomsbury Press.

Sommerfeldt, E.J. (2013). The civility of social capital: Public relations in the public sphere, civil society, and democracy. *Public Relations Review*, 39, 280–289.

Specter, M. (2014). The gene factory. *New Yorker*, 6 January, pp. 34–43.

Valenzuela, S., Arriagada, A., and Scherman, A. (2012). The social media basis of youth protest behavior: The case of Chile. *Journal of Communication*, 62, 299–314.

Voynick, S.M. (1996). *Climax: The history of Colorado's Climax Molybdenum Mine*. Missoula, MT: Mountain Press Publishing Company.

Youmans, W.L., and York, J.C. (2012). Social media and activist toolkit: User agreements, corporate interests, and the information infrastructure of modern social movements. *Journal of Communication*, 62, 315–329.

12 Conclusion

Within this final chapter we map out the conceptual themes we have explored in our discussions of the relationships between social media and public relations. We also critically reflect on future directions for public relations and social media. A series of problematizations were posed at the outset of the book to analyze how social media has impacted on public relations, and how public relations practice affects the use and usefulness of social media as a means for community dialogue:

- What is the nature of the relationship between public relations and social media?
- How do power relations play out within the practices of public relations in social media?
- What are the implications of public relations practices within social media contexts for identity and relationships?
- In what ways does social media open up or reconfigure discursive possibilities for public relations?
- Does social media increase transparency or merely give it one more kaleidoscopic twist?

The notion that social media has somehow magically transformed public relations into an improved, engaged practice has been interrogated as part of a broader agenda that questions whether it is actually possible for professional public relations to change, beyond adapting to and sometimes even exploiting media to serve narrow, elitist interests

Such problematics focus attention on how public relations practitioners use a medium, social media in this case, for purposes that narrowly serve some elite and not the community. That bias cannot be addressed merely by advocating the virtue of two-way communication. Even the assumption, which may be questionable, that social media fosters dialogue is a theme that is constantly being tested.

Our conclusion is that although social media poses a fundamental challenge to professional public relations and there has been a shift in the power wielded by publics, overall, public relations continues to function as a socializing influence and agent for promotional culture (see Moloney, 2006). Although we call for a new praxis that is oriented towards creativity, engagement and social good, we also recognize that professional public relations can only do so within the constraints of its commercial, sociopolitical foundation and rationale. Fundamentally the challenges are to determine whether an ethical understanding of public interest through dialogue can be used as a tool in the planning box of practitioners. And whether they can convince managements that engagement is not only valued, but imperative with increased utilization of social media which differs from more linear standard media.

Navigating cultural clashes: Socialization, promotion and politics

Superficially, social media and public relations seem to enjoy an ideal partnership—at least in potential. As our discussion has explained, social media and public relations are both discursive-related constructs. However, it is not that simple. Social media comprises the multiple spaces for the interactions of diverse individuals, organizations, discursive networks and communities. Public relations, in contrast, is actively involved in discourse technologization—the creation, transformation and promotion of elite discourses (Fairclough, 1992, Motion and Leitch, 1996, Edwards, 2011). A goal of public relations professionals is to gain acceptance for discourses that advance particular meaning systems, power relationships, and sociocultural practices that are prioritized to serve their clients' interests rather than those of social media communities or some broader public interest.

Advancing particular interests means that discourse technologization often involves a social engineering role that seeks "attitudinal change" and "behavioural compliance" (Moloney, 2006, p. 167)—which in and of themselves are not inherently unethical or dysfunctional—in line with the outcomes favored by political or corporate elites. A key to ethics, we argue, is the interests that are favored.

Successful promotion of elite discourses is by no means a straightforward task within social media. Theorizing public relations as a socialization agent focuses attention on the sociopolitical and promotional objectives that are pursued through discourse transformation efforts. Reactions to socialization may vary depending on the cultural context of particular social media sites. As individual views on social, political, economic, and relational matters are shared and considered, they become embodied in cultural zones of meaning in which engagement occurs, decisions are made and a form of social order prevails.

Cultural zones of meaning guide social media users when they share perspectives, values, and actions. Some social media networks act as cultural settings for the exploration and critique of contemporary issues and organizational practices. Interventions by outsiders in these sites that violate the existing social order and which are perceived as social engineering, promotional, or inauthentic may be exposed and fail. Indeed, some social media sites explicitly advance critiques and counterarguments to expose or directly attack the social engineering efforts of professional public relations. For a profession that often seeks to render itself invisible and erase traces of its own efforts this risk of exposure is deeply concerning.

The socialization objectives of public relations are revealed (and often ridiculed) as a form of exploitation—appropriating social issues for commercial purposes is a risky strategy that calls for very sensitive engagement with publics. Perhaps, to call it appropriation of social issues is to understate the point—what is really happening is that public relations is appropriating culture for commercial or political ends. When detected, social media users typically resist such efforts to control or change culture. That is not to say, however, that all attempts at social engineering are unwelcome or fail.

Some public relations interventions that have the potential to make lasting positive change may be readily accepted and promoted by social media users when brand and social objectives are integrated within public relations campaigns to offer empowering identities and meaningful actions. Such campaigns have the potential to make a genuine social impact and transform existing power relations while at the same time strengthening brand awareness because they share common starting points with social media publics (Leitch and Motion, 1999; Motion and Leitch 2002). Each public relations effort at socialization within social media needs to establish shared meaningfulness, relevance and value. In this way, social media may be forcing public relations to think more carefully about the value of its offering. Yet, in spite of this pressure to operate differently within a critical participatory culture, it is important not to assume that the increased scrutiny and criticism of social media has resulted in changed public relations practices—a search for more engaged, deliberative ways of operating suggests that they are still extremely difficult to locate.

A key problem when discussing the relationship between public relations and social media is that they are each dynamic, complex, communicative systems that have pragmatic and moral implications regarding not only their legitimacy, but also the legitimacy of those who use them to communicate. Even the use of these terms, social media and public relations, is complicated. They are abstract concepts that encompass a multitude of ideas but also refer to a set of relations and practices that signify particular cultures. Attempts to bridge the differences between social media and public relations have resulted in public relations identifying conversations as a unifying activity. By focusing on conversation, public relations has misunderstood the fundamental shift in how our worlds are now shaped—we have entered a communicative epoch based on a fundamental shift to participatory cultures constituted by relational connections and sharing (John, 2012).

What this means in practice is that many of our everyday and professional communicative practices are now conducted in various social media arenas that have become key sites for engaging in relational activities and enacting our relationships. The notion that relationships are at the heart of public relations has been advanced by both academia and practice—yet the ways in which public relations constitutes and practices "relations" are very different to our everyday social media relations. As a paid agent of and for promotional culture, public relations faces a significant clash with the relational, participatory, sharing cultures of social media. Traditional public relations modes of operating are being called into question. For instance, the strategies of engaging with traditional media do not readily translate or transfer to social media.

Public relations has an interdependent relationship with traditional media which is based on cajoling or coopting media into circulating particular perspectives that perform or masquerade as news. However, unlike the symbiotic relationship between traditional media and public relations, social media relationships require a continual search for commonalities and each interaction is context specific. A number of strategic options are open to public relations professionals who seek to work in social media. Instrumental approaches focus on the affordances or utility of various social media platforms and how public relations may best operate in the various discursive spaces to achieve its objectives. The problem, however, is that simply concentrating on understanding the affordances of social media ignores the complexities of social media as culturally constituted discursive spaces.

Drawing upon critical theories that conceive of cultures as sites of contested meanings, identity politics, issues of power, ideology and difference (Bardhan and Weaver, 2011), we argue that public relations interventions in social media are complicated by cultural clashes. Within social media cultures, disorganized connecting, messaging and sharing predominates whereas professional public relations is an agent of commercialized, promotional culture that seeks to minimize contested meanings, downplay identity politics and differences, promote particular power relations and advance ideologies that advantage clients. The direct, personal and voluntary character of the communication between organizations and their publics that is enabled by social media stands in stark contrast to the traditional media which social media has replaced. Many social media corporations have struggled to successfully commercialize and monetize the potential of their investments because users resist the commercialization of their everyday online communication and attempts to brand consumer-generated content. As a consequence, a delicate balance of power persists that provides users with a modicum (or illusion) of control over commercial intrusions. Thus, to enter social media sites public relations must carefully moderate promotional strategies and offer some form of value.

Public relations offers value for traditional media by generating content; however, that value has been usurped by the shift to user-generated content in social media. Therein lies one of the fundamental challenges of engagement: the nature of social media changes content contribution from carefully tailored messages that are transmitted through standard media to means by which information is truly shared and publically vetted. The challenge for public relations, then, is to offer something of value to individual users, networks and communities. To further complicate the challenge, social media relationships are predicated on participatory cultures that have sharing as their foundational practice.

Membership and influence within such arenas are driven by protocols that allow for inclusion and exclusion. Both options are driven by norms that often are idiosyncratic to each arena. The benefits and costs of membership depend on how well the individual supports the arena by sharing information in various forms, complying with persuasive themes that can enlighten choices, and commenting (perhaps in ways that are protocol driven by response time and type) so that the communication commons truly become a shared communication space. For public relations, this requires a change in its fundamental business model. As an agent for client interests, professional public relations is tasked with promotion which is usually a one-way process.

The shift to a sharing ecology/economy raises questions about how exactly public relations may participate and reciprocate. One of the key themes of communication is that the place where it happens shapes how it transpires. This can be conceptualized as a discourse arena. With conventional media, some organizations (including media corporations) tend to shape the discourse arena by how they allow various voices access (often called gatekeeping) to the arena and to the voices in the arena.

Social media (as mediated interpersonal communication) allows individuals with shared interests and identities to shape their own discourse arena. Others may have access to this arena (as in the case of traditional media, public relations, and marketing) but they operate in a space that is controlled by the users of the arena. Users establish their own social media cultures with particular expectations, norms and rules. For public relations this requires a shift from promoting and pushing messages to engaging with those cultures by listening and sharing. Entertainment and sociability may work in some social media settings, political content in other settings and other settings are varied and unpredictable. Social media is a risky, dangerous space for public relations, particularly when it seeks to operate with stealth and self-interested control. Navigating these diverse expectations requires nuanced insights into the cultural contexts and settings of social media zones of meaning.

In many ways social media has afforded myriad new communication opportunities such as the increasing centrality of social media for communicating corporate identity and for developing the social capital associated with a particular corporate identity. A possibility for sidestepping expectations of sharing and reciprocity is to concentrate on "owned" social media sites, such as an organization's own Facebook page, which offers some control over content. However, the moment that participation is invited an organization loses control. This is a fundamental shift in discursive power. The role of traditional media as a gatekeeper, intermediary and power broker now has to be juggled with direct interactions with multiple publics.

Mass communication strategies that are translated into social media in an attempt to present a unified identity may be negated within social media because identity results from the multiple identity enactments across streams rather than a more centralized, controlled range of media outlets. The multiple identity enactments of each social media interaction have the potential to enhance or very quickly undermine reputational capital. Identity presentation must be grounded in authenticity—aspirational or fake representations of a branding are frequently exposed and ridiculed in social media. For corporate identity strategies to succeed organizations have to align with the common starting points of various social media cultures and then attempt to ensure that the multiple identity interactions are positive. This challenge requires an organization to move beyond promoting itself to genuine engagement with stakeholders. The challenge of navigating multiple social media cultures requires a very different set of strategies and power relations. The starting point is social media cultures, not public relations goals and strategies.

Mitigating vulnerabilities: Power/knowledge struggles

The use of social media for promotional purposes is not without significant risks and corporate identity work is no exception. Indeed, a new industry has sprung up around the need to protect corporate reputations and rescue damaged reputations from attacks that occur within social media contexts. Social media may just as easily provide a means for damaging reputations as they do for developing reputations. Despite the apparent dangers, many organizations have been slow to engage with social media. Opting out of engagement may not prove to be the wise option, especially when the conversation relates to issues of high importance to the organization. Nondialogic adaptation—the assumption that the organization cannot or need not participate in the discourse—opens up the risk of renewed and intensified scrutiny.

Misunderstandings of social media create significant vulnerabilities for public relations. A key vulnerability is the marked shift from power/knowledge modalities that are driven by power elites to participatory approaches. These shifts from the traditional power/knowledge relations that permitted public relations to indirectly promote clients' interests to more open, vigilant and vocal social media arenas have complicated risk, crisis, issues and policy communication. Not only does public relations have to develop risk communication strategies that address the usual types of political, technical, economic and cultural risks, now the discursive challenges and risks that arise from working in social media must also be addressed. A further complication is that social media increases the complexity of multistakeholder communication and the level of public scrutiny. The existence of multiple social media publics suggests that there are multiple interests that give voice to concerns and convey or deny legitimacy. For example, risk creators and arbitrators engage in precautionary contestation to determine how safety and fairness are determined and evaluated. Social media thus allows communities and networked publics to independently define and engage with risk, crises and issues and problematize traditional power relations. For public relations this poses a considerable challenge—social media are less subject to power/knowledge controls and multiple voices are likely to participate.

That is not to say, however, that all voices in social media have equal weight and legitimacy—but they do have public policy effects in terms of raising concerns and questions about what risks are safe and fair and examine the impact on daily lives. Social media enhances the capacity of communities to assess risk. As a consequence, a number of important implications for public relations arise when struggles over power/knowledge form the basis of risk, crisis, issues and policy debates. Although public relations has inherent discursive advantages when it comes to communicating knowledge, it has experienced a radical shift in terms of power relations. Contestation within social media over fact, value, policy and identification open society to the opportunity for a generalized distrust, the development of alliances, critical and subaltern counter-public participation and the recreation of society as an iterative process through public discourse.

Although social media functions as arenas for contestation over risk they do not necessarily produce consensus or even agreement; discussions are more usually indications of a range of responses and tendencies. It is also important to understand that although organizations and public relations professionals may gain access to a social media network that does mean that they are authentically engaged in dialogue or have any control over the types of information sharing and discussions that take place.

Notions of power and control are therefore central to our analysis of the relationship between social media and public relations. Power is understood, here, as multilayered, discursive and relational. Social media cultures, defined within social media texts and practices, shape the conditions and legitimacy of voices and allow multiple and diverse opinions to circulate. Stake seekers and stakeholders jostle for influence and control within a discursive dialectic of stake exchange that underpins various social media configurations of power relations. Within social media, power is practiced as inclusion and exclusion, sharing and nonsharing, praise and criticism, exposure, disclosure and calls for action. As our discussion has confirmed, social media reduce the ability to control discourse and increase the incentive for organizations and their public relations to adapt to and participate with public discourses.

Such participation needs to address conflicts of need and listen to marginalized stakeholders—we argue that communicative empathy is central to legislative and regulatory decision-making. To work effectively each partner needs to presume that they must listen first, and acknowledge points of view rather than turn the discourse to their interests. Failure to do so, we have suggested, is likely to result in a process we have labeled "critical public engagement." Social media publics assume a form of power and communicate to organizations in ways that are labeled "activist" but may equally be understood as a form of engagement. Institutional determinism, power and intentionality are all called into question as publics seek to reconfigure power relations. Although deliberative communication is posited as a panacea to foster mutual understanding what is first needed is thoughtful planning, navigation of issues and considerations of concerns about public interest. Quality policy and business practices occur when the competing voices of the powerful and less powerful are heard, understood and appreciated. New forms of corporate planning, operations and communication are called for that are necessary to understand and facilitate the types of discussion that are now possible with social media. The politics of change necessitate power sharing or empowerment processes that render collaborative outcomes possible The challenge, in this changed environment, is to be engaged without presuming the ability to control process and outcomes.

Public interest rationales

For participation and engagement to succeed public interest needs to inform policy decisions. The old notion of mass-mediated communicators affecting the agenda and content of issue discussions and gatekeepers has become reshaped. Discourse should serve the social media community's interests—not just those of an organization—and public policy deliberations should result from authentic and collaborative engagement. Social media are central to the formation and enactment of sociopolitical change. Of course, not all social media interactions become a metanarrative or inform policy. However, public relations can have a role in building a fully functioning society by having sharing and reciprocity as foundational principles.

In what we have concluded, and argued, we do not, and should not, presume that social media do not have a "one-way" value. Intent and meaning, not directionality, matter. Increasingly, news organizations and corporations are embracing social media as a means for getting information quickly into the minds of users. These "one-way" streams may provide information on traffic, weather, and emergency response. High-risk industries are adding social media to their toolboxes for warning and alerting near neighbors to some emergency. Because users are often keenly alert to their social media, they may, for instance, get a warning about a huge and dangerous brush fire more quickly and based on GPS options, with specific shelter in place or evacuation instructions.

Meaning grows in social media by a kind of consensus model among the users. Thus, to engage in discussions requires an understanding of protocols and meanings that are idiosyncratic to various social media arenas.

In interaction, dialogue, and even one-way emergency management communication it is important to note the threads, chains, of messaging. These can be, in the emergency response context, updates. In other contexts, such as routine uses of social media, they are like a conversation that evolves (repeats or devolves) as is the case of traditional face-to-face interpersonal interaction. In conversations, such chains or threads, are enacted through normative patterns that are learned social engagement. Several options, perhaps an almost infinite list, are apparent. One occurs as individuals add to and comment favorably on the theme of a thread. In conversation, actors often add details, clarification, encouragement, affirmation, and such, as some thread develops. Presentation of pictures (trips, children, and cats) is sure to spark comment, and predict that others in the chain are prone to add their content over time. We might call this an affirmation thread. Conversely, a thread might have the discourse trajectory of being disaffirmation. Some initiation might encounter rejection, doubt, contradiction, and even hostile rejection. One of the ultimate threads is cyber bullying. Another thread might play out as identity engagement. Each person variously in sequence interacts by reflecting as the rationale for identity engagement on what others have said. "That happened to me." "That makes me happy." "That angers me and makes me doubt the potential goodness of humans." "I can't believe that a pet owner could be so awful." "Grandmothers are the greatest people in the world." "As an X, I think that all of us are in varying degrees of danger."

Threads chain out in narrative form. Individuals contribute their own stories or versions of narrative themes as a way of sustaining the thread. By the same token, new chain links can take the emerging narrative off in a different direction. Each chain link can become a new thread, and enjoy affirmation or an ever-extending line of contribution. As such, it is unwise to presume that merely the spirit of interaction, and even engagement, lead to resolution. There is nothing inherent in discourse, dialogue, that predicts that opposing points of view will be resolved or that some conclusion can be derived on some issue that is mutually satisfying. That is the case, in social media, as it is in conversation. And, therefore, the study of social media must acknowledge the strength, trajectories, and dysfunctions of conversation as discourse continues. Finally, one of the discourse options is discontinuation. People leave the field in discussion, debate, advocacy, and even seemingly supportive decision-making if some resolution and/or decision is not forthcoming or satisfying.

Perhaps some of the most important elements of social media are both its efficiency, and its inefficiency. Western managerial models for more than a century have championed efficiency as a virtue. Sometimes social media are highly efficient. They are extremely effective in emergency management. A trend on social media, such as Twitter, can quickly produce a "collective" sentiment, moral judgment, or some other outcome. But, because the dynamics of social engagement are not driven by efficiency, but by something more like the vetting and sharing of information and opinion for collective judgment, they can move slower than glaciers, but perhaps, as it is the case of glaciers, the mark/residue of the process is profound and lasting. Thus, independent of external institutional influence, social media networks might conclude that sexual preference and same sex marriage is not as objectionable as mainstream thought would prefer. Thus, as "mainstream" thinkers seek to engage with participants in a social media arena on such topics, the institutional users might be like the boulders that get ground into sand by glaciers. Such processes and outcomes have profound pragmatic, and ethical, implications because of the deterministic nature of social media.

Meanings and policy change preferences have always been heavily influenced by interpersonal contact and conversation. Over the years media outlets (and politicians, as well as companies) have operated on the assumption that they shape opinions and define the public interest. We suggest, however, that really, the public—or various publics—define their own interests. So, each social media network or arena is a meaning generation and identity formation "apparatus." Public relations practitioners, rather than boldly believing they can control and shape interests, especially with the help of media gatekeepers, can be starkly startled by the narrowly dynamic leadership that occurs through engagement among social media users. Practitioners are wise to realize that they are playing in other folks' playgrounds—and that they will be perceived as fake friends when they behave deterministically. Speculation about the future of public relations in social media suggests a number of scenarios—business as usual; an adaptive model for promoting clients' interests; or a radically changed profession. Failure to adapt or change, we argue, is likely to render public relations powerless and eventually irrelevant to social media. It is our hope, instead, that public relations will be compelled to embrace change as social media publics seek to safeguard how their everyday lives may play out in social media. Public relations has the opportunity to discard the more negative aspects of practice and meaningfully engage with online publics by advancing democratic aims, promoting equity practices, taking into account what matters to various publics and serving the broader public interest.

References

Bardhan, N. and Weaver, C.K. (eds.) (2011). Introduction: Public relations in global cultural contexts. In *Public Relations in Global Cultural Contexts: Multi-paradigmatic Perspectives*, pp. 1–28. New York, NY: Routledge.

Edwards, L. (2011). Public relations and society: A Bourdieuvian perspective. In L. Edwards and C. Hodges (eds.). *Public Relations, Society and Culture: Theoretical and Empirical Explorations*, pp. 61–74. London and New York: Routledge.

Fairclough, N. (1992) *Discourse and social change*. Cambridge: Polity Press.

John, N.A. (2012). Sharing and web 2.0: The emergence of a keyword. *New Media & Society*, 15(2), 167–182.

Leitch, S. and Motion, J. (1999). Multiplicity in corporate identity strategy. *Corporate Communications: An International Journal*, 4(4), 193–199.

Moloney, K. (2006). *Rethinking Public Relations: PR Propaganda and Democracy*. Routledge.

Motion, J. and Leitch, S. (1996). A discursive perspective from New Zealand: Another worldview. *Public Relations Review*, 22(3), 297–309.

Motion, J. and Leitch, S. (2002). The technologies of corporate identity and branding. *International Studies of Management and Organization*, 32 (3), 46–64.

Index